Question&Answer

EVIDENCE

Develop your legal skills with Longman

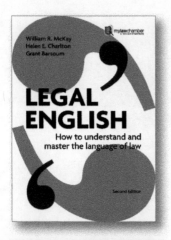

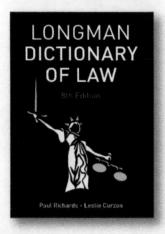

Written to help you develop the essential skills needed to succeed on your course and prepare for practice.

Longman is an imprint of

Available from all good bookshops or order online at:
www.pearsoned.co.uk/law

Question&Answer
EVIDENCE

Rita D'Alton-Harrison
University of Hertfordshire

Longman
is an imprint of

Harlow, England • London • New York • Boston • San Francisco • Toronto • Sydney • Singapore • Hong Kong
Tokyo • Seoul • Taipei • New Delhi • Cape Town • Madrid • Mexico City • Amsterdam • Munich • Paris • Milan

Pearson Education Limited
Edinburgh Gate
Harlow
Essex CM20 2JE
England

and Associated Companies throughout the world

Visit us on the World Wide Web at:
www.pearson.com/uk

First published 2012

ISBN: 978-1-4082-6667-0

British Library Cataloguing-in-Publication Data
A catalogue record for this book is available from the British Library

Library of Congress Cataloging-in-Publication Data
D'Alton-Harrison, Rita.
  Law express question and answer : evidence / Rita D'Alton-Harrison
      p. cm. -- (Law express question & answer)
  Includes bibliographical references and index.
  ISBN 978-1-4082-6667-0 (pbk.)
  1. Evidence (Law)--England--Outlines, syllabi, etc. I. Title. II. Title: Question and answer : evidence. III. Title: Evidence.
  KD7499.6.D35 2012
  347.42'06076--dc23

                                                                    2011040032

Typeset in 10pt Helvetica Condensed by 30

Contents

Supporting resources

Visit the Law Express Question & Answer series companion website at
www.pearsoned.co.uk/lawexpressqa to find valuable learning material including:

- Additional **essay and problem questions** arranged by topic for each chapter give you more opportunity to practise and hone your exam skills.
- **Diagram plans** for all additional questions assist you in structuring and writing your answers.
- **You be the marker** questions allow you to see through the eyes of the examiner by marking essay and problem questions on every topic covered in the book.
- Download and print all **Attack the question** diagrams and **Diagram plans** from the book.

Also: The companion website provides the following features:

- Search tool to help locate specific terms of content.
- Online help and support to assist with website usage and troubleshooting.

For more information please contact your local Pearson sales representative or visit
www.pearsoned.co.uk/lawexpressqa

Acknowledgements

My thanks go to Zoe Botterill the commissioning editor at Pearson Education for the opportunity to write this text. I would also like to thank everyone at Pearson Education who contributed to the production of this edition.

This book is dedicated to the memory of my sister Angela, whose smile and laughter we all miss.

I also wish to thank all my past students, whose constant search for simple explanations and key concepts in this area of law has, I hope, informed my writing style.

Finally, but not least, I wish to thank my husband and children for their patience during the writing of this book.

Publisher's acknowledgements

Our thanks go to all reviewers who contributed to the development of this text, including students who participated in research and focus groups which helped to shape the series format.

What you need to do for every question in the Law of Evidence

Books in the *Question and Answer* series focus on the *why* of a good answer alongside the *what*, thereby helping you to build your question answering skills and technique.

This guide should not be used as a substitute for learning the material thoroughly, your lecture notes or your textbook. It *will* help you to make the most out of what you have already learned when answering an exam or coursework question. Remember that the answers given here are not the *only* correct way of answering the question but serve to show you some good examples of how you *could* approach the question set.

Make sure that you refer regularly to your course syllabus frequently, check which issues are covered (as well as to what extent they are covered) and whether they are usually examined with other topics. Remember that what is required in a good answer could change significantly with only a slight change in the wording of a question. Therefore, do not try to memorise the answers given here, instead use the answers and the other features to understand what goes into a good answer and why.

The law of evidence requires analytical and problem-solving skills but most importantly students need to be able to see how key concepts interrelate rather than learning each topic in isolation. In the case of both essay and problem-solving questions you should produce a structured, reasoned and well balanced answer supported by case law. Avoid repetition and be concise in your answers and ensure that you relate your answer back to the question. There is a limit to the amount that you can write in the exam time so limit your answer to what is relevant to the question. The answers in this book are intended to reflect what a student could realistically write within the time constraints of an examination.

When answering problem-solving questions you should relate the law to the facts given and this should be done throughout the question rather than at the end. You should also focus on the current law rather than discussing the historical development of the law in that particular area.

However, for essay questions you would be expected to analyse the historical development of the law and to examine whether the current law meets its purpose. References to important reports such as Law Commission reports would be expected as well as reference to judicial commentary or any academic opinion or journal articles in the area.

Guided tour

What you need to do for every question in the Law of Evidence

What to do for every question – Find out the key things you should do and look for in any question and answer on the subject in order to give every one of your answers a great chance from the start.

HOW TO USE THIS BOOK

Books in the *Question and Answer* series focus on the *why* of a good answer alongside the *what*, thereby helping you to build your question answering skills and technique.

This guide should not be used as a substitute for learning the material thoroughly, your lecture notes or your textbook. It *will* help you to make the most out of what you have already learned when answering an exam or coursework question. Remember that the answers given here are not the *only* correct way of answering the question but serve to show you some good examples of how you *could* approach the question set.

Make sure that you refer regularly to your course syllabus frequently, check which issues are covered (as well as to what extent they are covered) and whether they are usually examined with other topics. Remember that what is required in a good answer could change significantly with only a slight change in the wording of a question. Therefore, do not try to memorise the answers given here, instead use the answers and the other features to understand what goes into a good answer and why.

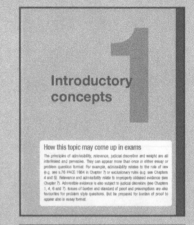

Introductory concepts

How this topic may come up in exams

The principles of admissibility, relevance, judicial discretion and weight are all interlinked and pervasive. They can appear more than once in either essay or problem question format. For example, admissibility relates to the role of raw (e.g. see s.78 PACE 1984 in Chapter 7) or exclusionary rules (e.g. see Chapters 4 and 5). Relevance and admissibility relate to improperly obtained evidence (see Chapter 7). Admissible evidence is also subject to judicial discretion (see Chapters 1, 4, 6 and 7). Issues of burden and standard of proof and presumptions are also favourites for problem style questions. But be prepared for burden of proof to appear also in essay format.

How this topic might come up in exams – Learn how to tackle any question on this topic by using the handy tips and advice relevant to both essay and problem questions. In-text symbols clearly identify each question type as they occur.

 Essay question

 Problem question

Attack the question – Attack attack attack! Use these diagrams as a step by step guide to help you confidently identify the main points covered in any question asked.

Answer plans and Diagram plans – Clear and concise answer plans and diagram plans support the planning and structuring of your answers whatever your preferred learning style.

Diagram plan

Answer plan
→ Explain the difference between the evidential and the legal burden.
→ Explain the general principle of who bears the burden and standard of proof.
→ Explain, using case law, how and when a reverse burden occurs.
→ Analyse the rationale for this.
→ Does the approach offend against Art.6?

Answer with accompanying guidance – Make the most out of every question by using the guidance to recognise what makes a good answer and why. Answers are the length you could realistically hope to produce in an exam to show you how to gain marks quickly when under pressure.

Case names clearly highlighted – Easy to spot bold text makes those all important case names stand out from the rest of the answer, ensuring they are much easier to remember in revision and in the exam.

Make your answer stand out – Really impress your examiners by including these additional points and further reading to illustrate your deeper knowledge of the subject, fully maximising your marks.

Don't be tempted to – Avoid common mistakes and losing easy marks by understanding where students most often trip up in exams.

Bibliography – Use this list of further reading to really explore areas in more depth, enabling you to excel in exams.

---

1 INTRODUCTORY CONCEPTS

4 Reaching a final view is necessary as you have been asked to consider whether the decision is capable of appeal. This shows that you are able to understand what the question requires of you.

5 This demonstrates a deeper knowledge on your part as the examiner can see that you have understood that different presumptions have different evidential value.

6 An ability to recognise errors in the decision demonstrates that you have a command of the subject area necessary for the correct application of the law to the facts.

7 Comparing and contrasting cases in this way will earn you more marks as it shows

enquiries that were made particularly following the husband's sighting in Marbella. In the circumstances the judge was wrong to apply the presumption.[4]

(b) With regard to the second extract, this appears to be a negligence case and the judge has applied the presumption of negligence known as *res ipsa loquitur*. As shown in the case of **Scott v London and St Katherine Docks Co** (1865) 3 H & C 596, this means that the claimant may rely on this principle to show that the relevant matter was under the control or management of the defendant and that the accident would not have happened if the defendant had taken proper care. In the absence of any evidence to the contrary a presumption will arise. However, it is a rebuttable presumption.[5] On the facts it would appear that it was reasonable for the judge to allow this presumption as it is reasonable to suggest that the bale of hay was under the control or management of the defendants as it had their name and address on it. The judge is wrong to suggest that it is still necessary for the defendant to prove the absence of negligence. The claimant in fact bears the legal burden to show the relevant matter was in the control of the defendants.[6] However, the defendant only bears the evidential burden to produce sufficient evidence to rebut the presumption as seen in cases such as **Ng Chun Pui v Lee Chuen Tat** (1988) RTR 298. It is fair to say that the case law is conflicting in this area with previous cases, such as **Ward v Tesco Stores Ltd** [1976] 1 WLR 810, suggesting that the defendant bears a legal burden. However, recent cases such as **Ng Chun** and **Ratcliffe v**

✓ Make your answer stand out

■ Discuss in detail the factors that the court should consider when deciding whether to uphold a reverse burden as identified by Lord Steyn in *R v Johnstone* (above), e.g. the seriousness of the offence.
■ Mention additional cases involving reverse burdens such as *L v DPP* [2002] 3 WLR 863 and *R v All*; *R v Jordan* [2001] 2 WLR 211.
■ Develop the discussion relating to s.101 Magistrates' Court Act 1980.
■ Discuss Lord Clyde's argument in *Lambert* that reverse burdens should be upheld where the offence is regulatory in nature.

! Don't be tempted to...

■ Write everything you know about burden and standard of proof – avoid lengthy definitions and moot points about how the standard of 'beyond reasonable doubt' and 'on a balance of probabilities' should be explained. The question requires you to focus on the issue of reverse burdens.
■ Ignore the quotation given in the question – whilst a brief mention of the facts is permissible you need to analyse whether or not Parliament should legislate in this area rather than leaving the courts to use statutory interpretation.
■ Discuss the facts of *R v Hunt* in detail simply because it is mentioned in the quotation – focus on the meaning of Lord Griffiths' words and the legal principle arising from the case.

Bibliography

Advisory Group on Video-Recorded Evidence (1989), Report ('Pigot Report'). London: Home Office
Auld LJ (2001), *A Review of the Criminal Courts of England and Wales*
Birch, D. (1995), 'Corroboration: goodbye to all that', Crim LR 525

Guided tour of the companion website

 Book resources are available to download. Print your own **Attack the question** and **Diagram plans**.

 Additional **Essay and Problem questions** with **Diagram plans** arranged by topic for each chapter give you more opportunity to practise and hone your exam skills. Print and email your answers.

 You be the marker gives you a chance to evaluate sample exam answers for different question types for each topic and understand how and why an examiner awards marks. Use the accompanying guidance to get the most out of every question and recognise what makes a good answer.

All this and more can be found when you visit **www.pearsoned.co.uk/lawexpressqa**

Table of cases and statutes

■ Cases

Al Fayed v Commissioner of Police of the Metropolis [2002] EWCA Civ 780 242

Al-Khawaja v UK (2009) App No. 26766/05, EctHR 70, 79

Allen v UK (2002) App. No. 76574/01 217, 222

Ashburton v Pape [1913] 2 Ch 469 218

Associated Provincial Pictures Houses v Wednesbury Corporation [1947] 1 KB 223 141, 187, 193, 197, 206, 244, 249

AT & T Istel Ltd v Tully [1992] 3 All ER 523 220

Attorney General v Hitchcock (1847) 1 Exch 91 51, 245

Attorney General's Reference (No.1 of 2004) [2004] EWCA Crim 1025, [2004] 1 WLR 2111, CA 6

Attorney-General's Reference (No.2 of 2001) [2003] UKHL 68 21

Attorney-General's Reference (No.3 of 2000) [2001] 1 WLR 2061 132

Averill v UK (2000) App. No. 36408/97 174

Balabel v Air India [1988] 2 WLR 1036, CA 216

Balfour v Foreign and Commonwealth Office [1994] 2 All ER 588 216

Beckford v R (1993) 97 Cr App R 409 (PC) 152, 157, 161, 162, 167

Benedetto and Labrador v R [2003] 1 WLR 1545, PC 198

Blunt v Park Lane Hotel [1942] 2 KB 253 213, 217, 220, 222

Blyth v Blyth [1966] 2 WLR 634 242

Brannigan v Davison [1997] AC 238 221

Brown v Stott [2001] 2 WLR 817 220, 221

Butler v Board of Trade [1970] 3 WLR 822 241

C plc v P (Secretary of State for the Home Office Intervening) [2007] 3 WLR 437 221

Calcraft v Guest [1898] 1 QB 759 22, 216, 241, 242

CG v UK (2001) App No. 43373 48

Chard v Chard [1956] P 259 19

Chief Adjudication Officer v Bath [2000] 1 FLR 8 240

Condron v UK (2001) 31 EHRR 1 173, 177, 178

Conway v Rimmer [1968] 2 WLR 998 211, 213, 215, 216, 225

Crescent Farm (Sidcup) Sports v Sterling Offices Ltd [1972] 2 WLR 91 241

Den Norske Bank ASA v Antonatos [1999] QB 271 219, 220

Doorson v The Netherlands (1996) App. No. 14448/88 (ECtHR) 78

DPP v Boardman [1974] 3 WLR 673 109

DPP v Kilbourne [1973] AC 729, HL 21, 139

DPP v M [1998] 2 WLR 604 34

DPP v P [1991] 3 WLR 161, HL 109

DPP v Stonehouse [1978] AC 55 16

Duncan v Cammell Laird & Co Ltd [1942] AC 624 213

Edwards v R [2006] UKPC 23 152

Freemantle v R [1994] 1 WLR 1437, PC 152, 157, 161, 167, 193

Funke v France [1993] 16 EHRR 297 221

Garton v Hunter (1969) 2 QB 37 22

Goddard v Nationwide Building Society [1986] 3 WLR 734, CA 217

Guinness Peat Properties v Fitzroy Robinson Partnership [1987] 1 WLR 1027 241

▄ Statutes

■ Statutory Instruments

■ Practice Directions

■ Conventions

■ Other jurisdictions

Introductory concepts

■ Attack the question

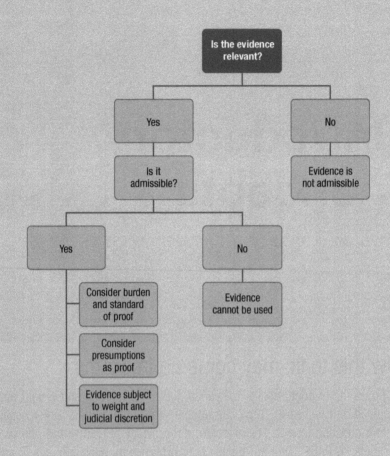

Question&Answer

EVIDENCE

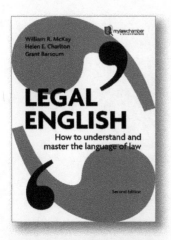

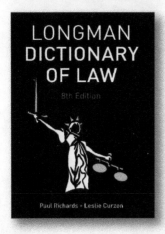
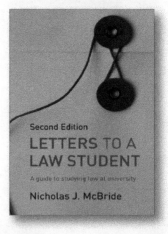

Question&Answer
EVIDENCE

Rita D'Alton-Harrison
University of Hertfordshire

Longman
is an imprint of

Harlow, England • London • New York • Boston • San Francisco • Toronto • Sydney • Singapore • Hong Kong
Tokyo • Seoul • Taipei • New Delhi • Cape Town • Madrid • Mexico City • Amsterdam • Munich • Paris • Milan

Pearson Education Limited
Edinburgh Gate
Harlow
Essex CM20 2JE
England

and Associated Companies throughout the world

Visit us on the World Wide Web at:
www.pearson.com/uk

First published 2012

© Pearson Education Limited 2012

ISBN: 978-1-4082-6667-0

British Library Cataloguing-in-Publication Data
A catalogue record for this book is available from the British Library

Library of Congress Cataloging-in-Publication Data
D'Alton-Harrison, Rita.
  Law express question and answer : evidence / Rita D'Alton-Harrison
      p. cm. -- (Law express question & answer)
  Includes bibliographical references and index.
  ISBN 978-1-4082-6667-0 (pbk.)
  1. Evidence (Law)--England--Outlines, syllabi, etc. I. Title. II. Title: Question and answer :
evidence. III. Title: Evidence.
  KD7499.6.D35 2012
  347.42'06076--dc23

                                                                2011040032

Typeset in 10pt Helvetica Condensed by 30

Contents

Supporting resources

Visit the Law Express Question & Answer series companion website at
www.pearsoned.co.uk/lawexpressqa to find valuable learning material including:

- Additional **essay and problem questions** arranged by topic for each chapter give you more opportunity to practise and hone your exam skills.
- **Diagram plans** for all additional questions assist you in structuring and writing your answers.
- **You be the marker** questions allow you to see through the eyes of the examiner by marking essay and problem questions on every topic covered in the book.
- Download and print all **Attack the question** diagrams and **Diagram plans** from the book.

Also: The companion website provides the following features:

- Search tool to help locate specific terms of content.
- Online help and support to assist with website usage and troubleshooting.

For more information please contact your local Pearson sales representative or visit
www.pearsoned.co.uk/lawexpressqa

Acknowledgements

My thanks go to Zoe Botterill the commissioning editor at Pearson Education for the opportunity to write this text. I would also like to thank everyone at Pearson Education who contributed to the production of this edition.

This book is dedicated to the memory of my sister Angela, whose smile and laughter we all miss.

I also wish to thank all my past students, whose constant search for simple explanations and key concepts in this area of law has, I hope, informed my writing style.

Finally, but not least, I wish to thank my husband and children for their patience during the writing of this book.

Publisher's acknowledgements

Our thanks go to all reviewers who contributed to the development of this text, including students who participated in research and focus groups which helped to shape the series format.

What you need to do for every question in the Law of Evidence

Books in the *Question and Answer* series focus on the *why* of a good answer alongside the *what*, thereby helping you to build your question answering skills and technique.

This guide should not be used as a substitute for learning the material thoroughly, your lecture notes or your textbook. It *will* help you to make the most out of what you have already learned when answering an exam or coursework question. Remember that the answers given here are not the *only* correct way of answering the question but serve to show you some good examples of how you *could* approach the question set.

Make sure that you refer regularly to your course syllabus frequently, check which issues are covered (as well as to what extent they are covered) and whether they are usually examined with other topics. Remember that what is required in a good answer could change significantly with only a slight change in the wording of a question. Therefore, do not try to memorise the answers given here, instead use the answers and the other features to understand what goes into a good answer and why.

The law of evidence requires analytical and problem-solving skills but most importantly students need to be able to see how key concepts interrelate rather than learning each topic in isolation. In the case of both essay and problem-solving questions you should produce a structured, reasoned and well balanced answer supported by case law. Avoid repetition and be concise in your answers and ensure that you relate your answer back to the question. There is a limit to the amount that you can write in the exam time so limit your answer to what is relevant to the question. The answers in this book are intended to reflect what a student could realistically write within the time constraints of an examination.

When answering problem-solving questions you should relate the law to the facts given and this should be done throughout the question rather than at the end. You should also focus on the current law rather than discussing the historical development of the law in that particular area.

However, for essay questions you would be expected to analyse the historical development of the law and to examine whether the current law meets its purpose. References to important reports such as Law Commission reports would be expected as well as reference to judicial commentary or any academic opinion or journal articles in the area.

Guided tour

What you need to do for every question in the Law of Evidence

What to do for every question – Find out the key things you should do and look for in any question and answer on the subject in order to give every one of your answers a great chance from the start.

How this topic might come up in exams – Learn how to tackle any question on this topic by using the handy tips and advice relevant to both essay and problem questions. In-text symbols clearly identify each question type as they occur.

 Essay question

 Problem question

Attack the question – Attack attack attack! Use these diagrams as a step by step guide to help you confidently identify the main points covered in any question asked.

Answer plans and Diagram plans – Clear and concise answer plans and diagram plans support the planning and structuring of your answers whatever your preferred learning style.

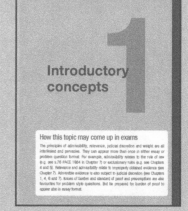

Introductory concepts

How this topic may come up in exams

The principles of admissibility, relevance, judicial discretion and weight are all interlinked and pervasive. They can appear more than once in either essay or problem question format. For example, admissibility relates to the role of law (e.g. see s.78 PACE 1984 in Chapter 7) or exclusionary rules (e.g. see Chapters 4 and 5). Relevance and admissibility relate to improperly obtained evidence (see Chapter 7). Admissible evidence is also subject to judicial discretion (see Chapters 1, 4, 6 and 7). Issues of burden and standard of proof and presumptions are also favourites for problem style questions. But be prepared for burden of proof to appear also in essay format.

1 INTRODUCTORY CONCEPTS
Attack the question

Answer plan

→ Explain the difference between the evidential and the legal burden.
→ Explain the general principle of who bears the burden and standard of proof.
→ Explain, using case law, how and when a reverse burden occurs.
→ Analyse the rationale for this.
→ Does the approach offend against Art.6?

Diagram plan

Answer with accompanying guidance –
Make the most out of every question by using
the guidance to recognise what
makes a good answer and
why. Answers are the
length you could
realistically hope to
produce in an exam
to show you how to
gain marks quickly
when under pressure.

Case names clearly highlighted – Easy to
spot bold text makes those all important case
names stand out from the rest of the answer,
ensuring they are much easier to remember
in revision and in the exam.

Make your answer stand out – Really
impress your examiners by including these
additional points and further reading to
illustrate your deeper knowledge of the
subject, fully maximising your marks.

Don't be tempted to – Avoid common
mistakes and losing easy marks by
understanding where students most often trip
up in exams.

Bibliography – Use this list of further
reading to really explore areas in more depth,
enabling you to excel in exams.

---

1 INTRODUCTORY CONCEPTS

[4] Reaching a final view is necessary as you have been asked to consider whether the decision is capable of appeal. This shows that you are able to understand what the question requires of you.

[6] An ability to recognise errors in the decision demonstrates that you have a command of the subject area necessary for the correct application of the law to the facts.

[7] Comparing and contrasting cases in this way will earn you more marks as it shows

enquiries that were made particularly following the husband's sighting in Marbella. In the circumstances the judge was wrong to apply the presumption.[4]

(b) With regard to the second extract, this appears to be a negligence case and the judge has applied the presumption of negligence known as *res ipsa loquitur*. As shown in the case of **Scott v London and St Katherine Docks Co** (1865) 3 H & C 596, this means that the claimant may rely on this principle to show that the relevant matter was under the control or management of the defendant and that the accident would not have happened if the defendant had taken proper care. In the absence of any evidence to the contrary a presumption will arise. However, it is a rebuttable presumption.[5] On the facts it would appear that it was reasonable for the judge to allow this presumption as it is reasonable to suggest that the bale of hay was under the control or management of the defendants as it had their name and address on it. The judge is wrong to suggest that it is still necessary for the defendant to prove the absence

---

[5] This demonstrates a deeper knowledge on your part as the examiner can see that you have understood that different presumptions have different evidential value.

[6] An ability to recognise errors in the decision demonstrates that you have a command of the subject area necessary for the correct application of the law to the facts.

[7] Comparing and contrasting cases in this way will earn you more marks as it shows

arise. However, it is a rebuttable presumption.[5] On the facts it would appear that it was reasonable for the judge to allow this presumption as it is reasonable to suggest that the bale of hay was under the control or management of the defendants as it had their name and address on it. The judge is wrong to suggest that it is still necessary for the defendant to prove the absence of negligence. The claimant in fact bears the legal burden to show that the relevant matter was in the control of the defendants.[6] However, the defendant only bears the evidential burden to produce sufficient evidence to rebut the presumption as seen in cases such as **Ng Chun Pui v Lee Chuen Tat** (1988) RTR 298. It is fair to say that the case law is conflicting in this area with previous cases, such as **Ward v Tesco Stores Ltd** [1976] 1 WLR 810, suggesting that the defendant bears a legal burden. However, recent cases such as **Ng Chun** and **Ratcliffe v**

✓ Make your answer stand out

■ Discuss in detail the factors that the court should consider when deciding whether to uphold a reverse burden as identified by Lord Steyn in *R v Johnstone* (above), e.g. the seriousness of the offence.

■ Mention additional cases involving reverse burdens such as *L v DPP* [2002] 3 WLR 863 and *R v Ali; R v Jordan* [2001] 2 WLR 211.

■ Develop the discussion relating to s.101 *Magistrates' Court Act 1980*.

■ Discuss Lord Clyde's argument in *Lambert* that reverse burdens should be upheld where the offence is regulatory in nature.

! Don't be tempted to...

■ Write everything you know about burden and standard of proof – avoid lengthy definitions and moot points about how the standard of 'beyond reasonable doubt' and 'on a balance of probabilities' should be explained. The question requires you to focus on the issue of reverse burdens.

■ Ignore the quotation given in the question – whilst a brief mention of the facts is permissible you need to analyse whether or not Parliament should legislate in this area rather than leaving the courts to use statutory interpretation.

■ Discuss the facts of *R v Hunt* in detail simply because it is mentioned in the quotation – focus on the meaning of Lord Griffiths' words and the legal principle arising from the case.

Bibliography

Advisory Group on Video-Recorded Evidence (1989), Report ('Pigot Report'). London: Home Office
Auld LJ (2001), *A Review of the Criminal Courts of England and Wales*
Birch, D. (1995), 'Corroboration: goodbye to all that', Crim LR 525

Guided tour of the companion website

 Book resources are available to download. Print your own **Attack the question** and **Diagram plans**.

 Additional **Essay and Problem questions** with **Diagram plans** arranged by topic for each chapter give you more opportunity to practise and hone your exam skills. Print and email your answers.

 You be the marker gives you a chance to evaluate sample exam answers for different question types for each topic and understand how and why an examiner awards marks. Use the accompanying guidance to get the most out of every question and recognise what makes a good answer.

All this and more can be found when you visit
www.pearsoned.co.uk/lawexpressqa

Table of cases and statutes

■ Cases

Al Fayed *v* Commissioner of Police of the Metropolis [2002] EWCA Civ 780 **242**

Al-Khawaja *v* UK (2009) App No. 26766/05, EctHR **70, 79**

Allen *v* UK (2002) App. No. 76574/01 **217, 222**

Ashburton *v* Pape [1913] 2 Ch 469 **218**

Associated Provincial Pictures Houses *v* Wednesbury Corporation [1947] 1 KB 223 **141, 187, 193, 197, 206, 244, 249**

AT & T Istel Ltd *v* Tully [1992] 3 All ER 523 **220**

Attorney General *v* Hitchcock (1847) 1 Exch 91 **51, 245**

Attorney General's Reference (No.1 of 2004) [2004] EWCA Crim 1025, [2004] 1 WLR 2111, CA **6**

Attorney-General's Reference (No.2 of 2001) [2003] UKHL 68 **21**

Attorney-General's Reference (No.3 of 2000) [2001] 1 WLR 2061 **132**

Averill *v* UK (2000) App. No. 36408/97 **174**

Balabel *v* Air India [1988] 2 WLR 1036, CA **216**

Balfour *v* Foreign and Commonwealth Office [1994] 2 All ER 588 **216**

Beckford *v* R (1993) 97 Cr App R 409 (PC) **152, 157, 161, 162, 167**

Benedetto and Labrador *v* R [2003] 1 WLR 1545, PC **198**

Blunt *v* Park Lane Hotel [1942] 2 KB 253 **213, 217, 220, 222**

Blyth *v* Blyth [1966] 2 WLR 634 **242**

Brannigan *v* Davison [1997] AC 238 **221**

Brown *v* Stott [2001] 2 WLR 817 **220, 221**

Butler *v* Board of Trade [1970] 3 WLR 822 **241**

C plc *v* P (Secretary of State for the Home Office Intervening) [2007] 3 WLR 437 **221**

Calcraft *v* Guest [1898] 1 QB 759 **22, 216, 241, 242**

CG *v* UK (2001) App No. 43373 **48**

Chard *v* Chard [1956] P 259 **19**

Chief Adjudication Officer *v* Bath [2000] 1 FLR 8 **240**

Condron *v* UK (2001) 31 EHRR 1 **173, 177, 178**

Conway *v* Rimmer [1968] 2 WLR 998 **211, 213, 215, 216, 225**

Crescent Farm (Sidcup) Sports *v* Sterling Offices Ltd [1972] 2 WLR 91 **241**

Den Norske Bank ASA *v* Antonatos [1999] QB 271 **219, 220**

Doorson *v* The Netherlands (1996) App. No. 14448/88 (ECtHR) **78**

DPP *v* Boardman [1974] 3 WLR 673 **109**

DPP *v* Kilbourne [1973] AC 729, HL **21, 139**

DPP *v* M [1998] 2 WLR 604 **34**

DPP *v* P [1991] 3 WLR 161, HL **109**

DPP *v* Stonehouse [1978] AC 55 **16**

Duncan *v* Cammell Laird & Co Ltd [1942] AC 624 **213**

Edwards *v* R [2006] UKPC 23 **152**

Freemantle *v* R [1994] 1 WLR 1437, PC **152, 157, 161, 167, 193**

Funke *v* France [1993] 16 EHRR 297 **221**

Garton *v* Hunter (1969) 2 QB 37 **22**

Goddard *v* Nationwide Building Society [1986] 3 WLR 734, CA **217**

Guinness Peat Properties *v* Fitzroy Robinson Partnership [1987] 1 WLR 1027 **241**

▉ Statutes

Statutory Instruments

Practice Directions

Conventions

Other jurisdictions

Introductory concepts

1

How this topic may come up in exams

The principles of admissibility, relevance, judicial discretion and weight are all interlinked and pervasive. They can appear more than once in either essay or problem question format. For example, admissibility relates to the rule of law (e.g. see s.76 PACE 1984 in Chapter 7) or exclusionary rules (e.g. see Chapters 4 and 5). Relevance and admissibility relate to improperly obtained evidence (see Chapter 7). Admissible evidence is also subject to judicial discretion (see Chapters 1, 4, 6 and 7). Issues of burden and standard of proof and presumptions are also favourites for problem style questions. But be prepared for burden of proof to appear also in essay format.

Attack the question

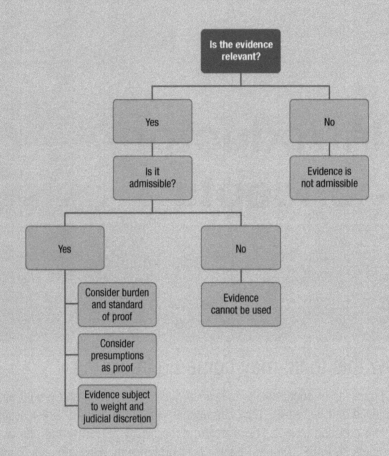

🖋 Question 1

'… wherever a burden of proof is placed upon the defendant by statute the burden should be an evidential burden and not a persuasive burden … My Lords, [this] fundamental change is, in my view, a matter for Parliament and not a decision of your Lordships' House.' (Lord Griffiths in *R* v *Hunt* [1987] AC 352, HL)

Critically evaluate the above quotation with reference to decided case law on the reversal of the burden of proof and consider whether the current approach offends Art.6 of the European Convention on Human Rights.

Answer plan

→ Explain the difference between the evidential and the legal burden.

→ Explain the general principle of who bears the burden and standard of proof.

→ Explain, using case law, how and when a reverse burden occurs.

→ Analyse the rationale for this.

→ Does the approach offend against Art.6?

Diagram plan

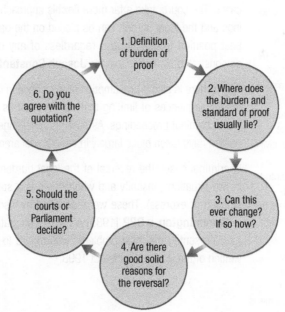

1. Definition of burden of proof

2. Where does the burden and standard of proof usually lie?

3. Can this ever change? If so how?

4. Are there good solid reasons for the reversal?

5. Should the courts or Parliament decide?

6. Do you agree with the quotation?

A printable version of this diagram plan is available from www.pearsoned.co.uk/lawexpressqa

[1]The question relates to the burden of proof, so start with a definition of this concept so that the examiner is aware that you understand there are two aspects to the burden of proof.

[2] It is not necessary to give the full case citation in an answer to an examination question and this would not usually earn you extra points. Usually the case name will suffice. However, some institutions will expect you to cite both the case name and the year. Full citations of cases appear throughout the answers in this book for reference purposes.

[3] It is important to explain the general principle before going on to deal with reverse burdens so that the examiner can see that you understand that reverse burdens are not the norm.

[4] Although the quotation relates to a criminal case (*R v Hunt*), the question itself is not restricted to criminal cases. You should therefore show the examiner that you understand that reverse burdens can happen in civil cases as well.

[5] If you intend to concentrate mainly on the criminal jurisdiction it is important to explain to the examiner why you have done this.

[6] It is important to now discuss when and how reverse burden occur in criminal proceedings as this is the focus of your answer.

Answer

The burden of proof has two elements: the legal (or persuasive) burden of proof is the obligation to prove a fact in issue whilst the evidential burden is the obligation to adduce sufficient evidence to justify the matter being left to the jury. The party who bears the legal burden will also bear the evidential burden.[1]

In criminal cases the 'golden rule' is that the prosecution will bear the legal burden of proof (per Viscount Sankey LC in **Woolmington *v* DPP** [1935] AC 462).[2] This principle is based on the presumption that an accused is innocent until proven guilty which has been established as a right under Art. 6(2) of the European Convention on Human Rights (ECHR). The standard of proof is 'beyond reasonable doubt'.[3]

In civil proceedings Lord Maugham in **Joseph Constantine Steamship Line v Imperial Smelting Corporation** [1942] AC 154, HL said 'he who asserts must prove'. Therefore, the claimant will normally bear the legal burden. The standard of proof is 'on a balance of probabilities'.[4]

It is possible for the legal burden to be reversed in civil and criminal cases. The courts take a far more flexible approach in civil proceedings and the legal burden can be placed on the party who is in the best position to discharge it regardless of any counterclaim, as demonstrated by the facts in the **Joseph Constantine** case.

Whilst there is also a presumption of innocence in civil proceedings, the consequences of limiting that right are not as extreme as they are in criminal proceedings. As such the challenges to the reverse burden have taken place largely in the criminal arena.[5]

In criminal cases the reversal of the legal burden of proof occurs in two situations, insanity and where there is a statutory exception (implied or express). These were identified by Viscount Sankey LC in **Woolmington *v* DPP** [1935] AC 462. The statutory exceptions have presented the most problems with regard to possible contravention of the Human Rights Act 1998.[6]

[7] The question asks you to consider reverse burdens in the context of Art.6 of the ECHR. It is necessary to mention the Human Rights Act 1998, which incorporates the Articles from the ECHR.

[8] The question asks you to evaluate the quotation with reference to decided cases and so you must make some attempt to compare and contrast cases in this area.

[9] As the quotation suggests that there is a movement that favours treating reverse burdens as evidential burdens, you need to discuss whether case law has followed this majority view.

[10] You must put Lord Griffiths' quotation into some context and start to evaluate the next part of the question, which is whether the quotation reflects the modern day approach to reverse burdens.

Since the 1998 Act came into force there have been a number of conflicting decisions in relation to whether an express or implied legal burden on the defendant should be upheld. The consensus is no longer that the legal burden should always be treated as an evidential burden as suggested in Lord Griffiths' quotation.[7]

In the case of **R v Lambert** [2001] 3 WLR 206, HL, which was heard before the 1998 Act came into effect, Lord Steyn observed that certain defences were so closely linked with the *mens rea* that it would be unfair to transfer the legal burden to the defendant. **Lambert** followed the approach in **Salabiaku v France** (1998) 13 EHRR 379 of considering whether the limitation of the Art. 6(2) right pursues a legitimate aim (this would involve looking at the mischief at which the statute was aimed) and satisfies the principle of proportionality. Their Lordships favoured a proactive approach and read down the legal burden in s.28(3) as being no more than an evidential burden.[8]

However, the legal burden has not in fact been read down in all cases. For example, in the case of **Sheldrake v DPP, Attorney-General's Reference (No. 4 of 2002)** [2004] 3 WLR 976, whilst the court approved the 'legitimacy' and 'proportionality' approach in **Lambert**, they felt that a reverse burden did not always prevent a fair trial and it was recognised that Art. 6 is not an absolute right. The protection of members of the public was considered equally important to the outcome of this case.[9]

Lord Griffiths' quotation recognises that a blanket principle that a legal burden on the defendant should not apply would be a fundamental change that only Parliament should make.[10] This recognises the need for judges to avoid making law. It is worth noting that Lord Griffiths' comments in **R v Hunt** [1987] AC 352, HL relate in particular to s.101 of the Magistrates' Court Act 1980. This is an example of an attempt by Parliament to legislate on the issue of implied statutory exceptions in the magistrates' court. The 1980 Act places a legal burden on the defendant where there is reliance on 'any exception, exemption, proviso, excuse or qualification'. Yet, despite this, the provisions have been largely ignored or the courts have

[11] Because Lord Griffiths' quotation suggests that only Parliament should make the fundamental change, it is helpful to look at whether Parliament has ever attempted to legislate in this area before.

[12] You need to start reaching a view following your evaluation. It does not matter to the examiner which view you take as long as you can support that view with convincing arguments. A short summary of the strengths and weaknesses will help to lead into your conclusion.

circumvented the Act. See, for example, **Hirst v Chief Constable of West Yorkshire** (1986) 85 Cr App R 143. As stated in **Hunt**, when deciding whether the 1980 Act should apply, each case will turn on the construction of statute relating to the offence itself.[11]

In fact s.3 of the Human Rights Act envisages a statutory interpretation approach to all UK statutes followed by a declaration of incompatibility before Parliament intervenes. However, there are some disadvantages to statutory interpretation such as the scope for inconsistency.[12] For example the 'legitimacy' and 'proportionality' approach in **Lambert** was not followed in the case of **R v Johnstone** [2003] 1 WLR 1736, where Lord Nicholls favoured a more cautious approach. His view was that when interpreting a statute the court should only reach a different view from Parliament about the incidence of the legal burden if it seemed Parliament had not paid enough consideration to the presumption of innocence. In the case of **Attorney-General's Reference (No. 1 of 2004)** [2004] 1 WLR 2111 Lord Woolf CJ stated that the approach in **Johnstone** rather than **Lambert** should be followed. However, **Sheldrake** did not consider that the two decisions were incompatible, just that they dealt with different kinds of statutes.

The advantage of statutory interpretation is that it also provides flexibility. It is because Art.6 is not an absolute right that the courts are arguably better able than Parliament to consider matters on a case-by-case basis. It is also because each statute is different that a flexible approach is required.

The Human Rights Act has enabled the courts to take a fresh look at various offences and to apply statutory interpretation. This avoids the need for multiple legislation to review every statute bearing an express or implied reverse burden. Reverse burdens operate in many jurisdictions and Art.6 cases such as **Salabiaku** favour consideration of Art.6 in the process of statutory interpretation rather than eliminating reverse burdens altogether. The modern approach is that there should not be a fundamental rule on reverse burdens and each case should be looked at based on interpretation of the statute relating to the offence.

Make your answer stand out

■ Discuss in detail the factors that the court should consider when deciding whether to uphold a reverse burden as identified by Lord Steyn in *R* v *Johnstone* (above), e.g. the seriousness of the offence.

■ Mention additional cases involving reverse burdens such as *L* v *DPP* [2002] 3 WLR 863 and *R* v *Ali*; *R* v *Jordan* [2001] 2 WLR 211.

■ Develop the discussion relating to s.101 Magistrates' Court Act 1980.

■ Discuss Lord Clyde's argument in *Lambert* that reverse burdens should be upheld where the offence is regulatory in nature.

! **Don't be tempted to...**

■ Write everything you know about burden and standard of proof – avoid lengthy definitions and moot points about how the standard of 'beyond reasonable doubt' and 'on a balance of probabilities' should be explained. The question requires you to focus on the issue of reverse burdens.

■ Ignore the quotation given in the question – whilst a brief mention of the facts is permissible you need to analyse whether or not Parliament should legislate in this area rather than leaving the courts to use statutory interpretation.

■ Discuss the facts of *R* v *Hunt* in detail simply because it is mentioned in the quotation – focus on the meaning of Lord Griffiths' words and the legal principle arising from the case.

❓ Question 2

Consider the various standard and burden of proof and presumptions that arise in the following situations:

(a) Toby is charged with the murder of Vanessa. Toby pleads not guilty due to diminished responsibility under s.2(2) of the Homicide Act 1957 (as amended by s.52 of the Coroners and Justice Act 2009). Advise Toby.

(b) Jay is being sued for personal injury in the civil courts following a road traffic accident when he is alleged to have hit a pedestrian whilst driving at speed. Jay was convicted in the local magistrates' court of dangerous driving. Advise Jay.

(c) In a civil case brought by Aesthetics Ltd against the owners of a warehouse, Storage Elite Ltd, Aesthetics Ltd allege that Storage Elite are in breach of their contract because they failed to deliver valuable art works stored by them to a major gallery exhibition. Storage Elite argue that the contract was frustrated due to a fire at the warehouse which meant they were unable to deliver the art works in time. Aesthetics Ltd claim that the fire was self-induced and caused by the negligence of Storage Elite. Advise Aesthetics Ltd.

(d) Holly is charged under s.137(1) of the Highways Act 1980 on the basis that she wilfully obstructed the highway without lawful excuse by sitting in the road during a peaceful demonstration against the use of GM products by a well known supermarket. Holly's case is to be heard in the magistrates' court and Holly will say that she had lawful excuse as the demonstration was on an issue of public concern. The Act is silent as to which party bears the burden of proof. Advise Holly.

Answer plan

→ Consider issues of reverse burden of proof in criminal cases for Toby.

→ Discuss issues of presumptions under s.11 Civil Evidence Act 1968 for Jay.

→ Examine issue of reverse burdens in contract cases for Aesthetics Ltd.

→ Consider issues of implied statutory exceptions under s.101 Magistrates' Court Act 1980 for Holly.

→ Provide relevant advice to all four characters.

Diagram plan

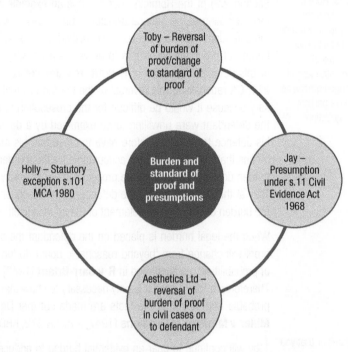

Toby – Reversal of burden of proof/change to standard of proof

Holly – Statutory exception s.101 MCA 1980

Burden and standard of proof and presumptions

Jay – Presumption under s.11 Civil Evidence Act 1968

Aesthetics Ltd – reversal of burden of proof in civil cases on to defendant

A printable version of this diagram plan is available from www.pearsoned.co.uk/lawexpressqa

[1] Your introduction should show the examiner that you are aware of all the evidential issues covered by the problem question and therefore the topics you will be addressing are burden and standard of proof and presumptions. This is a good structure and will ensure your answer remains focused.

[2] Explain the general principle here so that the examiner is aware that you have appreciated that reverse burdens only occur in certain situations.

Answer

In order to advise the various parties it is necessary to consider who bears the burden of proof and whether any presumptions of proof apply. It is also necessary to consider the standard of proof.[1]

Toby

In criminal proceedings the burden and standard of proof normally rests with the prosecution, as observed by Viscount Sankey LC in **Woolmington v DPP** [1935] AC 462. The case of **R v Bentley (Deceased)** [2001] 1 Cr App R 307 also confirmed that the judge should direct the jury as to where the burden of proof lies.[2]

[3] You should always refer back to the facts. Here it is necessary to show the examiner that you understand that when the legal burden is reversed in criminal proceedings the standard of proof also changes otherwise you will only have partially addressed the question.

Toby intends to plead not guilty due to diminished responsibility. Section 2(2) of the Homicide Act 1957 is an example of a statutory exception to the general principle.[3] Under this provision when the defendant raises a defence of diminished responsibility the legal burden of proof will be on him to prove the necessary ingredients of this defence. The case of **R v Ali**; **R v Jordan** [2001] 2 WLR 211, CA rationalised this reversal of the burden of proof as necessary because it would be difficult for the prosecution to disprove if the defendant were unwilling to be examined by a doctor. Toby or his defence team will therefore have to prove that his mental state means that he cannot be held accountable for the murder. The legal burden does not move from the prosecution but is simply placed on Toby at the stage of proving the defence. The prosecution still bears the burden of proving every element of the offence itself.

When the legal burden is placed on the defendant the standard of proof will change from 'beyond reasonable doubt' to 'on a balance of probabilities', as confirmed in **R v Carr-Briant** [1943] 1 KB 607. Therefore, in Toby's case it is only necessary to show that 'it is more probable than not' that the facts are made out (per Denning J in **Miller v Minister of Pensions** [1947] 2 All ER 372, KBD).

[4] Show the examiner that you are aware that the reversal of proof involves the legal (persuasive) rather than the evidential burden.

Toby will continue to bear an evidential burden to adduce sufficient evidence to leave the defence of diminished responsibility to the jury to consider. This will mean that Toby will have to either testify or call witnesses on his behalf.[4]

Jay

[5] Set out the relevant statutory provision when discussing presumptions and show the examiner that you are aware which exception applies.

It is possible for Jay's criminal conviction in the magistrates' court to be used in the civil proceedings. This is because under s.11 Civil Evidence Act 1968 a criminal conviction can be used in civil proceedings and it will raise a persuasive presumption of law.[5] The party relying on the presumption (in this case the claimant who is suing Jay) will still have to prove the presumed fact and this can be done by producing a record of the conviction.

[6] This shows the examiner that you are aware that the presumption you are discussing is a rebuttable rather than an irrebuttable presumption.

The burden will be deemed to have been discharged. It will then be for Jay to rebut the presumption by showing why the conviction is not conclusive.[6] This will be difficult unless he can show the conviction has been successfully appealed. The standard of proof will be on a balance of probabilities.[7]

Aesthetics Ltd

[8] This alerts the examiner to the fact that you are aware of the general principle, so the examiner can see that you have identified what makes your advice different.

As Aesthetics Ltd are bringing the action they will be the claimants and ordinarily in civil proceedings the legal burden of proof will be on the claimant.[8] In **Joseph Constantine Steamship Line v Imperial Smelting Corporation** [1942] AC 154, HL Lord Maugham stated that 'he who asserts must prove'. However, in civil proceedings there are also exceptions to the general principle of which party bears the legal burden.[9] In contract cases it is possible to expressly state where the burden of proof is to lie. The facts are silent as to whether this is the case here. The facts here are similar to the facts in the case of **Joseph Constantine** (above).[10] In that case the plaintiffs alleged that frustration could not be relied upon if the explosion had been caused by the ship owner's negligence. The issue was who had to prove or disprove negligence on the part of the ship owners. The House of Lords held that it was for the plaintiffs to prove that the ship owners had been negligent. In the circumstances as Aesthetics Ltd are alleging that the fire was caused by the negligence of Storage Elite the burden of proof rests on them. The standard of proof will be on a balance of probabilities.

[9] Show the examiner you are aware that an exception applies.

[10] As the facts in the case are similar to the problem it is fine to discuss the facts of the case briefly here. Ordinarily you would only focus on the legal principle arising from the case.

Holly

[11] The examiner will know that you have understood from the facts that Holly has to prove a negative element of the offence.

It is necessary to consider whether Holly bears the legal burden of proving the negative element of the offence under s.137(1) of the Highways Act 1980,[11] namely that she had lawful excuse to obstruct the highway. As the Act is silent[12] and the matter is to be heard in the magistrates' court then s.101 of the Magistrates' Court Act 1980 is of importance. This provides that where a defendant relies on an exception, exemption, proviso, excuse or qualification in a statutory offence the burden of proving the exception rests on the defendant. This would suggest that Holly bears a legal burden of proof to show that she was acting with lawful authority and the standard of proof will be on a balance of probabilities.

[12] Here you have identified that this is an important issue because it allows s.101 to be considered.

However, the case law in this area is far from clear cut, with a number of cases showing that, despite the wording of s.101 of the 1980 Act, judges have nonetheless maintained that the legal

[13] Showing that you understand that this area of law is unclear, with conflicting cases on the application of s.101, demonstrates some analysis by you and will gain higher marks.

[14] Show the examiner that you know the facts in the problem are similar to those in the *Hirst* case but also that the case does not help you because s.101 was ignored in that case.

[15] Offer some explanation as to how the court might deal with Holly's case in the absence of clear guidelines.

burden of proof should remain with the prosecution in such cases.[13] Whilst the facts are similar to the case of **Hirst v Chief Constable of West Yorkshire** (1986) 85 Cr App R 143, DC, s.101 of the 1980 Act was ignored in this case and so is not of help here.[14]

Lord Griffiths in the case of **R v Hunt** [1987] AC 352 reconfirmed that it is for the courts to interpret and construe the statute to decide whether a defence is an exception or not. It is possible that the court will consider that imposing a legal burden on Holly would offend against the Human Rights Act 1998.[15]

In conclusion, Toby would bear a legal burden of proof but only on the defence of diminished responsibility; Jay would be able to rely on a persuasive presumption under s.11 of the Civil Evidence Act 1968. Aesthetics Ltd would bear the burden of proving the contract was frustrated by negligence. In respect of Holly, the court would use statutory interpretation of s.137 of the Highways Act as well as consideration of the Human Rights Act in deciding whether to apply the principle in the 1980 Act.

 Make your answer stand out

- In respect of Toby, you could also discuss the fact that the judge is likely to direct the jury on the standard of proof by using the sure test as set out in *R v Summers* [1952] 1 All ER 1059, CCA or the wording in the Judicial Studies Board guidelines on directions (*Crown Court Bench Book*).

- In respect of Jay you could discuss the case of *Stupple v Royal Insurance Co Ltd* [1970] 3 WLR 217 and the conflicting views between Buckley LJ and Lord Denning MR as to the value of the presumption under s.11 of the 1968 Act.

- In respect of Aesthetics Ltd you could refer to additional cases such as *Munro Brice & Co v War Risks Association* [1918] 2 KB 78 or more current cases to illustrate the reverse burden in civil cases.

- In respect of Holly you could discuss cases such as *Jaggard v Dickinson* [1981] 2 WLR 118 where, despite s.101 of the 1980 Act, the burden of proof remained with the prosecution.

📋 Question 3

Evaluate the extent to which the functions of a judge and jury remain separate and distinct in the case of jury trials in the UK adversarial system.

Answer plan

→ Explain the traditional role of the judge and jury.

→ Give examples of how and when the role of the judge crosses over into considerations of fact.

→ Rationalise why this is necessary.

→ Can this approach be defended?

Diagram plan

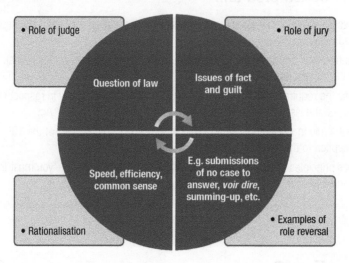

A printable version of this diagram plan is available from www.pearsoned.co.uk/lawexpressqa

Answer

[1] Outlining the roles of the judge and jury operating in the English legal system in the introduction shows that you have understood the roles are generally regarded as separate.

The English trial process is an adversarial system. The court does not conduct the search for relevant evidence to present at trial but instead relies on the parties to do this. The function of the judge will be based largely on questions of law and the jury will decide questions of fact.[1]

[2] You have been asked to evaluate the quotation and this involves looking at ways it may be true as well as ways it may be false. A reference to the quotation also shows the examiner that your answer is focused.

To some extent these functions are separate and distinct but in other respects the functions can converge as indicated in the above quotation.[2] The role of the jury can never cross into the role of the judiciary but the reverse cannot be said to be true. There are a number of stages during the trial when the judge is required to consider issues of fact.

[3] Try to support each argument with at least one case, more if you can.

The first example can be found when looking at submissions of 'no case to answer', when the judge will be required to decide whether the case should be left to the jury to decide. Under Lord Lane's test in **R v Galbraith** [1981] 2 All ER 1060[3] decisions as to the cogency or the probity of the evidence which would normally be dealt with by the jury are in fact decided by the judge at an early stage where the evidence is tenuous or weak. The evidence is then

4 By looking at safeguards you balance your analysis as it shows that whilst the roles may sometimes converge this is not necessarily detrimental.

dismissed by the judge before consideration by the jury. However, there are safeguards[4] within the **Galbraith** test to ensure that the jury's role is not usurped completely. Lord Lane made it clear that where the strength or weakness of a piece of evidence depends on for example the unreliability of a witness then such matters should be left to the jury.

The second area of convergence arises when the judge considers the relevance of evidence in order to decide on admissibility. Whilst evidence must be relevant in order to be admissible, not all relevant evidence will be admissible. This can be seen in cases such as **R v Leatham** (1861) 25 JP 468 reconfirmed in later cases such as **Jeffrey v Black** [1978] QB 490. The consideration of relevance involves a consideration of the cogency of the evidence which would normally be within the function of the jury.

Another example can be found in the *voir dire* process. The judge will effectively conduct a trial within a trial in the absence of the jury to decide on the admissibility of a piece of evidence. As part of this role the judge will also have to carry out a factual inquiry. Lord Goddard CJ expressed dissatisfaction with this practice in the case of **R v Reynolds** [1950] 1 KB 606 and was of the opinion that deciding preliminary facts in the absence of a jury should be confined to exceptional cases such as the admissibility of a confession.[5]

5 Highlighting cases such as *R* v *Reynolds* that challenge the role of the judge shows that you have attempted some critical analysis of this part of the judge's role and this will earn you additional marks.

A similar approach is taken in the case of decisions on the competency of a witness. The judge can hear factual evidence as to a witness's competence including medical evidence. In the case of **R v Deakin** [1994] 4 All ER 769 the Court of Appeal drew a strong line between where the question of competence is a matter of admissibility and where it is a matter of weight for the jury. Expert testimony that a witness is capable of telling the truth encroaches on the jury's role to consider the weight of the evidence.

It is also arguable that the summing-up by the judge at the end of the trial (whilst designed to assist the jury in recalling the evidence) can influence the jury's fact finding role if it is not conducted correctly. Whilst in the case of **R v Marr** (1989) 90 Cr App Rep 154 the Court of Appeal reiterated that judges cannot direct the jury to accept their version of disputed facts, cases such as **R v Everett** [1995] Crim LR 76, have highlighted the dangers of judiciary opinion seeping into the summing-up. The Judicial Studies Board

1 INTRODUCTORY CONCEPTS

[6] You should draw on published reports such as the Royal Commission's Report to support your answer as it shows evidence of a wider understanding of the subject and will earn you additional marks.

[7] Reference to comparative jurisdictions such as the United States shows evidence of analysis as well as wider reading and will help you to gain extra marks as it gives depth to your answer and marks you out as a good student.

[8] Show the examiner that you appreciate that the quotation is not clear cut and is capable of a contrary view as this shows critical thinking.

[9] This shows the examiner that you are attempting to challenge the statement in the question that the United Kingdom is a purely adversarial system.

Guidelines recommend that judges should tell the jury to disregard evidence as unimportant if they want to even if the judge has emphasised such evidence in the summing-up.

The Royal Commission on Criminal Justice in their report, *A Review of the Criminal Courts of England and Wales* (2001), ch. 10, para. 209[6] recommended that the judge should give the jury a fuller explanation of their task as jurors and the judge should support his summing-up with a written *aide-memoire* similar to the approach adopted in the Unites States.[7]

It is true that the one area the judge cannot encroach on during the summing-up is the jury's right to decide on the accused's guilt.[8] This can be seen in the case of **DPP v Stonehouse** [1978] AC 55, where the House of Lords held that even if on the facts a reasonably directed jury must reach a verdict of guilt the matter must still be left to the jury.

Another area in which the jury's fact finding role is weakened is in the case of presumptions where certain facts may be presumed to exist even in the absence of complete proof. The effect of applying a presumption is to remove the jury's fact finding role in relation to that particular issue. Whilst rebuttable presumptions such as the presumption of death and the presumption of legitimacy still enable juries to consider facts presented in rebuttal, irrebuttable presumptions such as the presumption of innocence of a child under 10 would not allow juries to consider any factual evidence to the contrary.

Judicial notice is another area where the judicial role crosses over to a fact finding role but has benefits for common sense and administrative efficiency. Judges are able to use their general knowledge of the world and dispense with the need for evidence on the basis that the facts are 'notorious'.

It is worth noting that civil and criminal proceedings have become more inquisitorial in nature since the introduction of the Civil Procedure Rules 1998 and Criminal Procedure Rules 2011.[9] The court through its case management powers now has far more control over the collection of evidence prior to trial.

[10] Reaching a final view is important for a well-structured answer. As long as your view is supported by convincing arguments it does not matter whether the examiner would have reached a different view.

It can therefore be seen that issues of fact are often present in issues of law and it is not always possible to separate the two. Wherever possible, judges must limit their role to questions of law and leave matters of fact for the jury. However, the proper administration of justice requires that for efficiency, speed and common sense removing factual issues from the trial proceedings avoids the jury being over-burdened with irrelevant weak or inadmissible evidence.[10]

 Make your answer stand out

- Discuss more examples of where the role of the judge and jury meet, such as in defamation cases on the meaning and usage of words.
- Refer to comparative jurisdictions, such as the United States, where advocates approach the bench to discuss some issues of admissibility with the judge whilst the jury remain in the courtroom.
- Use further cases on the role of the judge such as *R* v *Bentley (Deceased)* [2001] 1 Cr App R 307.
- Refer to academic opinion such as R. Pattenden, 'Pre-verdict judicial fact-finding in criminal trials with juries' (2009) 29 OJLS 1 when discussing the role of the jury.

! **Don't be tempted to...**

- Discuss the separate role of the judge and jury without attempting to analyse how these roles are not always separate and distinct.
- Discuss areas where there is clearly no convergence, such as in the judge's role in deciding questions of law.
- Avoid reaching a reasoned conclusion as to whether the functions are completely separate and distinct.

❓ Question 4

Consider the following extracts from the decisions of the fictional cases heard by his Honour Judge Pedigrin in a number of criminal and civil trials:

(a) 'The applicant seeks a remedy of specific performance against ABX Insurance Company on the basis that they have refused to pay out against her husband's insurance policy. Her husband has been missing for six years and 364 days and was last seen close to a beach in Marbella. I have found in favour of the applicant on the basis that her husband can be presumed to be dead and therefore the insurance monies should be paid despite the fact that they were separated.'

(b) 'The claimant has alleged in civil proceedings that there is no need to prove that the bale of hay which fell on the road and with which the claimant's vehicle collided fell from the defendant's tractor because even though the claimant did not see the tractor the bale of hay has the name of the defendant's farm written on it. However, in my view it is still necessary for the defendant to prove the absence of negligence.'

(c) 'The prosecution have addressed me on the fact that the charge of rape against the defendant took six years to reach trial and that I should dismiss the case on the basis that it is an abuse of process. I do not believe that I have the power to do this.'

(d) 'The claimant in her breach of contract action has produced a copy of the original contract. I have taken the view that whilst the contract is relevant a copy is not admissible as only the original can be regarded as admissible evidence.'

Consider whether the above decisions can be subject to appeal.

Answer plan

➡ Discuss the requirement for the presumption of death and why these do not apply on the facts.

➡ Examine the presumption of *res ipsa loquitur* and how this applies to the facts.

➡ Consider whether the delay is an abuse of process.

➡ Discuss the best evidence rule.

Diagram plan

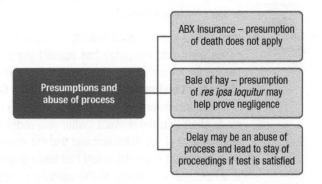

A printable version of this diagram plan is available from www.pearsoned.co.uk/lawexpressqa

Answer

When considering the various decisions of Judge Pedigrin it is clear that he has made a number of errors, which may lead to those decisions being appealed. The errors relate to the application of presumptions, abuse of process and admissibility.

(a) With regard to the first extract the judge is asked to apply the presumption of death. Presumptions are a rule of law whereby proof of the primary fact will also be taken to have proved the secondary fact (which in this case is death).[1] The claimant bears an evidential burden. However, before the presumption can be applied there must be an absence of any evidence to suggest that the person was alive during a continuous period of seven years. In this case the claimant's husband was sighted six years and 364 days ago on a beach in Marbella. The seven-year condition has not been satisfied.[2] In addition, it must be shown that there is likely to be someone who would have heard from him but has not. In the case of **Chard v Chard** [1956] P 259 this was considered to be a necessary requirement. Therefore, as the applicant was separated from her husband she cannot necessarily be said to be a person likely to have heard from him.[3]

The final requirement is that it is necessary to show that all necessary enquiries have been made to locate the husband without success. There is no information that suggests the nature of the

[1] Providing a definition of presumptions in this way alerts the examiner to the fact that you have a basic level of understanding of the subject area and this is a good basis upon which to develop your answer.

[2] By recognising an important clue in the question you demonstrate an ability to select and apply the relevant law to the facts and this in turn demonstrates practical skills on your part.

[3] Stating an important legal principle arising from a case and then applying it to the facts demonstrates an ability to recognise and apply case law.

[4] Reaching a final view is necessary as you have been asked to consider whether the decision is capable of appeal. This shows that you are able to understand what the question requires of you.

enquiries that were made particularly following the husband's sighting in Marbella. In the circumstances the judge was wrong to apply the presumption.[4]

(b) With regard to the second extract, this appears to be a negligence case and the judge has applied the presumption of negligence known as *res ipsa loquitur*. As shown in the case of **Scott v London and St Katherine Docks Co** (1865) 3 H & C 596, this means that the claimant may rely on this principle to show that the relevant matter was under the control or management of the defendant and that the accident would not have happened if the defendant had taken proper care. In the absence of any evidence to the contrary a presumption will arise. However, it is a rebuttable presumption.[5] On the facts it would appear that it was reasonable for the judge to allow this presumption as it is reasonable to suggest that the bale of hay was under the control or management of the defendants as it had their name and address on it. The judge is wrong to suggest that it is still necessary for the defendant to prove the absence of negligence. The claimant in fact bears the legal burden to show the relevant matter was in the control of the defendants.[6] However, the defendant only bears the evidential burden to produce sufficient evidence to rebut the presumption as seen in cases such as **Ng Chun Pui v Lee Chuen Tat** (1988) RTR 298. It is fair to say that the case law is conflicting in this area with previous cases, such as **Ward v Tesco Stores Ltd** [1976] 1 WLR 810, suggesting that the defendant bears a legal burden. However, recent cases such as **Ng Chun** and **Ratcliffe v Plymouth & Torbay Health Authority** [1998] Lloyd's Rep Med 162, CA suggest otherwise.[7]

[5] This demonstrates a deeper knowledge on your part as the examiner can see that you have understood that different presumptions have different evidential value.

[6] An ability to recognise errors in the decision demonstrates that you have a command of the subject area necessary for the correct application of the law to the facts.

[7] Comparing and contrasting cases in this way will earn you more marks as it shows an ability to critically evaluate the law.

(c) With regard to the third extract, the judge is wrong to state that he does not have power to dismiss a case for abuse of process. The judge has an inherent jurisdiction to stay proceedings for abuse of process if the defendant cannot receive a fair trial or it would be unfair for the accused to be tried (see **R v Horseferry**

Road Magistrates' Court, ex parte Bennett [1993] 3 WLR 90, HL. However, a stay of proceedings is regarded as an extreme remedy as indicated in **Attorney-General's Reference (No. 2 of 2001)** [2003] UKHL 68. In the case of delay not all examples of delay will be sufficient to warrant a stay of proceedings. For example, there was no stay in the case of **R v Sawoniuk** [2000] 2 Cr App Rep 220, where the defendant was tried for war crimes some 58 years after the offences occurred. The trial was not dismissed as an abuse of process as there were sufficient eyewitnesses and documentation to ensure that the evidence given was reliable. As an alternative the judge can offer a public reproach to the prosecution regarding the delay or if the defendant is on remand release him on bail or expedite the hearing so that no further delay occurs.[8]

(d) With regard to the final extract, the judge was wrong to dismiss the use of a copy of a contract as evidence. Evidence is admissible if it is probative of some matter to be proved or disproved (see **DPP v Kilbourne** [1973] AC 729, HL) and does not fall foul of an exclusionary rule and is not excluded by the judge exercising his general discretion under s.78 or s.82(3) of the Police and Criminal Evidence Act 1984. Historically, the 'best evidence' rule required that primary rather than secondary evidence be admitted as proof.[9] The original contract would be regarded as primary evidence and the copy as secondary evidence. Whilst the rule has not been formally abolished it is no longer considered to apply. For example, in the case of **Springsteen v Masquerade Music Ltd** [2001] EMLR 654 the best evidence rule was expressed as 'dead'. However, if the original document is readily available but is not produced then the judge may comment on this and decide to give less weight to the copy produced. There is no need to formally exclude the document.

In the circumstances the claimants and the defendants in each case should be advised to consider appealing the decision of his Honour Judge Pedigrin.

[8] Suggesting alternative action shows that you are able to go beyond a basic answer which merely identifies weaknesses in the decision and actually offer solutions. This will earn you additional marks.

[9] Reference to the historical approach to admissibility of evidence is justified here because it provides a basis for showing that the judge's decision may be outdated. It also shows the examiner that you understand that the law has moved on.

Make your answer stand out

- With regard to the presumptions of death and negligence mention that cases such as *Royal Bank of Scotland* v *Etridge (No. 2)* [2001] UKHL 44 warned against attaching too much weight to presumptions and Lord Reid's comments in *S* v *S* [1972] AC 24 that presumptions should only be considered where the evidence is so evenly balanced that the court cannot reach a decision on it.

- When discussing the debate as to the usefulness of presumptions refer to journal articles such as C. Witting 'Res ipsa loquitur: some last words' (2001) 117 *Law Quarterly Review* 392–397 and D. Mendonca 'Presumptions' (1998) 11(4) *Ratio Juris* 399–412.

- When discussing the best evidence rule, elaborate by discussing the fact that there were so many exceptions to the rule that it became difficult to apply – mention cases such as *Saltern* v *Melhuish* (1754) Amb 246 and *Garton* v *Hunter* [1969] 2 QB 37.

! Don't be tempted to...

- Leave out discussion of how presumptions affect the issue of the legal and evidential burden as presumptions are part of the element of proof.

- When discussing extract (b) mention judicial notice – the facts (i.e. the name and address on the bale of hay) cannot be said to be notorious in any way.

- When discussing extract (c) do not confuse the test for using the remedy of a stay of proceedings for delay with the test for using a stay of proceedings for entrapment. Do not therefore discuss cases such as *R* v *Loosely* [2001] 1 WLR 2.

- Discuss cases such as *Calcraft* v *Guest* [1898] 1 QB 759 for extract (d) on the basis that privilege does not attach to a copy – the facts do not mention privilege as an issue.

Competence and compellability

2

How this topic may come up in exams

The topic of competence and compellability is often examined together with special measures. However, they can each be associated with other topics. For example, competence and compellability is also relevant to the examination of witnesses and special measures can also appear in hearsay questions when looking at s.116(2)(e) of the Criminal Justice Act 2003. Both topics are favourites for inclusion in mixed problem questions. However, it is not unusual to have essay style questions which focus for example on the effectiveness of the Youth Justice and Criminal Evidence Act 1999 and the Coroners and Justice Act 2009.

■ Attack the question

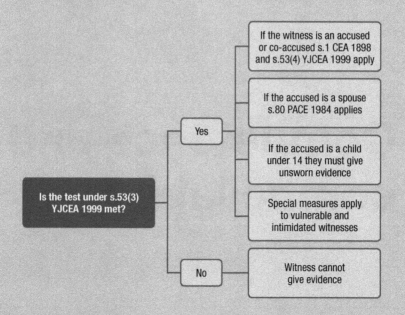

Is the test under s.53(3) YJCEA 1999 met?

Yes

If the witness is an accused or co-accused s.1 CEA 1898 and s.53(4) YJCEA 1999 apply

If the accused is a spouse s.80 PACE 1984 applies

If the accused is a child under 14 they must give unsworn evidence

Special measures apply to vulnerable and intimidated witnesses

No

Witness cannot give evidence

A printable version of this diagram is available from www.pearsoned.co.uk/lawexpressqa

Question 1

'The evidence of victims and other witnesses is crucial to the criminal justice process because prosecutions will founder, and guilty people thus escape justice, if victims and other witnesses are not prepared to make statements to the police and thereafter to give evidence.' (Royal Commission on Criminal Justice: Report Cm.2263 (1993) para.5.44)

Examine whether the Youth Justice and Criminal Evidence Act 1999 and subsequent legislation successfully protects vulnerable and intimidated witnesses.

Answer plan

→ Discuss ss.16 and 17 of the Youth Justice and Criminal Evidence Act 1999.

→ Give examples of the different types of special measures.

→ Discuss the effectiveness or otherwise of special measures for vulnerable and intimidated witnesses.

→ Identify any further powers in legislation since the 1999 Act.

→ Does legislation sufficiently protect such witnesses?

Diagram plan

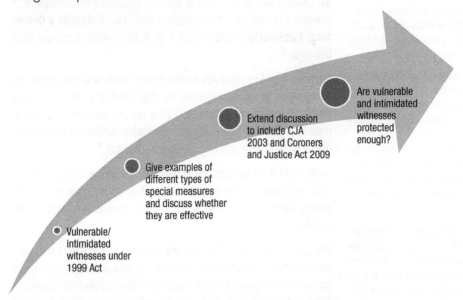

Are vulnerable and intimidated witnesses protected enough?

Extend discussion to include CJA 2003 and Coroners and Justice Act 2009

Give examples of different types of special measures and discuss whether they are effective

Vulnerable/ intimidated witnesses under 1999 Act

A printable version of this diagram plan is available from www.pearsoned.co.uk/lawexpressqa

Answer

In order to be able to give evidence at trial a witness must be competent. If a witness is competent they will also be compellable. Despite this, situations often occur when witnesses refuse to give evidence due to fear or because their age or mental condition would make them vulnerable during cross-examination. The court is able to deal with these difficulties by the use of special measures (under the Youth Justice and Criminal Evidence Act 1999) or anonymity orders (under the Coroners and Justice Act 2009).[1]

[1] A short introduction which mentions competence and compellability is helpful in setting the question in context before moving on to discuss issues of vulnerable and intimidated witnesses.

In the 'Pigot Report' (Report of the Advisory Group on Video-Recorded Evidence (1989) London: Home Office)[2] recommendations were made that the evidence-in-chief and cross-examination evidence of children should be given in a pre-recorded video. This was followed by the Home Office Report *Speaking Up for Justice* in 1998, which recommended further measures to protect vulnerable and intimidated witnesses. Some of these measures were brought into effect by the 1999 Act.

[2] You should make reference to reports such as the Pigot Report and any research in this area to demonstrate wider reading and understanding of the topic area.

The 1999 Act deals with special measures in criminal proceedings but special measures can also be used in civil proceedings despite the general rule in r.32(1)(a) of the Civil Procedure Rules 1998 that witnesses should give their evidence orally (see **Polanski v Condé Nast Publications Ltd** [2005] 1 WLR 637, which departed from this rule).[3]

[3] This shows the examiner that you understand special measures can be used in both criminal and civil proceedings but its use in civil proceedings is limited. This is important because the question does not focus simply on criminal issues.

Section 16 of the 1999 Act relates to vulnerable witnesses who are categorised as witnesses under the age of 17 or witnesses whose evidence is likely to be affected by a mental disorder or physical disability. Section 17 deals with vulnerable witnesses whose evidence is likely to be affected by 'fear or distress'.[4]

[4] Because the focus of the question is on vulnerable and intimidated witnesses, you should cite the statutory provisions which give the court powers to make orders relating to such witnesses. This ensures that your answer is detailed and focused.

Under s.32 the trial judge must also give the jury whatever warning is thought appropriate to ensure that they do not view the use of special measures in a way which might prejudice them against the defendant.

[5] Giving some examples of special measures shows the examiner that you are aware of the different types but avoid simply setting out a bare list of all the measures as this wastes space and time.

The provisions in the 1999 Act are effective to the extent that certain categories of witnesses such as children and complainants in sexual offence cases are automatically entitled to special measures. These include the use of screens, live television link or video related evidence-in-chief under ss 23–30 of the 1999 Act.[5] However, for other witnesses this is subject to judicial discretion. The use of judicial discretion is arguably necessary because of the potential 'inequality of arms' argument relating to breaches of Art.6 of the European Convention on Human Rights. In **R v Camberwell Green Youth Court** [2005] 1 WLR 393 the House of Lords also noted that the additional safeguards of s.20(2) and s.24(3) which allowed a judge to discharge or vary a special measures direction also gave the court an opportunity to ensure a fair trial.

A further advantage is that a combination of special measures can be used if this would best assist a witness to give evidence. This usually occurs in relation to the evidence of child witnesses where for example their evidence-in-chief might be pre-recorded but their cross-examination is given by live television link (see **R v H** [2006] EWCA Crim 853).

⁶ In examining whether special measures are effective you also have to look at any potential weaknesses in order to balance your answer.

Whilst the introduction of special measures was seen as a radical step and beneficial to witnesses, the 1999 Act has not been without problems.⁶ Witnesses must specifically fit into the definition of ss.16 and 17 to be entitled to special measures. To some extent this was addressed by s.51 of the Criminal Justice Act 2003, which extended the provisions of s.24 (live television link) to cover 'ordinary witnesses' if the court is satisfied that it is in the interests of justice and there are suitable court facilities. In addition, s.137 of the 2003 Act when in force will give the court discretion to permit video recording of a witness's evidence to be used as part of their examination-in-chief in cases involving serious crimes. However, the witness's recollection of events must have been significantly better at the time of the recording than at the trial and must be in the interests of justice to admit the recording.

In addition, s.99 of the Coroners and Justice Act 2009 extends the categories of witnesses who are automatically entitled to special measures to include witnesses in a relevant offence listed in Sched. 1A of the 1999 Act. These include offences involving knives and guns.

However, some restrictions remain. For example, the court cannot exclude certain members of the public from the court under s.25. The accused, legal representatives and at least one nominated media representative must be present. This can still create an intimidating atmosphere for a witness. With regard to s.27 the witness must still be called for cross-examination by the party using the recording unless a further special measures direction is made for cross-examination to be given by some other means. Also a witness can only in exceptional circumstances supplement their pre-recorded evidence with live oral evidence. However, this will change once s.103 of the 2009 Act comes into effect.

In addition, s.28 of the 1999 Act, which provided for cross-examination and re-examination of a witness to be carried out by video recording, has not been brought into effect and the Government announced in July 2004 that it would not be implemented in its present form.[7]

The inadequacies of the 1999 Act were accepted when the Government commissioned a review in 2004.[8] In addition, the 1999 Act did not make any provisions for the use of anonymity orders and the courts relied on the common law to do this until the Criminal Evidence (Witness Anonymity) Act 2008 came into force, which has now been replaced by the Coroners and Justice Act 2009.[9] An anonymity order can be made to ensure that the identity of the witness is not disclosed. Measures can include withholding a witness's name and other details and distorting the witness's voice or hiding the witness behind a screen. For such an order to be made the three conditions set out in s.88 must be met. The judge also has powers to vary or discharge such orders where appropriate. Anonymity orders were described in **R v Mayers** [2009] 1 WLR 1915 as a measure 'of last resort'.

Regardless of any weaknesses with the current statutory framework[10] for special measures, the judge retains an inherent jurisdiction to make orders to protect witnesses (see s.19(6) of the 1999 Act) which means that the judge does not have to be hampered by some of the limitations of the 1999 Act and the subsequent legislation.

Special measures and anonymity orders are vital for the protection of witnesses and some of the inadequacies in the 1999 Act have been addressed by subsequent legislation. However, there remain areas for improvement. A degree of flexibility is needed in this area given that the court must balance the protection of witnesses and ensuring the defendant has a fair trial and this can be addressed by the use of the judge's inherent jurisdiction.[11]

[7] Knowledge of which statutory provisions are or are not in force shows the examiner that your knowledge is up to date and also that you have wider knowledge. This in turn will help you to gain additional marks.

[8] This shows the examiner that you understand that the 1999 Act has been subject to review which shows that you are up to date in your knowledge and know more than just the basics.

[9] You should deal with the 2009 Act because anonymity orders are also regarded as special measures.

[10] You should start to form a view here as to whether you think the statutory provisions sufficiently protect vulnerable witnesses or not. This then leads into your conclusion.

[11] You should conclude by stating whether or not the statutory provisions protect vulnerable and intimidated witnesses as this is at the heart of what the question is asking. It does not matter which view you reach as long as you have supported your view with convincing arguments.

Make your answer stand out

■ Use journal articles such as D. Jones 'The evidence of a three year old child' [1987] Crim LR 677 or D. Cooper 'Pigot unfulfilled: video recorded evidence under section 28 of the Youth Justice and Criminal Evidence Act' [2005] Crim LR 456 when talking about special measures for children.

■ Briefly mention Home Office Research Study 283, *Are Special Measures Working? Evidence from Surveys of Vulnerable and Intimidated Witnesses* (published June 2004) which concluded that witnesses found the measures helpful and that 33% of witnesses said they would not have given evidence without them.

■ When discussing anonymity orders refer to views in articles such as L. C. H Hoyano 'Coroners and Justice Act 2009: special measures directions take two: entrenching unequal access to justice? [2010] 5 CLR 366 and D. Omerod, A. L. T Choo and R. L. Easter 'Coroners and Justice Act 2009: the "witness anonymity" and "investigation anonymity" provisions' [2010] 5 CLR 380 on the issue of potential breaches of Art.6.

! Don't be tempted to...

■ Discuss the rules on competence and compellability – the focus of the question is special measures.

■ Give a bare list of the special measures without attempting to analyse their effectiveness.

■ Ignore the Criminal Justice Act 2003 and the Coroners and Justice Act 2009 – the question asks you to consider 'subsequent legislation' as well as the 1999 Act.

? Question 2

Zac, aged 38, is standing trial on a charge of indecent assault of his two-year-old niece Lorraine. The prosecution wishes to call the following witnesses to give evidence:

(a) Lorraine, the alleged complainant.

(b) Sarah, who is Zac's estranged wife and who witnessed the incident. Sarah is concerned about facing Zac in court as she says that there is a history of domestic violence and she is afraid of Zac.

(c) Ed, who is a former acquaintance of Zac's and says that they met on the Internet and both shared an interest in child pornography. Ed has previously been convicted of possessing child pornography. He wishes to keep his identity secret during the trial because he is afraid of reprisals.

(d) Maxine, Zac's mother, who is 81 and suffers from senile dementia, who will testify that she has always suspected that Zac 'likes little girls'.

Advise Zac as to which of the above evidence is likely to be heard at his trial and why.

Answer plan

→ Discuss the presumption of competence in s.53(1) of the Youth Justice and Criminal Evidence Act 1999.

→ Consider the competence and compellability of each of the four main characters.

→ Examine the competence and compellability of children in relation to Lorraine.

→ Discuss special measures and anonymity orders in relation to Sarah and Ed.

→ Mention the issue of unsworn evidence in relation to Maxine.

→ Advise Zac as to the admissibility of each witness's evidence.

Diagram plan

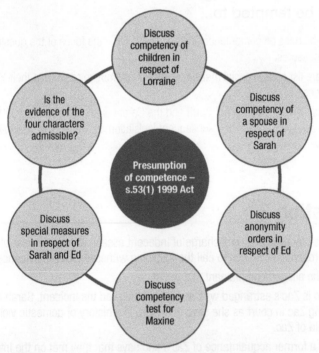

A printable version of this diagram plan is available from www.pearsoned.co.uk/lawexpressqa

Answer

[1] Show the examiner that you are aware that age may cause difficulties with competency and ensure that you quote the statutory provisions. This shows you are able to spot important clues in the question and will help you gain the available marks.

[2] Having explained that Lorraine's competency can be challenged you also need to explain how this can be done as this will earn you extra marks as it will show good application on your part.

[3] You should make the examiner aware that you understand that the standard of proof changes to the civil standard for the prosecution when competency is challenged as it shows a good level of understanding and will earn you more marks.

[4] Apply case law to explain how the judge might deal with the issue of Lorraine's competency as this shows application.

[5] You must not ignore how Lorraine's evidence will be given if she is competent or you will not have fully applied the law in this area.

[6] Don't ignore the issue of special measures for child witnesses or you will not have fully applied the law.

In advising Zac and his defence team it is necessary to consider the competence and compellability of each of the prosecution witnesses.

Lorraine

Lorraine is only two years of age and therefore an issue arises as to her competence to give evidence at the trial. Section 53(1) of the Youth Justice and Criminal Evidence Act 1999 provides that all persons, whatever their age, are competent to give evidence.[1] There is a presumption of competency which does not depend on the age of the witness. However, it is a rebuttable presumption. Zac and his defence team can object to the competency of Lorraine if they consider that she is likely to be unable to understand or properly respond to questions (s.53(3)). Lorraine's competency will be an issue for the trial judge to determine. The judge's ruling will take place at a *voir dire* in the absence of the jury (s.54(4)) but in the presence of the parties including Zac.[2]

It is for the prosecution to satisfy the court on a balance of probabilities[3] that Lorraine is competent to testify. If Lorraine is adjudged competent she will also be compellable and so can be forced to attend court.

In order to decide the issue of competency the judge may have to hear the whole of Lorraine's evidence first. In **R v Macpherson** [2005] EWCA Crim 3605 the Court of Appeal stated that infants who can only communicate with their mother in 'baby language' would not be competent.[4] Much will depend on Lorraine's understanding of basic English, which will be limited for a two-year-old child.

If Lorraine is considered to be competent then because she is under the age of 14 her evidence will have to be given unsworn under s.55(2).[5]

Lorraine would also be entitled to a special measures direction[6] under s.16 of the 1999 Act because she is under the age of 17. Such measures can include giving evidence by live television link (s.24). The judge can also order the removal of wigs and gowns (s.26). As the case involves a sexual offence, s.25 of the 1999 Act may also be applicable with Lorraine giving her evidence in private

31

and certain individuals being excluded from the court. Zac and his defence team cannot, however, be excluded under this section.

The judge would have to give a warning to the jury under s.32 of the 1999 Act that a special measures direction does not prejudice the defendant.[7]

Sarah

Sarah in this instance is both a competent and a compellable witness for the prosecution. This is because the exceptions under s.80(3) Police and Criminal Evidence Act 1984 apply as the case involves a sexual assault on a child under 16 (s.80(3)(b)).

[8] Because Sarah's reluctance to attend court is mentioned, you should briefly mention how she can be forced to attend court.

The prosecution can serve a witness summons on Sarah requiring her to attend the trial and if she fails to attend she will be in contempt of court.[8]

Sarah's fear of facing Zac in court can be dealt with by a special measures direction given by the judge under s.17 Youth Justice and Criminal Evidence Act 1999, which relates to intimidated witnesses. The court has powers under s.19 of the 1999 Act to make special measures directions. As Sarah's fear seems to be related to actually facing Zac in court then the most suitable measure would be the use of screens under s.23 of the 1999 Act. This would require the judge to exercise a 'balance of fairness test' and take into account not only Zac's interests but the interests of the prosecution and witnesses.

[9] Because you are told Sarah does not want to give evidence you also have to consider other ways in which her evidence can be heard without her being present at court – this is why it is important to also discuss hearsay statements of absent witnesses.

The judge would also have to give a warning to the jury under s.32 of the 1999 Act.

Alternatively, the prosecution could seek to admit Sarah's written statement into court either as a s.9 statement (if Zac and his defence team agree to its content) or as an exception to the hearsay rule under s.116(2)(e) Criminal Justice Act 2003[9] witness in fear. However, this would require leave of the court and the judge would consider factors in s.116(4) and such leave would only be given if it was felt that a special measures direction was not a viable alternative.

[10] Show the examiner that you have appreciated that Ed's special measures will be covered by a different statute. This shows a good level of knowledge on your part and will earn you the available marks

Ed

Ed may also be entitled to a form of special measures but under the Coroners and Justice Act 2009.[10] The prosecution would first have to obtain an order from the trial judge that Ed's identity can be concealed. Under s.88 various conditions (A–C) are imposed for making an order. The order must be necessary to protect Ed's safety and prevent harm to the public interest and the order must also be consistent with Zac receiving a fair trial. Section 89 further provides that the court must have regard to Zac's right to know the identity of witnesses. Cases such as **R v Davis** [2008] 3 All ER 461 has disapproved of the widespread practice of granting anonymity to intimidated witnesses on the basis that this compromised Art.6 and the common law principle that a defendant should be able to confront and cross-examine his accusers.

Under s.90 of the Act the judge must give a warning to the jury so they do not make assumptions which might be favourable to Ed or adverse to Zac.

Maxine

[11] This alerts the examiner to the fact that you have understood that mental capacity can affect the issue of compellability.

Maxine will be presumed competent and therefore compellable under s.53(1) of the Youth Justice and Criminal Evidence Act 1999. However, because she suffers from senile dementia[11] the defence may raise the issue of her competency under s.53(1) and it will be for the prosecution to prove on a balance of probabilities that she is competent to give evidence. The test under s.53(3) of the 1999 will again be used.

In **R v Sed** [2004] EWCA Crim 1294 the Court of Appeal held that the test of competency was satisfied even though the witness could not understand or give a coherent answer to 100% of the questions put to her, the evidence has to be taken as a whole. Maxine's evidence may still be admissible if she is coherent about the main issue on which her evidence is sought, namely Zac's preference for 'little girls'.

[12] A sophisticated answer which recognises the implications of a lack of competency alerts the examiner to the fact that you have understood that mental capacity can affect whether Maxine's evidence is admissible. This shows that you have a good level of understanding of the provisions of s.55 of the 1999 Act.

If the judge decides that Maxine is competent, a decision is needed as to whether her evidence is to be given sworn or unsworn. The test in s.55(2)(b) of the 1999 Act will be applied. It must be shown that Maxine 'has a sufficient appreciation of the solemnity of the occasion and of the particular responsibility to tell the truth which is involved in taking the oath'. There is a presumption that Maxine satisfies the test for competency if she is able to give intelligible testimony (s.55(8)). If Maxine is found to be mentally defective then she is not competent and cannot give either sworn or unsworn evidence.[12]

In conclusion, it is likely that the evidence of Sarah and Ed will be heard in court but with special measures. The evidence of Lorraine and Maxine, however, is more likely to fail the competency test.

 Make your answer stand out

- Refer to cases such as *R* v *Mayers* [2009] 1 WLR 1915 when discussing anonymity orders in relation to Ed.
- Give more examples of special measures for Lorraine.
- Consider the court's inherent powers under s.19(6)(a) of the 1999 Act to make further special measures such as voice modulation.
- Discuss further cases on child evidence, such as *DPP* v *M* [1989] 2 WLR 604, when discussing the evidence of Lorraine.

! Don't be tempted to...

- List every special measure under the 1999 Act – just discuss the measures which are likely on the facts.
- Repeat large sections of the 1999 Act – this is a waste of space and does not show application to the facts.
- State that Sarah is competent and compellable because she is no longer married to Zac – the facts state that they are separated (estranged).
- To be side tracked into discussing issues of expert evidence of a psychiatrist when discussing Maxine as it has not been flagged up that the issue is one of the admissibility of medical evidence.

 # Question 3

'...the material before us does not enable us to conclude that because a concession has been made to husbands and wives proper respect for family life requires that a similar concession be made to those in the position of a husband or a wife.' (Kennedy LJ in *R* v *Pearce* [2002] 1 Cr App R 39)

Analyse whether the current law on the compellability of a spouse hinders or advances the proper administration of justice.

Answer plan

→ Discuss when a spouse is regarded as competent and compellable.

→ Consider the historical basis of spousal compellability.

→ Examine recent legislation and the changes these brought about.

→ Analyse the difficulties/possibilities of extending the spousal exception.

→ Reach a final view as to whether you agree or disagree with the quotation.

Diagram plan

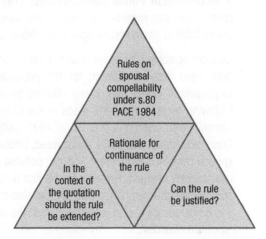

A printable version of this diagram plan is available from www.pearsoned.co.uk/lawexpressqa

Answer

[1] Referring your answer back to the quotation shows the examiner that your answer is focused and this in turn demonstrates a good command of the material.

Whilst s.53(3) of the Youth Justice and Criminal Evidence Act 1999 raises a presumption that all witnesses whatever their age are competent, special rules apply in the case of spousal compellability. As indicated in the quotation by Kennedy LJ in **R v Pearce** [2002] 1 Cr App R 39 a concession is made relating to the compellability of a spouse which is based on the right of respect for family life enshrined in Art.8 of the European Convention on Human Rights.[1] The spousal exception has historical roots based on the sanctity of marriage.

Before the passing of s.1 of the Criminal Evidence Act 1898 the defendant was not competent or compellable to give evidence against or on his/her own behalf. The view was that defendants could not be expected to tell the truth in their own defence. As the spouse was seen as an extension of the defendant then it was viewed as logical to extent this rule to spouses. However, by 1853 this view lost favour certainly as far as civil proceedings were concerned and spouses became competent as a result of the Evidence (Further Amendment) Act 1853. It was not until the 1898 Act that defendants in criminal proceedings became competent and compellable to give evidence and in turn the spouse became competent and compellable to give evidence on behalf of the defendant.[2] However, as can be seen by cases such as **Hoskyn v Metropolitan Police Commissioner** [1978] 2 WLR 695, a spouse was still regarded as rarely being competent and never compellable to give evidence against the defendant.

[2] Comparing and contrasting the different rate of change in this area between civil and criminal shows a deeper level of understanding of the historical development of the spousal exception and will earn you extra marks.

Concern remained, however, that the continuation of the exception could make it difficult for the prosecution successfully to prosecute cases particularly relating to domestic violence. Following recommendations made in the Criminal Law Revision Committee's Eleventh Report Cmnd 4991 s.80 of the Police and Criminal Evidence Act 1984 was passed. Under s.80(2) and (4) a spouse remained competent and compellable for the defendant unless jointly charged. However, for the first time under s.80(3) the spouse became competent and compellable for the prosecution and co-defendant to give evidence against the defendant in certain 'specified offences'.

[3] The question requires an analysis of the effectiveness of the provisions on spousal competence and therefore addressing criticisms flags up to the examiner that you are using analytical skills.

One of the criticisms of s.80 is in relation to the 'specified offences' chosen. The Criminal Law Revision Committee's recommendations were based on addressing domestic violence. However, the provisions are wider in that s.80(3)(b) relates to a sexual offence on any child under 16 and is not restricted to a child of the family.[3] Interestingly, sexual offences on minors come within the compellability range but not sexual offences against the spouse. It is arguable that s.80(3)(a) is sufficiently wide in the use of words 'assault, injury or threat of injury' to include sexual assault on the spouse but the Act does not give examples or expand on this.

A further criticism of the rules relating to spousal compellability is that the spouse is still given special protection from testifying against the defendant whilst protection for other members of the defendant's family such as children are ignored. In addition, the 1984 Act does not prevent a defendant from marrying a potential witness to prevent that witness giving evidence against the defendant.

The wording of s.80(2A) of the Act also presents difficulties where the defendant is charged with two or more offences but the spouse is only compellable for one of those offences. Confusion exists as to whether the compellable evidence of the spouse can still be used in those offences for which the spouse was not compellable. Academics such as Peter Creighton in his article 'Spouse competence and compellability' [1990] Crim LR 34 consider that the section should not be given this interpretation otherwise it would increase the need for separate trials and the use of s.78 discretion to exclude the spouse's evidence where it has been used unlawfully. The issue was raised in the case of **R v L** [2009] 1 WLR 626 but was not resolved by the Court of Appeal.

[4] By referring back to the quotation in the question you show the examiner that you are able to keep your answer focused and relevant and this is the essence of a good answer.

The quotation in the question highlights the fact that the spousal protection is not afforded to common-law partners who may consider themselves to be in the same position as a spouse. In **R v Pearce** (1979) 69 Cr App Rep 365 the Court of Appeal rejected an argument that cohabitees should be treated in the same way as spouses to ensure that their Art.8 rights were not breached.[4] The Court of Appeal was concerned not to restrict the number of witnesses who were compellable and felt that there would be problems in determining what was be considered a long-term relationship in order to allow certain cohabitees to come under the protection. Overall it was felt that the interests of the community should outweigh the interests of the family.

Some concession to the spousal protection was made when it was enlarged to include same-sex couples who had entered into a civil partnership (s.84 Civil Partnership Act 2004).

[5] By looking at counter-arguments you ensure that your answer is balanced and this again demonstrates to the examiner that you are attempting some analysis as required by the question.

Whilst the spousal exception has been criticised, it is important to note that despite the exception the spouse can voluntarily agree to give evidence against the defendant without being compelled to do so. Section 80 does not hinder the proper administration of justice in this respect.[5] If a spouse decides to waive his or her right to testify, according to **R v Pitt** [1983] QB 25 the judge should remind them of their right and that once that right is waived they will be subject to cross-examination like any other witness.

Section 17 of the Youth Justice and Criminal Evidence Act 1999 also protects a spouse who may be afraid to testify due to fear of the defendant by allowing the judge to make special measures which would, for example, enable them to give evidence behind a screen. Similarly, the hearsay provisions under s.116 Criminal Justice Act 2003 would allow a spouse's witness statement to be submitted in place or oral testimony if the spouse was shown to be in fear. These are all measures which would help spouses to give evidence voluntarily.

The spousal rule is, however, arguably archaic and one could argue of little value because it can be circumvented. Whilst a spouse may not be compellable, any statement that they have given to the prosecution can still be used according to cases such as **R v L** [2009] 1 WLR 626. The statement can be admitted as admissible hearsay under the courts' inclusionary discretion under s.114(1)(d) of the Criminal Justice Act 2003.

[6] Reference to comparative jurisdictions gives depth to your answer and will earn you additional marks.

It could be argued that one approach would be to follow the model in Australia and leave the issue of spousal compellability to the discretion of the judge.[6] The judge could then consider issues such as the seriousness of the offence when deciding on spousal compellability.

Spousal compellability has not evolved with society's forward-thinking views on marriage and relationships, particularly as cohabitees do not receive the same protection. However, the current rules do not hinder the proper administration of justice because of the ability of the spouse to give evidence voluntarily and for the prosecution to use the witness statement of a spouse. The rules do not, however, advance the historical view of the sanctity of a union because the rules do not extend the concept of family privacy to other situations beyond marriage or civil partnerships.

✓ Make your answer stand out

- Discuss cases such as *R* v *Khan* [1987] 84 Cr App Rep 44 with regard to marriages which take place overseas to show the exception can still apply if the ceremony is recognised under English law.
- Consider s.80A of the 1984 Act and cases such as *R* v *Naudeer* [1984] 3 All ER 1036, which suggest that the judge and prosecution should be careful about making any comments about the failure of a spouse to give evidence.
- When discussing Art.6 mention that it is a qualified right.

! **Don't be tempted to...**

- Discuss the law on competence and compellability generally – focus on compellability issues relating to a spouse.

- Forget to address the quotation – you must consider whether or not there should be an enlargement to the current rules.

- Focus simply on the spouse's ability to give evidence for a defendant. Reference in the question to 'proper administration of justice' also requires you to discuss whether a spouse can give evidence for the prosecution.

? Question 4

Consider the competence and compellability of the following witnesses:

(a) Alex, a 10-year-old child who wishes to give evidence in support of his mother's application for a residence order (custody).

(b) Xavier, a co-defendant in a drug trial who has information to suggest that the defendant had previously imported heroin into the country. The prosecution wish to call Xavier to give evidence against the defendant.

(c) Wayne and Marcos are civil partners having been through a civil partnership ceremony. Wayne is charged with assaulting Marcos. Marcos is reluctant to give evidence against Wayne because Wayne has threatened to kill him if he gives evidence.

(d) Anusha is a witness in a theft trial and suffers from a physical condition which means that her short-term memory is poor. The prosecution wish to call her as their main witness.

Answer plan

→ Discuss the civil test for competency in relation to Alex.

→ Examine the competence and compellability of co-defendants in relation to Xavier under s.53(4) and (5) of the Youth Justice and Criminal Evidence Act 1999.

→ Apply s.80(3) Police and Criminal Evidence Act 1984 in relation to Marcos.

→ Discuss the application of s.53(3) of the 1999 Act in relation to Anusha.

Diagram plan

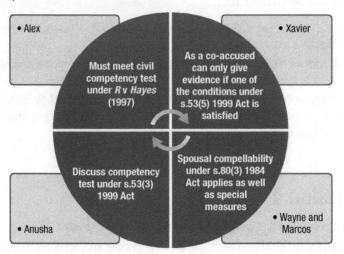

- Alex

Must meet civil competency test under *R* v *Hayes* (1997)

- Xavier

As a co-accused can only give evidence if one of the conditions under s.53(5) 1999 Act is satisfied

Discuss competency test under s.53(3) 1999 Act

Spousal compellability under s.80(3) 1984 Act applies as well as special measures

- Anusha

- Wayne and Marcos

A printable version of this diagram plan is available from www.pearsoned.co.uk/lawexpressqa

Answer

[1] This shows the examiner that you have immediately identified that different jurisdictions apply here and that therefore different rules will have to be considered. This shows a good command of the subject area.

In order to consider the competence and compellability of the various witnesses it will be necessary to consider the provisions of either the Youth Justice and Criminal Evidence Act 1999 in respect of criminal matters and the Children Act 1989 in respect of civil cases.[1]

(a) With regard to Alex, as he is a child giving evidence in a civil action the common law test is that found in **R *v* Hayes** [1977] 1 WLR 234, which still governs civil cases. He will be competent to give evidence as long as he understands the nature of the oath that must be given before his evidence. Alex must have a sufficient appreciation of the solemnity of the occasion in addition to the responsibility to tell the truth. The case of **Hayes** suggests children over 10 will be able to take an oath but each case will turn on its own facts. The judge must therefore be satisfied that Alex is sufficiently mature to understand the importance and meaning of taking an oath.[2] If Alex does not understand the oath then under s.96 of the Children Act 1989 he can give his evidence if he at least understands the duty to speak the truth and has sufficient understanding of the proceedings.

[2] This demonstrates that you are able to spot the clues in the question such as the age of the child and apply the relevant law.

(b) As Xavier is a co-defendant then ordinarily under s.53(4) of the Youth Justice and Criminal Evidence Act 1999 he would be neither competent nor compellable to give evidence against the defendant. However, under s.53(5) he will become compellable to give evidence for the prosecution if the prosecution drop the case against him, or if he pleads not guilty or he is tried separately.[3] The prosecution cannot, however, engineer one of these situations simply to make Xavier compellable. However, there is nothing stopping Xavier from voluntarily giving evidence against the defendant.

[3] Knowledge of the exceptions to the general rule of competency and compellability of a co-defendant demonstrates a deeper level of understanding.

(c) The rules relating to the competence and compellability of a spouse also applies to those in a civil partnership as a result of s.84 of the Civil Partnership Act 2004.[4] Under s.80 of the Police and Criminal Evidence Act 1984 Marcos is both competent and compellable to give evidence for the prosecution against Wayne because the offence involves an assault on Marcos and therefore is regarded as a 'specified offence' under s.80(3). Marcos is reluctant to give evidence but he should be advised that he could be forced to give evidence. However, Marcos may be regarded as an intimidated witness under s.17 of the Youth Justice and Criminal Evidence Act 1999 (as amended by the Coroners and Justice Act 2009).[5] This would entitle him to special measures if the court took the view that the quality of his evidence is likely to be diminished by fear or distress. The special measures would include giving evidence behind a screen under s.23 of the 1999 Act or giving evidence by live television link under s.24. The judge will have to give a direction to the jury under s.32 of the Act to ensure that Wayne is not prejudiced by the fact that Marcos's evidence is given under a special measures direction and this should be given at the time of Marcos's evidence rather than during summing-up (see **R v Brown** [2004] EWCA Crim 1620).

[4] You will earn more marks here if you are able to cite specific sections of relevant statutes.

[5] By going on to consider alternative ways in which Marcos's evidence may be received you demonstrate an ability to look at the wider issues and offer solutions to solve the problem. This will earn you additional marks.

(d) Whether or not Anusha can give evidence will depend on whether she passes the test of competency. Whilst all witnesses in a criminal trial are presumed to be competent under s.53(3) of the Youth Justice and Criminal Evidence Act 1999, Anusha must understand the questions put to her and give answers that can be understood. A poor short-term memory would not necessarily prevent Anusha being a competent witness but may affect the reliability of her evidence and this will be a matter of weight for the jury.[6]

[6] This shows the examiner that you understand that there are wider issues to be considered than simply competence and compellability when assessing a witness's evidence. This in turn demonstrates a deeper level of understanding on your part.

If the defence wish to raise an objection as to Anusha's competency this will be dealt with in a *voir dire*. The prosecution will bear the burden of proof to satisfy the court on a balance of probabilities that Anusha is competent. If competency is unclear (for example, because it is not known whether Anusha's short-term memory will affect her ability to understand the questions put to her), the judge must keep the issue under review throughout her evidence and make a ruling as to incompetency as soon as this becomes clear from her evidence. However, the case of **R v Powell** [2006] 1 Cr App Rep 31 states that if the witness is found to be incompetent and their evidence is crucial or likely to be prejudicial so that a conviction would be unsafe then the judge must withdraw the case from the jury.[7]

[7] This shows the examiner that you understand that competency remains an issue throughout the course of the trial and not simply before a witness gives evidence. This takes your answer beyond a basic one.

In the circumstances, Marcos will be competent and compellable but Alex and Anusha will have to first pass the competency test. Xavier will only be competent and compellable if one of the circumstances under s.53(5) applies.

✓ Make your answer stand out

■ When discussing the compellability of Marcos, mention s.3 of the Criminal Procedure (Attendance of Witnesses) Act 1965 in relation to the fact that failure to attend will amount to contempt of court as well as cases such as *R v Yusuf* [2003] 2 Cr App Rep 32.

■ When discussing the provisions on intimidated witnesses, mention s.116(2) Criminal Justice Act 2003 relating to hearsay statements of a witness in fear – any previous statement made by Marcos could be admitted in place of his oral evidence.

! Don't be tempted to...

■ Discuss special measures when discussing Alex – these are unlikely to apply on the facts in civil proceedings.

■ Confuse the rules on competence and compellability of a defendant with that of a co-defendant when discussing Xavier.

■ Assume Anusha suffers from a mental disorder as you are told that her condition is a physical one – there is no need to discuss the issue of unsworn evidence.

■ Confuse civil and criminal rules in this area – you must show that you are aware of the difference between the tests on competency for both civil and criminal cases.

Examination of witnesses at trial

3

How this topic may come up in exams

Examination of witnesses at trial can be tied into problem questions relating to competence and compellability and special measures as mentioned in Chapter 2. However, this topic contains a number of areas which would be examinable in a multi-issue question; for example, previous consistent and inconsistent statements (s.120 and s.119 Criminal Justice Act 2003), refreshing memory (s.139 Criminal Justice Act 2003) and submissions of 'no case to answer'. Previous consistent and inconsistent statements also relate to the topic of hearsay (Chapter 4).

■ Attack the question

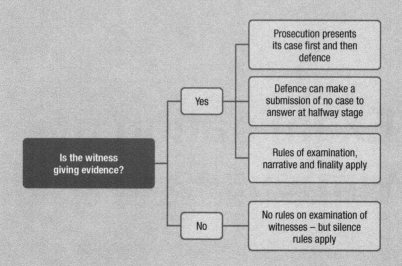

Question 1

'Not even the abuses, the mishandlings, and the puerilities which are so often associated with cross-examination have availed to nullify its value... It is beyond any doubt the greatest legal engine ever invented for the discovery of truth.' (J. Wigmore, *Evidence*, revised ed. 1974, Boston, MA: Little, Brown, para. 1367)

Critically evaluate this statement with reference to the efficacy of cross-examination in the adversarial trial system in the United Kingdom.

Answer plan

→ Explain purpose of cross-examination.

→ Examine weaknesses.

→ Examine strengths.

→ Discuss rules of examination, e.g. rule of finality.

→ Is the quotation a fair assessment of cross-examination?

Diagram plan

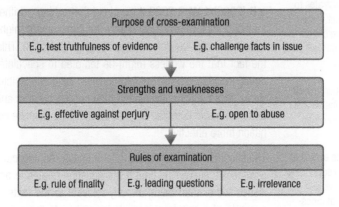

A printable version of this diagram plan is available from www.pearsoned.co.uk/lawexpressqa

Answer

Cross-examination of witnesses is regarded as an important tool to test the truthfulness of evidence given by the opposing party's witness. Under Art.6 of the European Convention on Human Rights the defendant is entitled to examine witnesses who are giving evidence against him. In an adversarial system where the judge relies on the collection of the evidence by the parties, cross-examination is an opportunity for that evidence to be thoroughly tested.[1]

Advocates are allowed a greater degree of flexibility in cross-examination as leading questions may be asked and as a general rule witnesses should answer any questions put to them during cross-examination.

The area of cross-examination has seen the emergence of a number of evidential rules which are designed to help the jury elicit facts that are relevant to the issues in dispute.[2]

The first is the common law rule derived from **R v Treacy** [1944] 2 All ER 229, CCA that witnesses should not be asked questions that are irrelevant or otherwise inadmissible. However, in the case of **R v B** [2003] 1 WLR 2809 it was held that asking a witness whether they can think of any reason why the complainant might lie is permissible where the defence are alleging fabrication. This is despite the fact that the witness might be tempted to speculate or provide opinion evidence which would normally be inadmissible.[3] The rule exists as a rule of convenience to speed up the trial and focus the trial on matters in issue. In this sense it helps to make cross-examination more effective.[4]

The second rule is that of the rule of finality. An advocate must take a witness's answer as final if the question relates to any collateral issues rather than being directly relevant to the facts in issue. An example of a collateral issue is in relation to the credibility of the witness. However, there are exceptions to this general rule. For example, if a case turns on the credibility of a prosecution case then evidence which would undermine the witness's credibility is admissible. As the rule does not apply to cross-examination on matters directly relevant to the facts in issue it cannot be said to hamper cross-examination.[5]

Sidebar notes:

[1] Your introduction should make some reference to the importance of cross-examination in the trial system and alert the examiner to your understanding that cross-examination of witnesses is part of the requirements of a fair trial under Art.6 of the ECHR to tie in with the quotation. This shows that your answer is focused.

[2] In order to discuss the effectiveness of cross-examination it is necessary to discuss the evidential rules in this area and whether the rules hamper or increase the effectiveness of cross-examination.

[3] Showing a contrary approach to the general principle demonstrates to the examiner that you are attempting some critical evaluation and this will earn you extra marks.

[4] This relates your answer back to the quotation that cross-examination is an effective tool.

[5] This shows the examiner that you are still supporting the view put forward in the quotation that cross-examination is a great invention and begins to reveal the direction that your argument is taking and therefore what your final view will be. This adds clarity to your answer and is an example of good structure which will earn you the available marks.

[6] Showing the examiner that you have appreciated that civil and criminal proceedings have separate rules relating to cross-examination demonstrates an ability to compare and contrast the two jurisdictions and therefore good analytical skills.

[7] You should refer back to the quotation wherever possible in your answer. The quotation suggests cross-examination has some weaknesses and so you need to discuss these weaknesses. This ensures your answer remains balanced and focused.

[8] The use of journal articles such as Stone demonstrates wider reading and greater depth of understanding which will earn you extra marks.

In civil proceedings[6] the overriding objective under Part 1 of the Civil Procedure Rules 1998 provides that cross-examination can be limited to ensure cases are dealt with justly and proportionately. In criminal cases the judge has discretion to curtail prolonged cross-examination of questions designed to annoy or bully a witness.

However, cross-examination can lead to abuses and mishandlings, as identified in the quotation.[7] For example, whilst cross-examination is a useful tool there are issues relating to its effectiveness when considering the quality of the evidence given the ability for witnesses to refuse to answer questions.

Cross-examination cannot circumvent the defendant's right of silence under s.35 of the Criminal Justice and Public Order Act 1994 or indeed the privilege against self-incrimination. In those circumstances the defendant may refuse to answer questions put. Equally, questions cannot be asked of those matters protected by legal professional privilege.

Also under s.41 of the Youth Justice and Criminal Evidence Act 1999 in sexual offence cases questions cannot be asked relating to the claimant's sexual behaviour without leave of the court.

Cross-examination of child witnesses is also problematic. Despite the provision of special measures cross-examination may not be the best way to establish the truth where children are concerned. Children can often feel intimidated by questions and anxiety might be taken by the jury to be a sign of a lying witness. As stated by Marcus Stone in his article 'Instant lie detection? Demeanour and credibility in criminal trials' [1991] Crim LR 821–830, 'truthful witnesses may be anxious, and liars may be, or seem to be, relaxed'.[8]

The role of the judge in cross-examination can also make the process problematic. The judge is given the position of an impartial umpire yet is also allowed to question and even call witnesses. The judge's impartiality can be compromised if the style or content of the questions suggest that the witness is not to be believed. Whilst guidelines are provided in cases such as **R v Mitchell** [2003] EWCA Crim 907 that questions by the judge should be aimed at clarifying matters, a number of appeal cases have shown that this power can often be abused. For example, in **R v Murray** [2004] EWCA Crim 2416 a conviction was quashed on the basis that the judge had completely taken over the cross-examination of the

[9] The use of human rights cases shows the examiner that you have considered the broader implications of an extension of the rules of cross-examination and gives depth to your answer.

[10] Having discussed the weaknesses you also need to discuss the strengths. This demonstrates that you are evaluating the issues and building an argument and brings you back to your main view which was evident earlier on in your answer.

[11] Discussion of safeguards takes your answer further and shows a wider understanding of the use of previous inconsistent statements which are in themselves a powerful tool in cross-examination.

witness. In **CG v United Kingdom** (2001) App. No. 43373 the European Court of Human Rights held that a judge's intervention could render a trial unfair if it was frequent and had the effect of challenging the defendant's case.[9]

However, there are also benefits with cross-examination[10] which arguably outweigh the disadvantages. Cross-examination can be effective in a number of areas. The use of previous inconsistent statements is one example. Previous inconsistent statements can be used to cross-examine a witness on matters where they have provided contradictory evidence and therefore is useful in counteracting perjury. Such statements can be both oral and written (see ss.4 and 5 Criminal Procedure Act 1865). Under s.119 of the Criminal Justice Act 2003 the statement can be used to prove the truth of the assertions contained in it. This could prove to be disadvantageous to the witness; however, safeguards are in place such as the fact that the witness must be allowed to see the statement before it is used so that any discrepancy can be explained. A statement is also not admissible under s.119 if made by a person who would not have been competent to give evidence at the time the statement was made. The judge also has discretion as to whether to allow the jury to see the entire statement or just parts. The admission of the statement remains a matter of weight for the jury.[11]

Under s.6 Criminal Procedure Act 1865 where during cross-examination a witness denies having a conviction, the cross-examining party is permitted to prove the conviction. This allows the witness's credibility to be challenged effectively.

The interests of justice are further served by protecting witnesses from certain types of cross-examination. For example, under s.34 of the Youth Justice and Criminal Evidence Act 1999 a defendant charged with a sexual offence cannot cross-examine in person a witness who is a complainant in the same proceedings.

[12] You should conclude by summarising whether you agree or disagree with the quotation. It does not matter which view you take but you must support it with strong arguments.

In summary, the quotation adequately reflects the fact that cross-examination as a tool is effective despite its limitations and possible abuses in some areas.[12] It continues to be an effective way to elicit evidence in an adversarial trial system. Whilst there are some restrictions on cross-examination, such as matters of privilege, these are necessary to balance the protection of the rights of the defendant.

Make your answer stand out

- Mention journal articles such as L. Ellison 'Cross-examination in rape trials' [1989] Crim LR 866 to support your discussion of the limitations of cross-examination.
- Use additional cases such as *R* v *Kepple* [2007] EWCA Crim 1339 on the importance of unfettered cross-examination.
- Mention cases such as *R* v *Treacy* [1944] 2 All ER 229, CCA on questions based on irrelevant or inadmissible evidence.

! Don't be tempted to...

- Discuss only the strengths of cross-examination just because the quotation suggests it is 'the greatest legal engine ever invented ...' You are asked to evaluate the statement and this means looking at some potential weaknesses as well.
- Discuss in any great detail examination-in-chief and re-examination as the question requires you to focus on cross-examination.
- Write everything you know about cross-examination without attempting to put it into context – your answer should focus on the efficacy of the process in an adversarial system.

? Question 2

His Honour Judge Feltham is presiding over a fictional trial for rape brought against David. Consider the following issues arising from the examination of prosecution witnesses:

(a) The prosecution witness, Laura, who is also the alleged complainant, gives evidence that she was raped following a date with the defendant. The defence ask Laura during cross-examination whether she had previously dated the defendant before and she answers 'no'. The defence wish to call Laura's work colleague Tina to prove that Laura had told her during a conversation about the rape that she had in fact dated the defendant twice before.

(b) Halfway through her testimony Laura states that she cannot now remember what happened on the crucial night and refuses to give any details of the rape.

(c) A medical expert is called on behalf of the prosecution and the expert asks to be able to refresh his memory from notes made following an examination of Laura.

(d) The defence allege that there is insufficient evidence for the case to proceed against the defendant.

Discuss with reference to statute and decided case law how Judge Feltham is likely to deal with each of the above issues as they arise at trial.

Answer plan

→ Discuss the rule of finality in relation to the further evidence of Laura's colleague Tina.

→ Consider whether Laura is a hostile or a favourable witness.

→ Discuss s.139 of the Criminal Justice Act 2003 in relation to refreshing memory.

→ Discuss submissions of no case to answer in relation to the defence.

→ Advise Judge Feltham on the admissibility of the evidence in each case.

Diagram plan

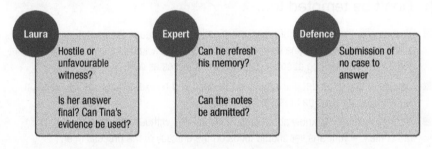

A printable version of this diagram plan is available from www.pearsoned.co.uk/lawexpressqa

Answer

[1] Your introduction should show that you have identified the relevant evidential rules that arise from the question. This is good structure and ensures that you remain focused on the issues.

In considering the evidential issues at trial Judge Feltham will have to be mindful of the rules of examination of witnesses including the rule against narrative and the rule of finality. In addition, Judge Feltham may have to consider a submission of no case to answer on the part of the defence.[1]

Tina

The first issue that arises involves whether the prosecution can call Tina to disprove Laura's evidence that she had never dated the defendant before. Laura has denied an allegation put to her on cross-examination. The rule of finality states that a witness's answer to collateral issues must be treated as final. The issue of credibility is usually regarded as a collateral issue in the sense that it is not necessary to prove it to establish the elements of the offence. Therefore, the issue is whether Laura's answer of 'no' should be taken as her final answer.

There are exceptions to the finality rule.[2] In **Attorney-General v Hitchcock** (1847) 1 Exch 91 it was held that the test for deciding whether further evidence could be adduced was whether such evidence could have been called by the questioning party as part of their own evidence during examination-in-chief.[3] The credibility of the alleged complainant is often regarded as important in rape cases to the issue of consent. In the case of **R v Funderburk** [1990] 2 All ER 482[4] the Court of Appeal allowed cross-examination on the alleged complainant's previous inconsistent statement in a sexual offence case on the basis that it was important to the issue of whether the alleged complainant was a virgin. Similarly, in **R v Nagrecha** [1997] 2 Cr App Rep 401, CA evidence that the alleged complainant had made allegations of sexual assault against other men was admissible. It is therefore likely that Tina's evidence will be regarded as central to the facts in issue.

Laura

If Laura has simply forgotten crucial details about the rape but is not attempting to sabotage the prosecution itself then there is very little that the prosecution can do. She will be regarded as an unfavourable witness because she has not supported her earlier version of events.[5] The prosecution cannot challenge their witness's credibility or subject her to cross-examination. They can only call further evidence to attempt to repair any damage that Laura's evidence may have done to their case. However, if Laura is deliberately refusing to tell the truth the prosecution can apply to the judge for permission to treat Laura as a hostile witness. They will then be entitled to cross-examine her. In the case of **R v Thompson** (1976) 64 Cr App Rep 96[6] the silence of a witness was enough to make her hostile and therefore Laura's refusal to give any details of the rape is important.

[2] Having identified the rule of finality as important to the question you should discuss whether, and if so which, exception applies to ensure your answer to this part of the question is a full one.

[3] Give your answer depth by showing the examiner that you understand the test that the judge will have to apply in deciding whether to allow further evidence. This will ensure you gain any available marks.

[4] Use cases to help you to explain the approach the judge might take to the evidence of Tina. This adds depth to your answer.

[5] As the facts do not say whether Laura is being deliberately obstructive you must consider her position as both an unfavourable witness and as a hostile witness. This ensures that your discussion is a full one as it shows wider reading on your part which in turn will mark you out as a strong candidate.

[6] This case helps to suggest Laura's silence could make her hostile and therefore is worth quoting.

7 You should show the examiner that you know the statutory provision that relates to refreshing memory as this shows a level of detail that will earn you additional marks.

8 You should show the examiner that you understand the relevant test as this goes beyond a basic answer and shows greater understanding of the subject area.

9 This shows the examiner that you understand the relevance of the old common law rules in this area as well as showing your ability to use case law to reach a view. This illustrates that you have a good level of knowledge and will separate you from the weaker student.

10 You should also show the examiner that you know this area is covered by statute and that it links into hearsay. This shows an ability to interrelate topics and this will earn you additional marks.

11 You should show the examiner that you understand that if all of the notes are relied on then it will still be admissible hearsay but under a different section of the 2003 Act. This shows a good level of understanding and takes your answer beyond a basic one.

12 Showing the examiner that you have an appreciation that if all of the notes are relied upon then the test differs shows a greater level of detail.

Under s.3 Criminal Procedure Act 1865 the prosecution can either discredit Laura by calling other witnesses, cross-examining her or by the use of any previous inconsistent statements made by Laura (ss.4 and 5). It is likely the prosecution took a statement from Laura at the time the rape was reported and this statement can now be used against Laura. Section 119 of the Criminal Justice Act 2003 provides that such statements can be admitted to prove the truth of the assertions contained in them and therefore provides an exception to the hearsay rule.

The medical expert

Under s.139 of the Criminal Justice Act 2003[7] the medical expert can refresh his memory from his notes as long as those notes record his recollection of the matter at the earlier time and his recollection was significantly better and he states that this is the case when he testifies.[8] The notes must be shown to the defence on request and they can cross-examine based on the notes. The Criminal Justice Act has not abolished the common law rules in this area and therefore cases such as **Senat v Senat** [1965] P 172 remain important[9] and if the medical expert is cross-examined on parts of the notes that are not used to refresh his memory the prosecution can seek to have the documents put into evidence. In accordance with s.120(3) of the 2003 Act the notes will be admissible to prove the truth of any assertions contained within them.[10]

If the medical expert cannot recall any of the contents of his notes then the notes can still be admitted as evidence and s.120(4) provides that the notes will be admissible to prove the truth of any assertions contained within.[11] However, the test that must be satisfied is varied. It is necessary to show that the notes were made at a time when matters were fresh in the expert's memory but that he cannot now remember and cannot reasonably be expected to remember.[12]

The defence's allegation of insufficient evidence

[13] You have done two things here: you have shown the examiner that you understand the nature of the application the defence will have to make and that you know there is a common law test linked to it.

It is possible for the defence to make an application at the halfway stage of the trial that the prosecution have not met the burden of proof. This is known as 'a submission of no case to answer' and the test is set out in **R v Galbraith** [1981] 2 All ER 1060, CA.[13] This means that the defence's argument will succeed if they can show that the prosecution evidence taken at its highest is such that a properly directed jury could not properly convict based on it. However, if the evidence is merely weak but depends on the view taken of it by the jury (for example, the issue is one of contradictory evidence or the unreliability of a witness) then the trial can still continue. This is very much at the discretion of the trial judge. If Laura is the sole witness and does not give evidence and the prosecution are not able to question her as a hostile witness the jury would have trouble convicting on the evidence.[14]

[14] Use the facts (however sparse) to try to reach a view on whether such an application would be successful or tell the examiner that there is not enough information from the facts to reach a view. This shows a deeper level of understanding and will help you gain extra marks.

It is likely that the defence will be able to use the evidence of Tina and that the prosecution will be able to treat Laura as a hostile witness. In addition, the prosecution's medical expert will be able to refresh his memory from his notes. Whether or not the defence will succeed in their submission of no case to answer will depend on the degree of weakness of the prosecution evidence.

 Make your answer stand out

- Discuss additional cases relating to submissions of no case to answer such as *R* v *Pryer* [2004] EWCA Crim 1163.
- Point out that the judge has an inherent power to withdraw the case from the jury due to insufficient evidence even if a submission of no case to answer is not made.

! **Don't be tempted to...**

- Assume that Laura is a hostile witness — you must also consider the position if her reluctance to give evidence is due to honest loss of memory and therefore she is simply an unfavourable witness.
- Forget to discuss the effect of the admission of documents used to refresh memory — this area impacts on the topic of hearsay but is also important to this topic.
- Discuss the issue of expert evidence in general when discussing the medical expert — focus on the issue of refreshing memory.

Question 3

'The presumption is that no man would declare anything against himself unless it were true; but every man, if he was in difficulty, or in the view to any difficulty, would make declarations for himself.' (Eyre CB in *R* v *Hardy* (1794) 4 St Tr 1065 at p.1093)

Critically evaluate the above quotation and consider to what extent the rule against previous consistent statements can be said to be justified in the context of ensuring a fair trial?

Answer plan

→ Explain the nature of the exclusionary rule relating to previous consistent statements.

→ Compare and contrast the common law exceptions under s.120 Criminal Justice Act 2003.

→ Analyse any perceived difficulties with s.120 and whether there are sufficient safeguards to prevent an abuse of Art.6 rights.

Diagram plan

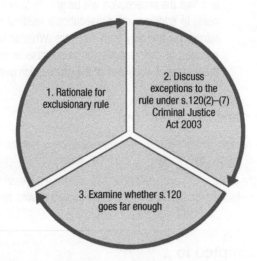

1. Rationale for exclusionary rule

2. Discuss exceptions to the rule under s.120(2)–(7) Criminal Justice Act 2003

3. Examine whether s.120 goes far enough

A printable version of this diagram plan is available from www.pearsoned.co.uk/lawexpressqa

Answer

The rule against previous consistent statements also known as the rule against narrative prevents the use of a witness's previous statement to bolster their oral testimony. The court will only admit relevant and reliable evidence and exclude evidence which is regarded as irrelevant or self-serving. The exclusionary rule operates largely in criminal proceedings as previous consistent statements are admissible in civil proceedings under ss.1 and 6 of the Civil Evidence Act 1995.[1]

The quotation from Eyre CB in the case of **R v Hardy** (1794) 4 St Tr 1065 highlights that the main difficulty with previous statements is that they are self-serving and can be manufactured.[2] For example in the case of **R v Roberts** [1942] 1 All ER 187 the defendant was prevented from supporting his defence of accidental shooting by repeating in evidence that he had told his father shortly after his arrest that there had been an accident.[3] Such statements are potentially unreliable. In addition such evidence would also offend the rule against hearsay.

Whilst such statements may be relevant to the collateral issue of credibility it does not go to the central issues involved in the trial. However, it is accepted that there may be certain instances when previous consistent statements may bolster the credibility of a witness to such an extent that such evidence cannot be ignored. The common law therefore recognised a number of exceptions to the exclusionary rule. The commom law exceptions related to previous statements which rebut an allegation of recent fabrication, which are used to refresh memory, used for identification, relate to a recent complaint or are exculpatory statements made in response to a criminal allegation.[4] These exceptions have been largely replicated in s.120 of the Criminal Justice Act 2003. The exceptions arguably assist in ensuring that the defendant has a fair trial by ensuring that relevant evidence is not excluded. However, there has been some inconsistency in the court's approach to the exceptions and this can equally have a negative impact on the right to a fair trial under Art.6 of the European Convention on Human Rights.[5]

---

[1] This explains to the examiner why your answer will focus largely on the criminal rules and therefore helps to put your answer in context for the examiner.

[2] Reference to the quotation in the question demonstrates that your answer is focused and this will earn you additional marks.

[3] It is acceptable to briefly refer to the facts of a case in this context if it is done to illustrate the operation of a rule but normally you should confine yourself to discussing the legal principles arising from a case.

[4] This shows a knowledge of the common law position which helps put your answer in context when you go on to discuss the changes under s.120.

[5] This ensures that your answer remains relevant to the question as you have been asked to consider whether the exclusion of such statements affects the right to a fair trial.

[6] A discussion of some of the potential problems with the common law exceptions shows the examiner that you are attempting some critical evaluation of previous consistent statements.

[7] Reference to law commission reports in this area demonstrates wider reading and will earn you additional marks.

[8] Reference to academic opinion of this kind demonstrates that you have undertaken wider reading of the topic area and that you have a deeper level of understanding. This will earn you additional marks.

[9] This continues your contrast of the old common law rules with the current rules and adds depth to your discussion. It also shows your ability to develop arguments, which in turn will give the impression that you have produced a good answer.

Section 120 was an opportunity to remove some of the inconsistent approaches to the common law exceptions. For example, one of the difficulties with the exception relating to recent complaints was that it was limited only to sexual offences rather than all offences and therefore not all defendants could take the benefit of this exception.[6] Following recommendations by the Law Commission in their report *Evidence in Criminal Proceedings: Hearsay and Related Topics* Cmnd 3670 (1997)[7] the law was changed with the introduction of s.120(4) and (7) of the Criminal Justice Act 2003 which extended the exception to all complaints. There is also no requirement that the complaint should be elicited using only natural rather than suggestive or leading questions. The requirement for the complaint to be 'recent' was also replaced with the words 'as soon as can reasonably be expected'. Diane Birch in her article 'Same old story, same old song' [2004] Crim LR 556 argues that this revised wording is still too open ended and that the courts might have to use the 'safety valve' of s.114(1)(d) of the 2003 Act to admit evidence of complaints that do not satisfy the promptness requirement.[8]

Cases such as **R v O** [2006] EWCA Crim 556 suggest that the court will take a more generous approach to what can be regarded as 'recent' and the court will look at the context in which the complaint was made and the person to whom the complaint was made. This can be seen in the case of sexual abuse cases which occurred some time ago (see **R v R (M)** [2007] EWCA Crim 518 where complaints made in 1998 were admitted in relation to sexual assaults which took place between 1991 and 1997).

With regard to the common law exception relating to previous statements used to rebut an allegation of recent fabrication s.120 removes the word 'recent' in response to the Law Commission's criticism of this requirement.[9]

The Criminal Justice Act, however, does not expressly abolish the common law rules on previous consistent statements and instead leaves two different rules in place. There would arguably be nothing preventing a defendant using the common law rules if those rules were more generous than s.120.

Only one of the common law exceptions previously fell into the exception to the hearsay rule and as such could be used to prove the truth of matters stated (namely certain exculpatory statements made in criminal proceedings). This presented an inconsistent approach to the use to which previous statements were put. The Criminal Justice Act, s.120 brought the remaining exceptions into line with the hearsay exceptions and under s.120(5) all previous consistent statements became admissible to prove the truth of the matters stated. This also brought such statements in line with civil proceedings where previous consistent statements can be used towards a witness's credibility as well as the truth of the matters stated. However, s.120 did not expressly refer to the common law exception relating to the admissibility of exculpatory statements made by the accused (which was also not included in the exceptions under s.120) and therefore an opportunity was missed to ensure a consistent approach to all the exceptions.

[10] By discussing the safeguards you balance your answer and counteract any weaknesses identified by you and this allows you to make a final assessment and reach a final view by the end of your answer. This gives your answer a good structure as well as being a good example of critical evaluation.

The 2003 Act does, however, have safeguards built in to ensure that previous consistent statements are limited wherever possible.[10] Under s.123 a previous consistent statement is not admissible if the maker of the statement would not have been competent to give evidence. This ensures that only statements from witnesses with the necessary capability are used in evidence. Previous statements can still be excluded using the courts' powers to exclude hearsay evidence under s.126. Also under s.122 (as confirmed in cases such as **R v Hulme** [2006] EWCA Crim 2899) a previous consistent statement produced as an exhibit cannot accompany the jury into the jury room unless the judge gives permission.

[11] By offering a final view in your conclusion you complete your evaluation and this ensures a good structure, which makes for impressive reading and in turn demonstrates that your answer has remained focused and this will earn you any available marks.

The exceptions to the rule against previous statements permits evidence to be admitted in circumstances where the likelihood of fabrication is regarded as small and where it would support the witness's evidence. The rule can be justified in that it ensures that only relevant and reliable evidence is admitted. The Law Commission themselves rejected any suggestion that previous consistent statements should be admissible generally. It is arguable, therefore, that sufficient safeguards are written into the 2003 Act to ensure that only statements which would advance the case and ensure a fair trial are admitted.[11]

Make your answer stand out

- When discussing the exception of recent complaints discuss some of the problems under the common law exception such as the definition of 'first reasonable opportunity' using cases such as *R* v *Valentine* [1996] 2 Cr App Rep 213.

- Use comparative jurisdiction to support your answer e.g. the US Federal Rule of Evidence 801(d)(1)(B), which excludes previous consistent statements as hearsay and only provides one exception which relates to statements to rebut an allegation of fabrication.

- When discussing the exception relating to statements to rebut an allegation of recent fabrication, discuss cases such as *R* v *Ali* [2004] EWCA Crim 2735 and *R* v *Oyesiku* (1971) 56 Cr App Rep 240.

- Mention that previous consistent statements can always be used in the defence's favour if made by a prosecution witness and it bolsters the defence's case – see *R* v *Evans* [2001] EWCA Crim 730.

! Don't be tempted to...

- Discuss previous inconsistent statements under s.119 Criminal Justice Act 2003 – the quotation clearly refers to previous consistent statements only.

- Confuse the exceptions in s.120 Criminal Justice Act 2003 with the common law exceptions found in s.118 – they are different.

- Ignore the central focus of the question – you must discuss previous consistent statements in the context of a fair trial.

❓ Question 4

Alfonso is charged with the rape of Felicity a masseuse aged 35. The rape is alleged to have taken place at a hotel. Alfonso denies the charge and says that Felicity consented to sex. Alfonso alleges that he has used Felicity's services before and that sex was part of the service and they often played sexual games in which Felicity pretended that she was not a willing participant. Alfonso is not represented and during the trial wishes to cross-examine Felicity about her previous sexual behaviour. Alfonso says that before the alleged incident they had last had sex two weeks ago. During cross-examination Felicity says that she has never met Alfonso before and that before the rape she was a virgin. The defence wish to use a previous statement made by Felicity to the police in which she admits that Alfonso is a client of hers. The prosecution also have a witness who is the hotel manager who identified

Alfonso during a video identification procedure as the man who ran out of the hotel moments before the rape was reported. However, the hotel manager is unable to remember whom he picked out during the identification procedure and the prosecution wish to call PC Walsh, who was in charge of the video identification, to give evidence about which suspect the hotel manager selected.

Advise the defence in respect of the evidential issues arising at trial.

Answer plan

→ Discuss how ss.34 and 41 of the Youth Justice and Criminal Evidence Act 1999 will apply with regard to Alfonso's wish to cross-examine Felicity.

→ Apply s.119 of the Criminal Justice Act 2003 to Felicity's previous statement to the police.

→ Consider whether the evidence of the hotel manager can be admitted as a previous consistent statement under s.120(4) and (5) of the Criminal Justice Act 2003.

Diagram plan

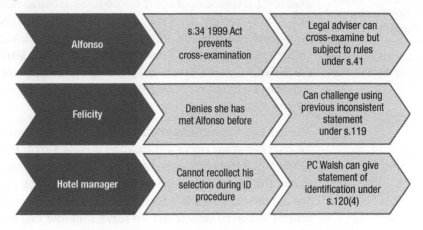

Alfonso	s.34 1999 Act prevents cross-examination	Legal adviser can cross-examine but subject to rules under s.41
Felicity	Denies she has met Alfonso before	Can challenge using previous inconsistent statement under s.119
Hotel manager	Cannot recollect his selection during ID procedure	PC Walsh can give statement of identification under s.120(4)

A printable version of this diagram plan is available from www.pearsoned.co.uk/lawexpressqa

Answer

The defence should be advised that in order to successfully prosecute the case against Alfonso the prosecution will have to overcome
a number of evidential issues at trial and these will involve rules of
cross-examination.

[1] Reference to the Criminal
Procedure Rules shows the
examiner that your knowledge
is up to date on the way the
courts apply the statutory
provisions and this will earn
you extra marks.

[2] Section 41 is central to this
answer and it is important
that you identify this section
and discuss its implications in
order to obtain decent marks.

[3] This shows the examiner
not only that you are aware
of the relevant statutory
provisions but that you have
an understanding of the
limitations imposed by the
section. This demonstrates
that you have a good level of
knowledge of the subject area
and are able to correctly apply
the law to the facts. This will
earn you the available marks.

The first issue that arises is Alfonso's wish to cross-examine Felicity
the complainant. Under ss.34–36 of the Youth Justice and Criminal
Evidence Act 1999, Alfonso will be informed by the judge that he
will not be permitted to cross-examine Felicity himself (s.38).
However, his legal representative can do this on his behalf and the
procedure is contained in Part 31 of the Criminal Procedure Rules
2011.[1] Under s.39 of the Act the judge must give the jury a warning
against drawing any adverse inferences against Alfonso because he
is prevented from questioning Felicity himself. Whilst Alfonso's legal
representative can cross-examine Felicity, s.41 of the Youth Justice
and Criminal Evidence Act 1999 limits the extent to which questions
can be asked about her previous sexual behaviour.[2] The questions
must relate to specific instances of alleged sexual behaviour rather
than general questions about Felicity's sexual behaviour (s.41(6)).
Such questions will not be allowed if the purpose is to damage
Felicity's reputation (s.41(4)).[3] However, cases such as **R v Martin**
[2004] EWCA Crim 916 have held that s.41(4) will not apply unless
impugning the complainant's credibility is 'the purpose' or 'the main
purpose' rather than merely one of a number of purposes.

Alfonso's legal representative would first need to seek permission of
the court to question Felicity and according to cases such as **R v F**
[2005] 1 WLR 2848 this will be heard in private in the absence of
Felicity. The criteria for admissibility are found in s.41(3) of the Act.
The question must relate to 'a relevant issue in the case' other than
consent unless the consent and the sexual behaviour took place
at or about the time of the rape or is similar to any sexual behaviour that took place as part of the rape that it cannot be explained
as merely a coincidence. On the facts the defence wish to use
Felicity's past sexual behaviour with Alfonso to prove the issue of
consent. The wording of s.41 would prevent this. However, following the House of Lord's decision in **R v A (No. 2)** [2001] 2 WLR
1546 it was accepted that s.41 was potentially in conflict with Art.
6 of the European Convention on Human Rights. The court therefore

[4] Knowledge that the provisions of s.41 have been given a different interpretation as a result of the decision in *R* v *A* is central to answering this part of the question and separates the stronger students from the weaker ones.

[5] This demonstrates that you are able to spot important clues in the question and use the information to reach a conclusion as to how the law might be applied by the trial judge.

[6] An ability to recognise that other sections in the Youth Justice and Criminal Evidence Act 1999 are potentially relevant on the facts demonstrates thought on your part leading to a considered answer which in turn will create an overall impression that your answer is a good one.

[7] Using case law such as *R* v *Hayes* to illustrate the use of previous consistent statements gives authority and in turn force to your answer and will earn you the available marks.

used its powers under s.3 of the Human Rights Act to interpret s.41 in such a way to make it compatible with Art.6.[4] This was done by interpreting s.41(3)(c) to permit evidence of sexual behaviour, even if it related to consent, as long as its probative value to the question of consent was so high that to exclude it would lead to an unfair trial. In the circumstances, Alfonso may be able to adduce specific allegations of past sexual behaviour involving himself and Felicity even if this touched on the issue of consent and did not occur at or about the time of the rape, as long as its probative value to consent is high. This may be the case as the suggestion is that refusal of consent was part of the sexual role-play between him and Felicity.[5]

In addition, s.41(5) would allow Alfonso's legal representative to ask questions about Felicity's sexual behaviour if this was done to rebut any evidence of sexual behaviour which had already been put forward by the prosecution. This section does not exclude questions designed to damage Felicity's credibility.[6] Sexual behaviour is given a wide definition and includes any sexual behaviour with the accused or another person but will exclude the actual rape for which Alfonso is charged. According to cases such as **R** **v E** [2004] EWCA Crim 1313 the test is an objective one. The question of whether or not the complainant was a virgin would, according to the decision in **R** **v Rooney** [2001] EWCA Crim 2844, fall within the meaning of sexual behaviour for the purposes of s.41(5).

In respect of both s.41(3) and (5) the court will only grant permission if it is satisfied that a refusal would mean that conclusions reached on any relevant issue in the trial could be unsafe.

With regard to Felicity's denial that she has ever met Alfonso before, under s.119 of the Criminal Justice Act 2003 it is permissible to use the previous inconsistent statement of a witness to contradict what that witness has said during cross-examination. This occurred in the case of **R** **v Hayes** [2004] EWCA Crim 2844, where the judge allowed the defendant to be cross-examined on a plea bargaining letter by his solicitor.[7] In the circumstances, the defence would be permitted to put to Felicity the previous statement made by her to the police. In addition, s.5 of the Criminal Procedure Act 1865 permits previous written statements to be used. Felicity must be allowed to see the sections of the statement that will be used to contradict her before the cross-examination begins. The inconsistency in the

[8] Referring to s.5 of the 1865 Act demonstrates to the examiner that you understand the procedure relating to the admission of previous consistent statements and this shows a deeper level of understanding which will earn you extra marks.

statement must be relevant to the issues in the trial.[8] This can be said to be the case here, as Felicity denies prior knowledge of the defendant which may in turn be important to the issue of consent. In addition, if it goes to the issue of credibility then cases such as **Tiwari v The State** [2002] UKPC 29 suggest that previous inconsistent statements can be used even though credibility is regarded as collateral rather than a central issue in a trial. Under s.119 such statements may be admissible as an exception to the hearsay rule and may be used to prove the truth of the matters stated.

The hotel manager is unable to recall whom he selected during an identification procedure and this requires another person (PC Walsh) to give evidence regarding this. Ordinarily this would fall foul of the rule against the admission of hearsay evidence, given that it is second-hand evidence used to prove the truth of matters stated as well as the rule against narrative given that it involves a previous statement.[9] However, under s.120(4) and (5) of the Criminal Justice Act 2003 a witness's previous statement which 'identifies or describes a person, object or place' is admissible as evidence of any matter stated. However, the hotel manager would need to indicate, whilst giving his own evidence, that to the best of his belief he made the statement of identification and it is true. The statement would be admissible as an exception to the hearsay rule and may be used to prove the truth of the matters stated.

[9] An ability to consider other exclusionary rules that may apply again shows that you have a wider understanding of the subject area in general.

The defence should therefore be advised that it is likely that they will be able to cross-examine Felicity about her past sexual behaviour under s.41 and that Felicity's previous inconsistent statement can also be used to challenge Felicity's credibility during cross-examination. The identification evidence of the hotel manager will also be admissible.

Make your answer stand out

- Discuss the effects of Art. 6(3)(d) on a judge's refusal to allow a defendant to cross-examine a complainant in a sexual offence case and how s.38 is a safeguard against a breach of Art. 6(3)(d).

- When discussing s.41 of the 1999 Act, refer to Lord Steyn's criticisms in *R* v *A (No. 2)* [2001] (above) of the 'outmoded beliefs' that a woman's previous sexual history suggests that she is more likely to have consented to the act in question.

- Refer to views contained in journal articles such as N. Kibble, 'The sexual history provisions: charting a course between inflexible legislative rules and wholly untrammelled judicial discretion?' [2000] Crim LR 274 or G. Young, 'The sexual history provisions in the Youth Justice and Criminal Evidence Act 1999 – a violation of the right to a fair trial' [2001] 41 *Medicine, Science and the Law* 217.

! Don't be tempted to...

- Ignore the operation of ss.34 and 38 of the 1999 Act – you are told that Alfonso is not represented but wants to cross-examine Felicity.

- Fail to mention the case of *R* v *A (No. 2)* [2001] cited above – this is important to s.41(3)(c), which applies on the facts of the scenario.

- Discuss the *Turnbull* warning or Code D of PACE 1984 when discussing the hotel manager's identification evidence – the facts relate to the admission of the evidence using a previous statement rather than the quality of the identification.

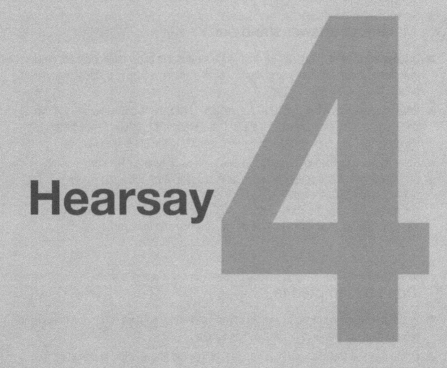

Hearsay

How this topic may come up in exams

Hearsay is an example of an exclusionary rule. It is common to see it examined as an essay question when looking at how exclusionary rules affect the principle of admissibility and the use of judicial discretion. In this context it would relate to issues in Chapter 1 as well as other exclusionary rules such as opinion evidence and previous judgments at trial (discussed in Chapter 5) and the rule against narrative (discussed in Chapter 3). However, hearsay equally appears in problem questions, in particular those where students are expected to identify when the exceptions under ss.116, 117 and 118 of the Criminal Justice Act 2003 might apply.

■ Attack the question

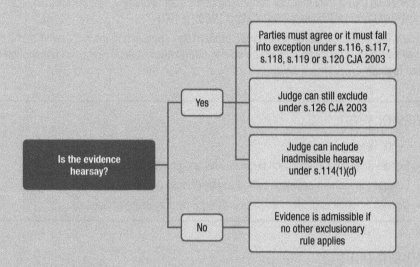

Is the evidence hearsay?

Yes
- Parties must agree or it must fall into exception under s.116, s.117, s.118, s.119 or s.120 CJA 2003
- Judge can still exclude under s.126 CJA 2003
- Judge can include inadmissible hearsay under s.114(1)(d)

No
- Evidence is admissible if no other exclusionary rule applies

Question 1

'To avoid exclusion the court searches for a convenient tag which may be given to this type of evidence so that it may pass for something other than hearsay…' (A. Zuckerman, *The Principles of Criminal Evidence* (OUP, Oxford 1989), p.197)

Analyse whether the quotation reflects the modern day approach to the admissibility of hearsay evidence. Can this approach be said to offend against Art.6 European Convention on Human Rights?

Answer plan

→ Define hearsay.

→ Explain difference in approach between civil and criminal proceedings.

→ Discuss the modern approach to hearsay by discussing the exceptions.

→ Discuss whether approach complies with Art.6 by discussing safeguards.

Diagram plan

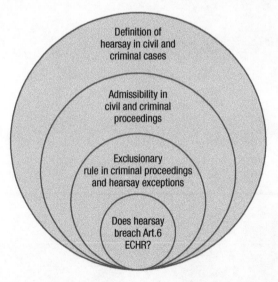

A printable version of this diagram plan is available from www.pearsoned.co.uk/lawexpressqa

Answer

Hearsay evidence is defined in civil proceedings in s.1(2)(a) of the Civil Evidence Act 1995 as 'a statement made otherwise than by a person while giving oral evidence in the proceedings which is tendered as evidence of the matters stated'.[1] In criminal proceedings a similar definition is found in s.114(1) of the Criminal Justice Act 2003. Hearsay evidence is admissible in civil proceedings[2] as long as the party wishing to use the evidence gives notice to the other party. However, in criminal proceedings an exclusionary rule continues to operate and hearsay evidence is generally inadmissible unless it falls into one of the exceptions identified in s.114 of the 2003 Act.

The modern day approach to hearsay evidence,[3] as re-confirmed in cases such as **R v Doherty** [2006] EWCA Crim 2716, is that it is possible for an accused to be tried and convicted in England and Wales on the basis of hearsay evidence which is the sole evidence against them regardless of whether or not the accused has had an opportunity to challenge the maker of the statement.

This approach is not thought to be in conflict with Art.6 of the European Convention on Human Rights because Art.6 is not regarded as an absolute right and the 2003 Act has a number of safeguards built into it.[4] This was confirmed in the case of **R v Horncastle** [2009] EWCA Crim 964.[5] This is despite the decision in **Tahery v United Kingdom** (2009) App. No. 22228/06 of the European Court of Human Rights that 'counterbalancing factors' could not justify a conviction based on untested hearsay evidence which was the sole or decisive evidence.

[1] You should show the examiner that you understand the meaning of hearsay by including a definition in your introduction and this will be expected and there will be marks awarded for this.

[2] As the question does not specifically ask you to deal with hearsay only in criminal proceedings you must show the examiner that you understand that hearsay is treated differently in civil cases and also explain why the remainder of your answer will concentrate on the criminal rules. This shows that you have a good level of understanding.

[3] The question asks you to discuss the modern day approach to hearsay and so you should address this in your answer as early as possible to show that your answer remains focused.

[4] The question also asks you to consider whether the approach offends against Art.6 and therefore you should also deal with this in the early stages of your answer.

[5] Show the examiner that you are aware of some of the Art.6 cases on hearsay as this demonstrates a familiarity and confidence with the material.

[6] As the cases on Art.6 state that the right is not breached if there are safeguards, you should show the examiner that you intend to identify and discuss the hearsay safeguards. This ensures that your answer is focused.

[7] Before identifying each safeguard it is helpful to discuss the hearsay exceptions briefly so that the examiner is aware that you understand the ways in which hearsay evidence will be admissible. You do not need to discuss the exceptions in great detail. This gives structure to your answer.

[8] Once you have identified that exceptions exist you can go on to discuss the safeguards that exist in the context of the exceptions so that your answer flows.

[9] You should separate out those safeguards that apply generally to the hearsay rules as opposed to being relating only to a specific hearsay exception. This gives good structure to your answer which in turn will help you to gain the available marks.

Safeguards are present throughout much of the hearsay provisions[6] in the 2003 Act and it is arguable that this would make it difficult for hearsay evidence to be freely admitted in the way suggested by the quotation. A party wishing to use the evidence must persuade the court (in the absence of agreement) that it falls into one of the exceptions under ss.116–118 of the 2003 Act.[7]

The most commonly used exception relates to absent witnesses under s.116. This exception includes a number of safeguards against the arbitrary admission of hearsay evidence.[8] Cases such as **R v Cole** [2007] 1 WLR 2716 and **R v Bailey** [2008] EWCA Crim 817 have confirmed that for the conditions set out in s.116(2) (a)–(d) the judge should refer to the factors set out in s.114(2) of the 2003 Act. These factors include the probative value of the statement, the circumstances in which the statement was made and the amount of difficulty involved in challenging the statement.

A further safeguard in s.116 is that s.116(2)(e) requires leave of the court before hearsay evidence can be adduced. Section 116(4) of the 2003 Act sets out factors to be taken into account by the court when considering whether the 'fear' provision should be used and these factors are similar to those found in s.114(2) but also include the possibility that a special measures direction could deal effectively with the issue of fear.

Further safeguards can be found in s.117 relating to business documents created or received in the course of a trade, business, profession or other occupation. The court can exclude such evidence under s.117(7) of the 2003 Act if the statement's reliability is in doubt.

A number of general safeguards also apply to the hearsay provisions.[9] For example, under s.123 of the 2003 Act the maker of the statement must have had the required capability at the time the statement was made. If capability is in doubt then the burden of proof lies with the party wishing to use the hearsay evidence. The standard of proof is on a balance of probabilities.

Under s.124 of the 2003 Act where hearsay evidence has been admitted the opposing party is entitled to adduce evidence to challenge the maker's credibility. This is an important provision to counter the potential injustice of hearsay evidence namely that the opposing party is not given the opportunity to cross-examine the original maker of the statement. This ensures that Art. 6(3)(d) of the Convention is taken into consideration.

In addition s.126 of the 2003 Act provides an exclusionary discretion where the case for excluding the evidence substantially outweighs the case for admitting it. In fact in **R v Xhabri** [2006] 1 Cr App Rep 413 the Court of Appeal stated that a judge might have a duty to exclude hearsay evidence under s.126 if it was necessary to ensure compliance with the Human Rights Act 1998 suggesting this exclusionary discretion is broad in nature.

In the case of **R v Singh** [2005] EWCA Crim 96 it was reiterated that when hearsay evidence is admitted the judge should give a direction to the jury warning them to take into account when evaluating the probative value of the evidence that it has not been subject to cross-examination. This therefore provides a further safeguard to the admission of hearsay evidence.

The issue is whether despite these safeguards the courts still make a determined effort to admit all forms of hearsay evidence when possible as suggested by the quotation.[10] It is arguable that the inclusionary discretion under s.114(1)(d) allows the courts to do just that[11] due to the fact that since 2005 otherwise inadmissible evidence can be admitted using judicial discretion if it is in the 'interests of justice'. Consideration of the interests of justice would seem to accord with Art.6 of the Convention and in addition the discretion covers evidence tendered by the defence as well as the prosecution. The Law Commission envisaged that the inclusionary discretion would be used liberally and would depend on the 'probative value' of the hearsay evidence. However, the wording of s.114(1)(d) is wider and omits any reference to probative value.[12]

The evidence from case law is that discretion is being used widely. For example, in the case of **R v Y** [2008] 1 WLR 1683, CA hearsay evidence was admitted using s.114(1)(d) even though it circumvented the rule in **R v Blastland** [1985] 2 All ER 1095 excluding third party confessions as hearsay.

[10] You should bring your answer back to the quotation itself as you have also been asked to what extend the quotation reflects the modern approach to hearsay.

[11] The quotation suggests that the courts find ways to admit hearsay evidence with ease and you need to assess whether this is true or not and give examples to support or disagree with the quotation – s.114(1)(d) is a good example to use.

[12] Discussing the Law Commission recommendations shows a greater level of analysis and critique as it shows the examiner you can see deficiencies based on recommendations not implemented. This gives depth to your answer and will help you gain additional marks.

The wide nature of s.114(1)(d) is curtailed by the fact that the court must have regard to the factors in s.114(2) mentioned earlier as well as any other factors considered to be relevant. In addition the case of **R v Taylor** [2006] EWCA Crim 260 confirms that the court should give a reasoned explanation for its decision to admit inadmissible hearsay evidence and make it clear which factors in s.114(2) have been taken into consideration.

[13] You should conclude by summarising whether the modern day approach to hearsay offends Art.6. There is no right or wrong view. The examiner just wants to see that you have used convincing arguments to support your final view.

In the circumstances[13] it is arguable that the modern day approach to the admissibility of hearsay evidence does not offend against Art. 6 because it is not an absolute right. Instead sufficient safeguards have been built into the hearsay provisions to counter any possible prejudice to the defendant.

 Make your answer stand out

- Refer to the Law Commission Report *Evidence in Criminal Proceedings: Hearsay and Related Topics* No. 245 (1997) when discussing s.116(2)(e).
- Discuss the use of the exclusionary discretion under s.78 PACE 1984 as a further safeguard or s.125 of the 2003 Act which allows the judge to stop the trial where 'unconvincing' hearsay evidence has been admitted.
- Consider further cases on hearsay and Art.6 such as *Luca* v *Italy* (2001) App. No. 33354/96, ECtHR, *R* v *Sellick* [2005] 1 WLR 3257 and *Al-Khawaja* v *United Kingdom* (2009) App. No. 26766/05.

! Don't be tempted to...

- Write everything you know on the hearsay provisions – you must restrict your answer to examining if and how the provisions offend against Art.6 and how the courts are currently interpreting the provisions.
- Discuss each and every hearsay exception in detail – you should discuss where the safeguards appear.
- Discuss the historical development of the hearsay provisions – the question requires you to focus on the modern day approach.

? Question 2

His Honour Judge Rosetti is presiding over a fictional criminal case involving the importation of drugs in which the following evidence has been presented:

(a) The defendant alleges that the bags which were detained at Customs contained poppy seeds from California destined for use in poppy seed oil. The prosecution wish to adduce labels from the bags to show that they were in fact imported from China.

(b) Transcripts of telephone calls between the defendant and a third party in which reference is made to 'the package' and 'keeping it below the radar'. The prosecution wish to adduce the statements made in the telephone conversation.

(c) A statement made by the defendant's associate at the time of being found in possession of three of the bags that 'he knew the plan was flawed and they would get caught'. He has since died in hospital after contracting a viral infection.

(d) A statement from the defendant's former girlfriend who overheard conversations between the defendant and his associates about the importation of the poppy seed to use in the production of heroin. She is living in South Africa and for this reason the prosecution do not intend to call her to give evidence.

Discuss the extent to which the above evidence is admissible.

Answer plan

→ Consider whether each piece of evidence meets the definition of hearsay.

→ Discuss the relevance of each piece of evidence.

→ Identify which hearsay exception applies to each piece of evidence.

→ Comment on whether the judge has a discretion to exclude the evidence if it is not admissible.

→ Consider whether the judge has a discretion to include the evidence if it is inadmissible.

→ Reach a conclusion as to which piece of evidence is admissible and why.

Diagram plan

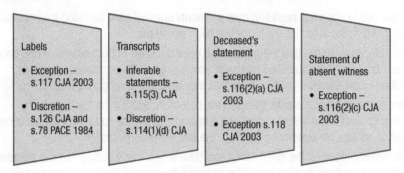

Labels	Transcripts	Deceased's statement	Statement of absent witness
• Exception – s.117 CJA 2003	• Inferable statements – s.115(3) CJA	• Exception – s.116(2)(a) CJA 2003	• Exception – s.116(2)(c) CJA 2003
• Discretion – s.126 CJA and s.78 PACE 1984	• Discretion – s.114(1)(d) CJA	• Exception s.118 CJA 2003	

A printable version of this diagram plan is available from www.pearsoned.co.uk/lawexpressqa

[1] Start your answer by summarising the evidential issues Judge Rosetti will need to consider so that the examiner is aware that you have understood the issues raised by the problem question. This is a good example of a focused and relevant introduction. As marks are awarded for structure you should always ensure that your introduction is relevant.

[2] As the case of *Patel* has similar facts, it is a good idea to mention it, but you should make the examiner aware that you understand that it pre-dates the 2003 Act and so cannot be used as a precedent.

[3] You should make the examiner aware that you understand that the case, whilst relevant, pre-dates the 2003 Act and so cannot be used as a precedent. This demonstrates an ability to sift out irrelevant information.

Answer

In order for Judge Rosetti to rule on the admissibility of the various pieces of evidence it is necessary to consider whether any exclusionary rules apply, as well as the relevance of each piece of evidence. The exclusionary rule to consider is hearsay.[1] A piece of evidence will be hearsay if made by a person otherwise than in oral evidence in the proceedings if it is tendered as proof of the matters stated.

Labels from the poppy seed bag

If the origins of the label are directly relevant to a fact in issue then it is necessary to examine whether the label is hearsay. Under s.115 of the 2003 Act for the purposes of hearsay a statement is any representation of fact or opinion made by a person 'by whatever means'. This extends to statements communicated in writing. In **Patel v Comptroller of Customs** [1965] 3 WLR 1222, which has similar facts,[2] the prosecution were not allowed to use statements on bags of coriander seeds to prove that they were from Morocco because it was inadmissible. However, this case was heard before the changes made by the Criminal Justice Acts of 1988 and 2003.[3] If the prosecution can argue that the requirements of s.117 of the 2003 Act are met then the labels may be admissible as an exception to the hearsay rule. The label must have been created or received in the course of a business, trade, profession or other occupation and the person who supplied the information contained in it must have had personal

[4] It is important to discuss the judge's exclusionary discretion so that the examiner knows that you understand the ways in which admissible hearsay evidence can still be excluded. You will not have fully applied the law in this area if you do not consider judicial discretion.

[5] The facts mention words such as 'the package' and these are clues that the words carry an inference. You need to show the examiner you have recognised the clue and that it points to inferable statements.

[6] It is OK to mention the case of *Kearley* simply to point out that the facts are similar but you must make the examiner aware that you realise the 2003 Act changes the decision in *Kearley*.

[7] Where you have suggested that it is uncertain whether or not the hearsay evidence will be admissible you must also discuss the inclusionary discretion so that the examiner is aware that you know that inadmissible hearsay evidence can still be admitted.

[8] This flags up to the examiner that you understand that the concept of relevance is still important in this area.

[9] Show the examiner that you appreciate that there is more than one way in which the confession can be admissible and refer to the statutory provision.

knowledge of the matters dealt with. If the criteria are met then the evidence will be automatically admissible. The judge still retains discretion to exclude the evidence under s.126 of the 2003 Act and can do this on the basis that the case for excluding the evidence substantially outweighs the case for admitting it.[4] This may be applied because the labels do not suggest a strong enough link to the crime.

Transcript of telephone calls

With regard to the transcripts of telephone calls made between the defendant and the third party the issue here is whether the statements are inferable statements.[5] The prosecution may allege that it can be inferred from the words 'package' and 'keeping it below the radar' that the defendant is involved in illegal drug supply or possession. The common law position of **R v Kearley** [1992] 2 WLR 656[6] (which had similar facts) that inferable statements are inadmissible hearsay is no longer applicable. Instead, under s.115(3) of the 2003 Act Judge Rosetti will have to consider whether the purpose of the person who made the statement was either (a) to cause another person to believe the matter or (b) to cause another person to act on the basis that the matter is as stated. Judge Rosetti essentially has discretion here. If neither purpose exists then the statements are not hearsay and are admissible. If one of the purposes exist then the statements are hearsay and must fall into one of the hearsay exceptions to be admissible. As the makers of the telephone call are not readily identifiable, s.116 is unlikely to apply here. Judge Rosetti could, however, exercise his discretion under s.114(1)(d) to include the evidence in the interests of justice.[7]

Statement of the defendant's associate

The statement of the defendant's associate is relevant[8] because it is an admission of involvement in an illegal activity. Confessions and admissions are an exception to the hearsay rule under s.118 of the 2003 Act and therefore admissible. As the associate is no longer alive, the statement could also be admitted under s.116.[9] It would first be necessary to show that if the associate had given oral evidence it would have been admissible and he must be identifiable to the court's satisfaction. The prosecution may then seek to rely on s.116(2)(a) that the person who made the statement is dead.

Statement from the defendant's girlfriend

[10] When mentioning s.116 you must ensure that you identify the correct sub-section rather than listing all five conditions.

With regard to the statement from the defendant's former girlfriend the prosecution may seek to admit it under s.116(2)(c)[10] on the basis that she is outside the United Kingdom. However, the prosecution must also show that it is not reasonably practicable to secure her attendance. Judge Rosetti will have to consider the importance of the evidence to the case overall as well as the degree of prejudice to the defendant if the statement is admitted (**R v Castillo** [1996] 1 Cr App Rep 438 approved in **R v Gyima** [2007] EWCA Crim 429).[11] This would require the judge to consider the steps the prosecution have taken or failed to take to secure the girlfriend's attendance (see **R v C** [2006] EWCA Crim 197) rather than the steps which should reasonably be taken, as this would be a matter to consider when deciding to exercise judicial discretion to exclude the evidence under s.126.

[11] Support your discussion of s.116(2)(c) with cases to help explain the approach Judge Rosetti may take in considering the practicalities of calling the defendant's girlfriend to give evidence.

In conclusion, it is likely that the evidence of the labels may be excluded because they do not suggest a strong enough link to the commission of a crime and the judge may therefore exercise his discretion to exclude the evidence. The admissibility of the transcript of the telephone calls and the statement of the defendant's associate will depend on s.115(3). As the seriousness of the offence warrants the girlfriend's attendance, it is unlikely that her hearsay statement will be admissible. In accordance with **R v Singh** [2005] EWCA Crim 96 the judge should give a direction to the jury to remind them that the hearsay evidence has not been tested in evidence.

Make your answer stand out

■ When discussing the labels, mention that they may be relevant to credibility – a brief reference to the rule of finality would be acceptable here.

■ Mention the discretion under s.78 PACE 1984 which can also be used for hearsay.

■ Briefly mention that the law on hearsay does not offend against Art.6 of the European Convention on Human Rights according to cases such as *R* v *Horncastle* [2009] EWCA Crim 964.

 Don't be tempted to...

■ Ignore s.114(1)(d) Criminal Justice Act 2003 when concluding that a piece of evidence is inadmissible hearsay because the court still has discretion to include the evidence in the interests of justice.

■ Select only one hearsay exception to use to admit the evidence without considering whether other exceptions might apply as well – it is possible to rely on more than one exception.

■ Ignore the facts of cases that are similar to the facts in the question.

■ Ignore the issue of relevance as this is also important to admissibility. Even if a piece of evidence is admissible hearsay, it must still be relevant.

Question 3

'Our provisional conclusion was that, insofar as a witness's demeanour does help the fact-finder to reach an accurate verdict, it is not so significant a fact in itself as to justify the exclusion of hearsay evidence.' (Law Commission, *Evidence in Criminal Proceedings: Hearsay and Related Topics*, Report No. 245, Cm. 3670, para 3.11)

Critically evaluate whether hearsay which is not subject to cross-examination can be regarded as a breach of Art.6 of the European Convention on Human Rights.

Answer plan

→ Define hearsay and explain the exclusionary rule.

→ Briefly discuss the exception to the rule.

→ Give examples of the difficulties with hearsay and the lack of cross-examination.

→ Examine some of the cases relating to hearsay and Art.6 European Convention on Human Rights.

→ Form a final view as to whether it leads to unfair trials.

Diagram plan

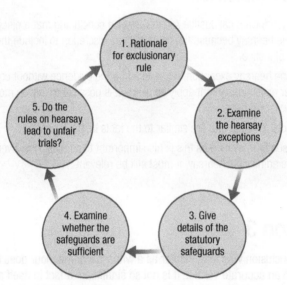

1. Rationale for exclusionary rule

2. Examine the hearsay exceptions

3. Give details of the statutory safeguards

4. Examine whether the safeguards are sufficient

5. Do the rules on hearsay lead to unfair trials?

A printable version of this diagram plan is available from www.pearsoned.co.uk/lawexpressqa

Answer

[1] An ability to offer a concise definition immediately demonstrates to the examiner that you have a good understanding of this topic area.

Hearsay evidence can be regarded as an out of court statement made by a person other than the person giving oral evidence and which is to be used to prove the truth of the matter stated.[1] In criminal proceedings hearsay evidence is subject to an exclusionary rule which makes it inadmissible unless it falls into one of the exceptions identified in s.114 of the Criminal Justice Act 2003, whereas

2 An ability to distinguish the different approaches in civil and criminal demonstrates a deeper level of understanding and takes your answer beyond a basic one.

3 Identifying the rationale for the hearsay rule provides a good starting point from which to go on to examine the effectiveness of the rule and therefore gives structure to your answer.

in civil proceedings all hearsay evidence is admissible under s.1 of the Civil Evidence Act 1995.[2]

The rationale for the exclusionary rule was set out by Lord Normand in **Teper v R** [1952] 2 All ER 447.[3] Hearsay evidence is regarded as unreliable because changes can be made in the repeating of the evidence and it is not regarded as the best evidence. However, the main difficulty with hearsay evidence is that the original maker of the statement will not be subject to cross-examination. This means that the truth of their evidence cannot be tested by rigorous questioning or observing their demeanour whilst they give evidence.

Lord Bridge in **R v Blastland** [1985] 2 All ER 1095 summarised the principal rationale for the rule as a concern that the jury would find it difficult to assess how much weight to give to such evidence.

However, the formulation of the common law exceptions such as *res gestae* (as codified in s.118 of the Criminal Justice Act 2003) acknowledged that hearsay evidence was often so closely linked to an event in question or could be the only available evidence that it could not be ignored. In **R v Andrews** [1987] AC 281 the House of Lords expanded on Lord Wilberforce's test in **Ratten v R** [1972] AC 378 as to when 'excited utterances' could be a statement forming part of the *res gestae*. In addition, statements made contemporaneously with the declarant's state of mind, health or conduct were also regarded as part of the *res gestae*. However, cases such as **Tobi v Nicholas** [1987] Crim LR 774 emphasise that *res gestae* should not be used as an excuse for not calling a witness who is available and should therefore be limited in its use.

4 This takes your answer back to the focus of the question, which is whether a lack of opportunity to cross-examine the witness of a hearsay statement affects the defendant's right to a fair trial. This shows the examiner that you are capable of keeping your answer focused.

Whilst there may be justifications for admitting hearsay evidence, there is no doubt that the inability to cross-examine the maker of the original statement cannot be ignored, particularly as the right to confront one's accusers is enshrined in Art. 6(3)(d) of the European Convention on Human Rights. According to decisions in the European Court of Human Rights such as **Luca v Italy** (2001) App. No. 33354/96, if such evidence is the sole or decisive evidence against the defendant it would then be a breach of Art.6.[4]

This issue was explored further in the case of **R v Horncastle** [2009] EWCA Crim 964 relating to the use of s.116(2)(e) statements. The Supreme Court held that the admission of hearsay

[5] Reference to cases in the European Court of Human Rights is important when addressing the part of the question relating to unfair trials and shows good application on your part.

[6] Reference to law reports demonstrates wider reading on your part and therefore an ability to put the law into its historical context which is essential in an essay style question. This will earn you additional marks.

evidence did not breach Art.6 rights because there were counterbalancing measures which safeguarded that right and ensured that admission of such evidence would be regarded as an abuse of process. The issue as stated in **Doorson v The Netherlands** (1996) App. No. 14448/88 is 'whether the proceedings as a whole, including the way the evidence was taken, were fair'.[5] Indeed, the view taken by the Law Commission in their 1997 report, *Evidence in Criminal Proceedings: Hearsay and Related Topics*, No. 245, Cm. 3670,[6] was that the demeanour of a witness is only one factor which should affect considerations about the admissibility of hearsay evidence.

With regard to s.116 the precondition relating to the maker's identity (s.116(1)) can be regarded as a counterbalancing measure. It is important because it provides the opposing party with an opportunity to find the human source of the statement and therefore find evidence to discredit that source.

Section 116 is not the only exception that poses problems as to lack of cross-examination, for example a business document under s.117 would also raise problems with regard to an inability to cross-examine the maker of the statement. However, there are counterbalancing measures here too. The court has discretion to exclude such documents under s.117(7) if there is doubt as to their reliability. This acts to ensure that the judge can examine closely the circumstances in which the document was made in a similar way to that which might have been done through cross-examination.

The main safeguard under the 2003 Act that addresses the problem of the lack of opportunity to cross-examine a witness can be found in s.124 of the 2003 Act, which provides that the opposing party may still call evidence to challenge the credibility of the maker of the statement such as a previous inconsistent statement or previous convictions. In this way the jury can be alerted to treat the evidence with caution.

In addition, if the maker of the statement could not have given evidence because they lacked capability then under s.123 of the 2003 Act the hearsay evidence will not be admissible.

In previous challenges to the UK laws on hearsay evidence, such as the case of **Trivedi v United Kingdom** [1997] EHRLR 520, the European Court of Human Rights has been influenced by the fact that there is a judicial discretion to exclude hearsay evidence. The court can rely either on its general exclusionary discretion under s.78 of the Police and Criminal Evidence Act 1984 or under s.126 of the Criminal Justice Act 2003.

The remaining risk is therefore that the admission of hearsay evidence would be a green light for juries to give such evidence too much weight. In civil proceedings before deciding how much weight to attach to such evidence a judge must consider factors under s.3 of the Civil Evidence Act 1995 such as whether it would have been reasonably practicable to have called the maker of the statement as a witness and whether any person might have a motive to conceal or misrepresent matters or whether the statement has been edited in any way.[7] In criminal proceedings safeguards are also in place in that, according to cases such as **R v Singh** [2005] EWCA Crim 96, the judge must give a direction to the jury warning them to have regard to the lack of cross-examination when deciding on the probative value of the evidence. If all these measures fail the judge can still stop the trial under s.125 of the 2003 Act if there is a danger of the jury convicting on 'unconvincing' hearsay evidence.

It has to be remembered that hearsay evidence can be used by either party in civil or criminal proceedings and the safeguards are designed to protect all parties where hearsay evidence is used. In the circumstances the counterbalancing measures lessen any potential prejudice which might be caused to a party by an inability to cross-examine the maker of the hearsay statement.

[7] Whilst hearsay evidence is readily admissible in civil proceedings, a discussion of safeguards here is still necessary and this will ensure that your answer is a full one.

✓ Make your answer stand out

- Mention *Al-Khawaja* v *United Kingdom* (2009) App. No. 26766/05, ECtHR, which involved absent witnesses and where the court held there was a breach of Art.6 and Art. 6(3)(d).
- Examine the fact that under s.116(2)(e) relating to a witness 'in fear' cross-examination can take place to the extent of deciding whether the witness is in fear and mention cases such as *R* v *Lobban* [2004] EWCA Crim 1099.
- Refer to academic opinion such as D. Birch, 'Hearsay: same old story, same old song? [2004] Crim LR 556 or R. Munday, 'The judicial discretion to admit hearsay evidence (2007) 171 *JP News* 276 when discussing the use of s.78 discretion and the discretion under s.126.

> ! **Don't be tempted to...**
>
> ■ Fail to critically evaluate the hearsay rule – you need to draw on some of the strengths and weaknesses.
>
> ■ Simply discuss all the exceptions to the hearsay rule without attempting to apply them to the issue of cross-examination.
>
> ■ Forget to mention Art.6 of the ECHR or the Human Rights Act 1998 – this is important to the issue of a fair trial.
>
> ■ Ignore the quotation taken from the Law Commission's report – you must put your answer in context.

? Question 4

The defendants, Robin and Abdul, are charged with robbery. At trial the prosecution wish to adduce the following evidence:

(a) A photofit picture of the 'mastermind' behind the drugs operation which fits Abdul's appearance and which was put together using the description provided by a former gang member. The maker of the photofit (the former gang member) has since died.

(b) The following statement made by Robin to Abdul as they got into the getaway car and overheard by Tess: 'Abdul did you empty all the safety deposit boxes?' The prosecution wish to use this statement to prove that Abdul was involved in the robbery.

(c) A report from a ballistics expert to show that gunpowder residue found at the bank matched a gun found at Robin's flat. The expert relied on tests carried out by the police forensic unit.

(d) The notes of PC Rance that, when arrested, Robin said in the police car: 'I don't know how I am going to get out of this one.' The remarks were made as a result of questioning by PC Rance. PC Rance has since retired but it is intended to use his notes as evidence.

Advise the prosecution as to the admissibility of the above evidence.

Answer plan

→ Discuss whether photofits form an exception to the hearsay rule.

→ Explain *res gestae* and apply to the statement overheard by Tess and consider whether s.114(1)(d) discretion can apply.

→ Discuss whether the expert evidence is hearsay and if so how it is admissible.

→ Consider admission of PC Rance's statement under s.117 Criminal Justice Act 2003.

Diagram plan

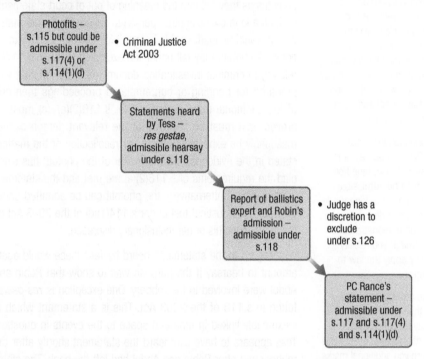

Photofits –
s.115 but could be
admissible under
s.117(4) or
s.114(1)(d)

• Criminal Justice
Act 2003

Statements heard
by Tess –
res gestae,
admissible hearsay
under s.118

Report of ballistics
expert and Robin's
admission –
admissible under
s.118

• Judge has a
discretion to
exclude
under s.126

PC Rance's
statement –
admissible under
s.117 and s.117(4)
and s.114(1)(d)

A printable version of this diagram plan is available from www.pearsoned.co.uk/lawexpressqa

Answer

In order to advise the prosecution as to each piece of evidence in the trial of Robin and Abdul it is necessary to consider the exclusionary rules relating to hearsay.

(a) With regard to the photofit picture which appears to fit Abdul's appearance this evidence may be regarded as hearsay if the person who made the photofit (namely the witness) does not come to court to give evidence. The definition of hearsay is found in s.114 and s.115 of the Criminal Justice Act 2003 and relates to statements made otherwise than in oral proceedings which are to be used to prove the truth of the matter stated.[1]

Prior to the Criminal Justice Act 2003 cases such as **R v Cook** [1987] 2 WLR 775 suggested that photofits might form a special exception to the hearsay rule. However, following the 2003

[1] Setting out a definition of hearsay allows the examiner to check that you have at least a basic understanding of the subject area.

2 Setting out the previous common law position and then the current position in this way allows you to show the examiner that you understand the law has moved on in this area and that you know how to select and apply the correct approach that the court will take.

3 Having identified that photofits are hearsay, it is necessary to examine how they might be admissible despite the exclusionary rule. Selecting and discussing an exception demonstrates to the examiner your ability to correctly apply the law to the facts.

4 If you are able to identify more than one possible hearsay exception that is relevant on the facts then this will earn you additional marks.

5 By selecting the correct exception and then using authority from the leading case of R v Andrews you show a good command of the material and an ability to apply the relevant law to the facts which will earn you additional marks.

Act, s.115 made it clear that the definition of hearsay included photofits as they fell into the meaning of out of court statements and if made to cause another person to believe the matter stated then it would be inadmissible unless it fell into one of the exceptions.[2] A photofit may fall under the exception found in s.117(4) relating to criminal investigation documents. If the photofit was prepared for pending or contemplated proceedings then one of the additional requirements under s.116(2)(a)–(e) must be proved or it must be shown that the relevant person cannot reasonably be expected to have any recollection of the matters stated in the evidence.[3] As the maker of the photofit has since died the requirements of s.116(2)(a) are met and the statement is admissible.[4] Alternatively, the photofit can be admitted under the 'interest of justice' test under s.114(1)(d) of the 2003 Act by the judge using his or her inclusionary discretion.

(b) With regard to the statements heard by Tess these would again amount to hearsay if the purpose was to show that Robin and Abdul were involved in the robbery. One exception is *res gestae* found in s.118 of the 2003 Act. This is a statement which is inextricably linked in time and space to the events in question. Tess appears to have overheard the statement shortly after the robbery and after Robin and Abdul had left the bank. The statement can be regarded as an 'excited utterance' which was made by Robin at the time of a dramatic event (escape from a bank robbery) and as such it can be regarded as reliable as Robin is unlikely to have had time to make up these remarks. Cases such as **R v Andrews** [1987] AC 281 state that an interval between the event and the making of the statement is acceptable as long as the trial judge is satisfied that the statement is an instinctive one and there has been no opportunity for reflection.[5]

(c) If the report of the ballistics expert is used as an expert report in the criminal trial it will be regarded as an exception to the hearsay rule under s.118. Cases such as **R v Abadom** [1983] 1 WLR 126 establish that even if an expert relies on statistics which have been compiled by a third party this will not make the evidence hearsay as experts can take other material into account as long as their report reveals the source and basis of the information. However, the fact that the tests on the gunpowder residue were carried out by the police forensic unit rather

6 Spotting clues in the
quotation and then explaining
how this may change your
advice demonstrates a
deeper understanding of the
topic and a good command of
the material.

than the expert is of importance as it does raise a query as to whether the expert's opinion is his own or whether he has relied too heavily on the results from the criminal investigation.[6] This may affect the weight the court attaches to the evidence or even whether the judge considers that the evidence should be admitted in the first place.

[7] Showing that you have recognised that, even if hearsay evidence is admissible under an exception, it can still be excluded ensures that your answer is a full one and will in turn ensure that you gain the available marks. It would also be permissible to mention s.78 of the Police and Criminal Evidence Act 1984 as an alternative exclusionary discretion.

The judge has discretion to exclude any admissible hearsay evidence under s.126 of the 2003 Act if the grounds for excluding it substantially outweigh the case for admitting it.[7] The judge will look at the value of the evidence and issues such as the danger that admitting the evidence could waste time or cause undue prejudice to the defendant.

(d) The notes of PC Rance reveal that Robin made an admission in the police car. This may again fall into the old common law exception under s.118 of the 2003 Act. An admission can be regarded as anything which is adverse to the maker of the statement and so Robin's statement can be taken to imply that he has something to hide. The rationale for its admission is the assumption that no one would make a statement adverse to their interest unless it was true. As the statement is contained in a notebook of PC Rance it may again fall under s.117(4) exception relating to documents created for the purpose of criminal investigation. It may still be necessary to show that PC Rance cannot attend court for one of the s.116 reasons. The absence of PC Rance due to retirement does not fall into one of the exceptions under s.116(2)(a)–(e). However, if PC Rance has forgotten the contents of the statement then it can still be admissible under s.117(4). Another possible exception is s.117 generally as it includes business documents created in the course of a profession or other occupation which would include the police service.[8]

[8] The ability to use the facts to explain why an exception cannot apply is an example of good application of the law as long as you go on to suggest other possible exceptions that might apply. This makes your answer a considered and detailed one and will give an overall good impression of the quality of your answer.

[9] A discussion of the inclusionary discretion is necessary where there is doubt as to the possible admissibility of hearsay evidence using an exception. This ensures your answer is a full one and demonstrates to the examiner that you have considered all possible methods of admissibility and so will earn you additional marks.

Even if the requirements of s.117 and s.117(4) are not met the prosecution should be reminded that the judge has an inclusionary discretion under s.114(1)(d) of the 2003 Act to include otherwise inadmissible evidence.[9] However, equally, the defence could ask the judge to exercise his discretion under s.117(6), (7) to exclude the evidence if the reliability of the statement is in doubt. This may apply here because the questioning took place in the police car rather than at the police station in breach of Code

C of the Police and Criminal Evidence Act 1984 and the confession could potentially be excluded under s.76 of the 1984 Act.[10]

[10] Spotting potential clues in the question shows perception and a good level of understanding which is necessary for problem solving questions and will earn you the available marks.

Before any of the evidence can be admitted it must be shown that the maker of the statement would have been competent to give evidence if called (see s.123 of the 2003 Act). The defence can also challenge the credibility of an absent witness such as Tess or PC Rance by producing evidence to challenge their credibility such as a previous inconsistent statement made by them or evidence of previous convictions of that witness (see s.124 of the 2003 Act).

Cases such as **R v Singh** [2005] EWCA Crim 96 have confirmed that once hearsay evidence is admitted the judge should give a warning to the jury reminding them that the lack of cross-examination should be taken into account when assessing the value of the hearsay evidence.

✓ Make your answer stand out

- Discuss the rationale for excluding hearsay evidence using cases such as *Teper* v *R* [1952] 2 All ER 447.
- When discussing *res gestae*, mention Lord Wiberforce's speech in *R* v *Ratten* [1971] 3 All ER 801 relating to the need for a 'close and intimate connection' between the statement and the event and how this approach was followed in *R* v *Andrews* (above).
- When discussing the inclusionary discretion under s.114(1)(d), mention the Law Commission's report, '*Evidence in Criminal Proceedings: Hearsay and Related Topics*' (Report No. 245 Cm. 3670, 1997) that the safety valve should only be used as an exception and in very limited circumstances.

! Don't be tempted to...

- Go into great detail about s.76 PACE 1984 when discussing Robin's admission – the focus of your answer should be on s.118 of the Criminal Justice Act 2003.
- Use old law – the 2003 Act changed some of the common law position on hearsay and an example is the reversal of the decision in *R* v *Cook* (above).
- Go into great detail about opinion evidence when discussing the ballistics expert – your answer should be given in the context of s.118 and therefore do not widen the debate by discussing expert cases such as *R* v *Turner* [1975] 2 WLR 56.

Opinion evidence and previous judgments

How this topic may come up in exams

Opinion evidence and previous judgments can be examined independently of each other as essay questions and also interrelate to the topic of hearsay, i.e. s.118 Criminal Justice Act 2003 (Chapter 4), presumptions, i.e. s.11 Civil Evidence Act 1968 (Chapter 1) and character, i.e. s.100 Criminal Justice Act 2003 (Chapter 6). Opinion evidence is also commonly found in problem questions in the form of discussions of the admissibility of expert evidence and in particular the *Turner* rule.

■ Attack the question

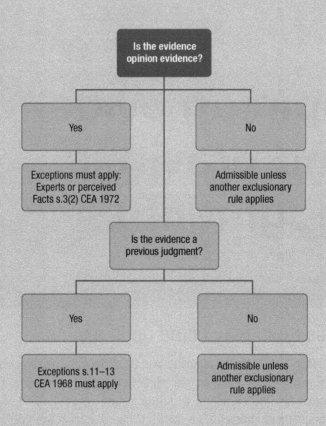

Question 1

'There is no more certain test for determining when experts may be used than the common sense inquiry whether the untrained layman would be qualified to determine intelligently and to the best possible degree the particular issue ...' (M. Ladd 'Expert testimony' (1952) 5 Vand LR 414 at p.418.)

Evaluate the veracity of the above statement with reference to the modern day approach to the admissibility of expert evidence.

Answer plan

→ Explain the general principle that opinion evidence is inadmissible and explain expert exception.

→ Discuss tests of admissibility of expert evidence and the rationale for each test.

→ Examine whether the quotation is a true reflection of the test of admissibility.

→ Analyse whether the current rules of admissibility are sufficient.

Diagram plan

A printable version of this diagram plan is available from www.pearsoned.co.uk/lawexpressqa

Answer

[1] Your introduction should explain who is regarded as an expert and how expert evidence is admissible to tie into the quotation.

An expert is regarded as a witness who is qualified due to study, training or experience to give evidence within their expertise. Expert evidence is admissible at trial by virtue of ss. 1 and 2 of the Civil Evidence Act 1972 (civil cases) and s.30 Criminal Justice Act 1988 (criminal cases).[1]

[2] This shows the examiner that you understand that expert evidence is treated differently in civil and criminal cases.

In criminal proceedings[2] expert evidence forms one of the exceptions to the exclusionary rule that opinion evidence is inadmissible to prove the truth of the matter. The exclusionary rule is based on the potential unreliability and irrelevance of opinion evidence but most importantly that it usurps the functions of the jury, who decide questions of fact. The expert exception is justified on the basis that the tribunal of fact cannot be expected to have knowledge of matters which touch on science and medicine or other disciplines outside the knowledge of a lay person. In both civil and criminal proceedings the admissibility of expert evidence is controlled by the trial judge.

[3] You should refer to the quotation in your answer as early as possible to highlight to the examiner that you are focusing on the question throughout.

M. Ladd's quotation correctly identifies that expert evidence will be admissible if it relates to matters beyond a layperson's expertise and that this is the primary test.[3] However, since 1952 the common law and statute have developed a number of additional tests relating to the admissibility of expert evidence.[4]

[4] This shows the examiner that you understand that there is more than one test for deciding on the admissibility of expert evidence.

The first test of admissibility is found in the case of **R v Turner** [1975] 2 WLR 56, CA and is similar to the test referred to in the quotation by Ladd.[5] An expert can give evidence on any relevant matters that are within their expertise and outside the knowledge and understanding of the jury. In **Turner** Lawton LJ stated that 'if on the proven facts a judge or jury can form their own conclusions without help, then the opinion of an expert is unnecessary'. The case of **Turner** focused largely on medical evidence from psychiatrists and psychologists. However, the principle extends beyond the field of medicine to include science.

[5] This shows the examiner that you understand that the central test mentioned in the quotation has a modern day version.

[6] As the legal principle in *Turner* was not followed in the case of *Lowery*, you need to address this.

The **Turner** approach conflicts with the approach taken in the earlier Privy Council case of **Lowery v R** [1974] 2 WLR 56, where expert evidence as to aggressive personality was held admissible. **Turner**, however, distinguishes **Lowery** on the basis that as one of the defendants had put forward his good character the expert evidence was also being used to rebut this and as such was not pure expert evidence.[6] The **Turner** approach is favoured where the issue is one of expert evidence rather than a challenge to the issue of the defendant's credibility.

[7] It is important to mention the civil and criminal procedure rules because they reproduce much of the common law position on experts which relates to the expert's duties and the form and content of their report.

The second test of admissibility can be found in Part 35 of the Civil Procedure Rules 1998 (civil cases) and Part 33 of the Criminal Procedure Rules 2011[7] (criminal cases), which state that an expert must give objective and unbiased opinion and that the duty of the

8 You should include a
selection of both civil
and criminal cases when
discussing experts as this
topic covers both jurisdictions.

9 This shows the examiner
that you also understand the
procedure for deciding on
the admissibility of an expert
and therefore goes beyond a
basic answer.

10 You should show the
examiner that you understand
this test is subject to some
debate and problems and is
an evolving area. This also
demonstrates your ability to
analyse the issues.

11 This shows the examiner
you are able to compare and
contrast cases and again
demonstrates an ability to
analyse the issues.

expert is to the court rather than to the party instructing them. Impartiality is therefore a further test for admissibility. In the case of **National Justice Cia Naviera SA v Prudential Co Ltd, The Ikarian Reefer** [1993] 2 Lloyd's Rep 68[8] guidance was given as to the roles of the expert, one of which was to provide independent assistance to the court and also to avoid assuming the role of an advocate. A judge may hold a *voir dire* to determine the suitability of an expert.[9] However, the case of **R v G** [2004] EWCA Crim 1240 states that to avoid satellite litigation this power should be exercised sparingly.

The third test relates to competency. It is not necessary for an expert to have formal qualifications as illustrated in the case of **R v Silverlock** [1894] 2 QB 766, CCCR where a solicitor who had a keen interest in the study of handwriting was accepted as an expert. The key requirement is expertise. However, this test can prove problematic in the areas of science or medicine that are not sufficiently developed. In **R v Gilfoyle (No. 2)** [2001] 2 Cr App Rep 57 a 'psychological autopsy' carried out on a deceased complainant was rejected as expert evidence on the basis that it was a developing and new field of science which had not been accepted by the scientific community as reliable. However, later cases such as **R v Dallagher** [2003] 1 Cr App Rep 195 and **R v Luttrell** [2004] Cr App Rep 520 took an opposing view and stated that the new field or technology in question need only be 'sufficiently well-established to pass the ordinary tests of relevance and reliability'. This approach is favoured rather than the approach in **Gilfoyle**.[10]

The fourth test relates to relevance and reliability and this is linked closely to the issue of an expert's competency. In the case of **R v Reed** [2009] EWCA Crim 2698 while reaffirming the position in **Dallagher** and **Luttrell**[11] the Court of Appeal also stated that the expert evidence would have to be sufficiently reliable to be left to the jury, thus also endorsing the **Gilfoyle** approach. This then leaves unclear the extent of the reliability test. That is whether it needs to be reliable to the extent it has been adopted by the scientific or medical community or whether a more basic test of reliability based on the judge's own acceptance of the expert's views suffice. At present there is no obligation for a judge to consider in depth the methodology or statistics which support an expert's evidence and this has led to some miscarriages of justice. For example, in the cases of **R v Clark (Sally) (No. 2)** [2003] EWCA Crim 1020 and

R v Cannings [2004] 1 WLR 2607, where data on probabilities of multiple cot deaths were subsequently rejected on appeal and the convictions quashed.

However, when considering whether to exclude expert evidence under the fairness test in s.78 of the Police and Criminal Evidence Act 1984 the judge can consider any weaknesses in the theory or methodology advanced by the expert. In addition, in both civil and criminal proceedings the court can order the use of a single joint expert, thereby eliminating any potential conflicts in approaches to the technology or methodology.

In conclusion, the modern day approach to the admissibility of expert evidence involves four main tests, all of which are sufficiently robust to ensure that expert evidence is only admitted where necessary. However, the reliability of the data used by experts requires more consideration and investigation by the trial judge to avoid miscarriages of justice.

✓ Make your answer stand out

- Briefly mention the Australian case of *R* v *Bonython* (1984) 38 SASR 45, SASC, which summarises the modern test on the admissibility of expert evidence.
- Mention academic opinion such as E. Butler-Sloss and A. Hall 'Expert witnesses, courts and the law' (2002) 95(9) *Journal of the Royal Society of Medicine* 431–4 or W. E. O'Brian, 'Court scrutiny of expert evidence' (2003) 7 Exp 172 when discussing the admissibility of expert evidence.
- Refer to the Law Commission Consultation Paper No. 190 (2009), *The Admissibility of Expert Evidence in Criminal Proceedings in England and Wales* when referring to the various tests.

! Don't be tempted to...

- Concentrate purely on criminal cases – you must also discuss the admissibility of expert evidence in the civil courts as the question is not limited to the consideration of just one jurisdiction.
- Be sidetracked into discussing whether an expert can give evidence on the ultimate issue – the focus of the essay is the test for admissibility of expert evidence.
- Be sidetracked into discussing experts and litigation privilege, as the issue here is the test for the admissibility of expert evidence rather than disclosure of expert evidence.

❓ Question 2

Christian and Peter are tried jointly on a single count of murder. Christian has confessed to being involved in the murder. Comment on the admissibility of the following evidence:

(a) Christian wishes to call Mr Nielson, an experienced psychologist, to give evidence that Christian's deprived childhood has made him more susceptible to peer pressure and therefore he is easily manipulated. This evidence is to support Christian's claim that Peter persuaded him to entice their victim, a ten-year-old boy to a nearby field and it was Peter who carried out the murder.

(b) Peter wishes to call Mr Darby, an experienced psychiatrist, to give evidence that Christian suffers from a personality disorder that makes him susceptible to lies and fantasies and that Christian's confession evidence cannot be trusted.

(c) The prosecution wish to rely on a judgement in a local county court in which the parents of the murdered 10-year-old boy sued Christian in a claim for unpaid business debts which eventually led to Christian's business going bankrupt. The prosecution allege that this is the motive for the murder.

(d) Peter wishes to call a friend of his who is interested in graphology, the study and analysis of handwriting. Whilst he has no qualifications in this area he has many years experience. He will show that the note found on the boy's body which read 'payback time' was not written by him.

Answer plan

➡ Explain the general principle on admissibility.

➡ Identify whether each piece of evidence is admissible on the facts and why.

➡ This will involve discussion of requirements of an expert and problems with evidence of psychiatrists and psychologists.

Diagram plan

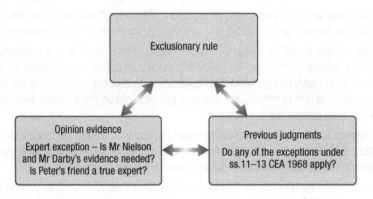

A printable version of this diagram plan is available from www.pearsoned.co.uk/lawexpressqa

¹ You should identify the evidential issues raised by the problem question so that the examiner is aware that you have broadly understood the nature of the advice you need to give.

² Shows the examiner that you understand that expert evidence is admissible as an exception to the exclusionary rule. This demonstrates a grasp of the basics.

³ This shows the examiner your understanding of the central test for admissibility which is crucial to answering the question.

⁴ Show the examiner that you are aware that the facts in the problem are similar to the case of *Lowery* and that therefore this requires you to look at whether the *Lowery* exception should apply here.

Answer

In considering whether the various pieces of evidence are admissible at Christian and Peter's trial it is necessary to consider the rules of evidence relating to opinion evidence and previous judgments at trial.¹

The evidence of Mr Nielson

Expert evidence is an exception to the rule that opinion evidence is generally inadmissible due to its unreliability, irrelevance and potential for bias.² The court must be satisfied that the expert has the necessary expertise to give evidence. As Mr Nielson is an experienced psychologist there should be no issue as to his expertise and ability to give evidence. However, the court will only receive expert evidence if it goes beyond what the tribunal of fact could decide for themselves (see **R v Turner** [1975] 2 WLR 56).³ Scientific and medical evidence would normally go beyond the knowledge of the jury. However, in this case the evidence is to be used to decide the *mens rea* for the offence and this would normally be part of the role of the jury. In the Privy Council case of **Lowery v R** [1974] AC 85, which had similar facts,⁴ expert evidence as to the propensity of the accused towards aggression was held to be relevant and admissible. However, **Turner** distinguished the facts of **Lowery** on the basis that Lowery had put forward his good character and the psychologist's evidence was needed to rebut it. Also the psychologist's evidence went beyond what the jury could be expected to decide for themselves. The fact that Christian had a deprived childhood does not in itself mean that he is easily manipulated and this would be a question of fact for the jury to decide.[5] However, if it is regarded as a personality trait (such as aggression) then the court may take the view that it is admissible. However, cases such as **R v Lodge** [2004] EWCA Crim 279 caution that such evidence should only be admitted in exceptional circumstances. The trial judge must not direct the jury to ignore or accept expert evidence. This is a matter for the jury (see **R v Lanfear** [1968] 2 QB 77).[6]

A further difficulty is that it could be argued Mr Nielson's evidence touches on the ultimate issue in the proceedings: who carried out the murder.[7] The case of **R v Stockwell (Christopher James)** 1993 97 Cr App Rep 260, CA confirms that as long as the judge tells the jury they are not bound by the expert's opinion then evidence on the ultimate issue will be allowed.

The evidence of Mr Darby

The evidence of personality disorders of an accused presents similar difficulties because personality disorders are not always regarded as mental illness.[8] However, in the case of **R v Ward** [1993] 1 WLR 619 the Court of Appeal held that if the personality disorder was so severe that it could be categorised as a mental disorder then expert evidence would be admissible to decide whether the accused's confession is reliable. Therefore, if Christian's personality disorder can be said to be severe enough to be categorised as mental disorder then Mr Darby's evidence will be admissible but only when assessing the reliability of Christian's confession. The Court of Appeal set out in **R v O'Brien** [2000] Crim LR 676 three conditions that must be satisfied namely: (1) the disorder must be of the type to render the confession unreliable – this would be the case here as Christian's personality disorder makes him susceptible to lies and fantasies; (2) the condition must be regarded as abnormal; and (3) the disorder must be shown to have existed before the confession was made. If these three criteria are met then Mr Darby's evidence will be admissible. The facts do not state when Christian developed his mental illness.[9]

[5] By using the facts in the problem question to help you decide which approach the court might take, you show the examiner that you are able to apply the law to the facts in a problem question.

[6] You have alerted the examiner to the fact that you understand that weight is a matter for the jury.

[7] It is important to discuss the 'ultimate issue' because the facts say Mr Nielson's evidence is to be used to show that it was Peter who committed the murder.

[8] This shows the examiner that you understand that the approach taken to expert evidence can differ between mental illness and personality disorder cases.

[9] There is not enough information from the facts to help you reach a firm conclusion as to whether the criteria have been met and you should say so.

The judgment of a local court

[10] This shows the examiner that you have identified that an exclusionary rule operates in this area.
[11] This shows that you have considered and rejected a possible exception to the exclusionary rule and that you understand that s.12 does not operate in reverse.

The common law rule in **Hollington v Hewthorn** [1943] KB 587, CA states that previous convictions and civil judgments are not admissible in later proceedings involving the same parties if it is to prove a factual issue in dispute.[10] Therefore, the judgment of the local county court may prove problematic. There are exceptions to the common law rule but as this is a civil judgment to be used in criminal proceedings rather than vice versa, s.12 of the Civil Evidence Act 1968 does not apply.[11]

The evidence of Peter's friend

Because the friend claims to be an expert in this field, it is necessary to consider whether his expert evidence is admissible. The issue here is that Peter's friend has no formal qualifications as an expert. However, cases such as **R v Silverlock** [1894] 2 QB 766, CCCR and **R v Dallagher** [2003] 1 Cr App R 12 suggest that expertise does not have to be acquired through formal qualifications or training. The judge will have to decide on the competency of Peter's friend to act as an expert and this will be done at a *voir dire* (see cases such as **R v G** [2004] EWCA Crim 1240). The judge will consider whether there is a formal scientific discipline for graphology and if so whether someone with formal qualifications could give more authoritative evidence than Peter's friend and whether Peter's friend is skilled and has adequate knowledge of the subject matter (see Lord Russell of Killowen's speech in **Silverlock**).

[12] This shows the examiner that you have considered the facts in broader terms than just expert evidence – it is helpful to look at s.8 here because Peter's friend may fail the competency test for an expert.

Section 8 of the Criminal Procedure Act 1865[12] allows witnesses to compare samples of handwriting and so Peter's friend could compare a sample of his handwriting and give evidence on this basis.

In summary the expert evidence of Mr Darby is likely to be admissible as expert evidence but the evidence of Mr Nielson and Peter's friend are more problematic. In the case of Mr Nielson's evidence it is more likely to be admissible if Christian has already put his good character in issue. In the case of Peter's friend the judge will have to hold a *voir dire* to decide on his competency. In respect of all the expert evidence, once admissible it will be for the jury to decide on the weight to attach to such evidence. The judge should give a warning to the jury that they are not bound by the expert evidence but no set wording is necessary (see **R v Fitzpatrick (Gerald)** [1999] Crim LR 832). The local county court judgment will be inadmissible.

Make your answer stand out

■ When discussing the judgment of the local court and the exceptions under the Civil Evidence Act 1968 you might point out that the judgment could arguably be used as evidence of bad character under s.100 of the Criminal Justice Act 2003 if it met the definition under s.98 and illustrate your point using the case of *R* v *Hogart* [2007] EWCA Crim 338, where a civil judgment in the High Court was admitted in criminal proceedings in support of the defendant's bad character to show he had been deceitful in similar circumstances.

■ Refer to academic opinion in this area such as L. Blom-Cooper 'Experts and assessors, past, present and future' (2002) 21 *Civil Justice Quarterly* 341 or T. Ward, 'Usurping the role of the jury? Expert evidence and witness credibility' (2009) 13 E & P 83 when discussing the role of the expert.

■ Refer to Part 33 of the Criminal Procedure Rules 2011 relating to experts to show knowledge of procedure.

■ Refer to further cases on the issue of an expert who has a skill rather than a qualification such as *R* v *Gilfoyle* [1996] 1 Cr App Rep 302, *R* v *Luttrell* [2004] 2 Cr App Rep 520.

■ Refer to the Judicial Studies Board Specimen Direction No. 33 in relation to warnings to juries on expert evidence.

! **Don't be tempted to...**

■ Confuse the criminal rules on opinion evidence with the civil rules where expert evidence is largely admissible.

■ Decide that Peter's friend is a non-expert and this therefore means his evidence is inadmissible – you must discuss the fact that this is a matter for the court and discuss the criteria the court will apply.

■ Spend time discussing the IQ cases such as *R* v *Masih* [1986] Crim LR 395 when discussing the evidence of Mr Darby – confine your answer to the issue of personality disorders.

■ Ignore the effect of the case of *Lowery*, as it has not been overruled and is still persuasive and has been recognised in post-*Turner* decisions.

Question 3

'... one purpose of jury trials is to bring into the jury box a body of men and women who are able to judge ordinary day-to-day questions by their own standards ...' (Roskill LJ in *R v Chard* (1971) 56 Cr App Rep 268)

Critically evaluate the above quotation with reference to the exceptions to the exclusionary rule of opinion evidence.

Answer plan

→ Briefly consider the role of the jury.

→ Consider how opinion evidence impacts on this role.

→ Explain and critically evaluate the exceptions to the exclusionary rule on opinion evidence, namely non-experts and experts.

→ Form a view as to whether the present rules are helpful or a hindrance to the role of the jury.

Diagram plan

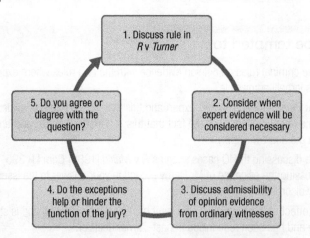

1. Discuss rule in *R v Turner*

2. Consider when expert evidence will be considered necessary

3. Discuss admissibility of opinion evidence from ordinary witnesses

4. Do the exceptions help or hinder the function of the jury?

5. Do you agree or diagree with the question?

A printable version of this diagram plan is available from www.pearsoned.co.uk/lawexpressqa

Answer

The role of jurors in the United Kingdom is largely confined to one of fact finding. The quotation in the question reflects the fact that jury members deal largely with ordinary and uncomplicated issues.[1] However, not all evidence will involve day-to-day questions and the jury will sometimes need assistance in understanding some of the factual issues at trial. Therefore, the views of a witness may play an important part in helping the jury carry out their fact-finding role.

[1] It is important to refer back to the quotation in the question to ensure that your answer is focused. Confining your answer to the relevant issues will earn you the available marks.

Witnesses are largely prevented from giving their own views and opinions in evidence. The exclusionary rule relating to opinion evidence is based on the principle that witnesses should confine their testimony to questions of fact as a witness's opinion is irrelevant and that opinion is a matter for a judge or jury rather than a witness.[2] There are, however, two important exceptions to the general rule which are influenced by a recognition that the jury may need some assistance. The first exception is found in the case of witnesses giving evidence based on perceived facts or the witness's own emotions or mental and physical condition. Where such evidence would enhance or clarify the testimony of the witness it is admissible. For example, s.89 of the Road Traffic Regulation Act 1984 allows witnesses to give an estimation of speed.

[2] Including some discussion of the rationale behind the exclusionary rule gives depth to your answer and takes it beyond a basic one.

However, the non-expert exception is not without its limitations.[3] A witness cannot testify on matters on which they have no expertise. Lord Parker CJ in **R v Davies** [1962] 1 WLR 1111 emphasised that whilst a non-expert witness might be able to give evidence that in their view the driver of a car had been drinking, only an expert could actually give evidence about whether the driver was in a fit state to drive. In addition, the opinion must be based on facts rather than hearsay evidence. There also remains an anomaly as to how the opinion evidence of a non-expert is treated. In criminal proceedings a non-expert cannot give evidence on the 'ultimate issue', namely the guilt or innocence of the defendant (see **R v Cleeland** [2002] EWCA Crim 293). However, in civil proceedings under s.3(3) Civil Evidence Act 1972 such evidence can go to any issue in the proceedings. This anomaly has not been removed despite recommendations made by the Criminal Law Revision Committee in their

[3] The question requires you to critically evaluate the exceptions to the exclusionary rule and this involves looking at the strengths and weaknesses and therefore it is important to discuss the limitations and constraints of the exceptions to the exclusionary rule of opinion evidence. Good evaluation will earn you additional marks.

[4] An ability to compare and contrast the civil and criminal jurisdiction demonstrates a good level of understanding that will earn you additional marks as it highlights to the examiner that you are aware that the question itself is not limited to the discussion of one jurisdiction but requires an evaluation of both. Reference to calls for change in this area such as the Law Revision Committee's recommendations gives authority to your arguments and will earn you additional marks.

[5] An ability to compare and contrast the difference in the limitations of the experts and non-experts is a good example of analysis and will give an overall good impression that your answer is a detailed and considered one which in turn will earn you additional marks.

[6] Certain topic areas will have key cases that the examiner is looking for. Your ability to mention key cases will ensure that you earn the available marks.

[7] An ability to state a legal principle arising from a case which is only persuasive in nature but then to identify where the same approach has been subsequently adopted in later cases in the national courts shows a sound knowledge of the case law in this area and will earn you additional marks.

Eleventh Report, Cmnd 4991 (1972).[4] It can sometimes be difficult to distinguish whether a witness's opinion does in fact touch on the ultimate issue. For example, in the case of **R v Haynes** [2008] EWCA Crim 1218 evidence that two defendants had been racing each other arguably touched on the ultimate issue of whether one of the defendants had aided and abetted death by dangerous driving. However, the Court of Appeal allowed the witnesses evidence on the basis that it was on the borderline between actual observation and opinion.

The second exception to the exclusionary rule is expert evidence. Such evidence involves opinion and, as seen in the case of **R v Abadom** [1983] 1 WLR 126, may also be based on hearsay evidence (unlike the position with non-expert evidence). In addition, according to cases such as **R v Stockwell** (1993) 97 Cr App R 260, an expert can give evidence on the ultimate issue.[5] However, the jury must be told that they are not bound to follow that opinion.

This exception has fewer limitations than non-experts because it is recognised that some issues call for special skill and knowledge which a juror may not have. However, one limitation that does exist comes from the case of **R v Turner** [1975] 2 WLR 56, in which Lawton LJ stated that expert evidence on matters within the competence of ordinary jury members is not admissible.[6] This includes issues of human nature and behaviour. Therefore, in the case of **R v Chard** (1971) 56 Cr App R 268 expert evidence was not permitted on how the defendant's mind operated at the time of the murder as there was no suggestion that the defendant was suffering from an abnormality of the mind.

One of the criticisms of the **Turner** rule is that it can lead to inconsistency of approach by the courts. In the case of **Lowery v R** [1973] AC 85, PC, a clinical psychologist was allowed to give evidence that the co-accused had an immature and easily dominated personality. This evidence was admissible to rebut good character evidence by the defendant but the Privy Council held that the evidence would have been admissible even if it had not been used as rebuttal evidence. This was because personality tests were regarded as scientific evidence and this approach was subsequently adopted in the case of **R v Randall** [2004] 1 All ER 467.[7] In addition, expert evidence has been admitted to provide helpful background rather than scientific evidence to the jury, for example in **R v Woods** [2003] EWCA Crim 1147.

Another difficulty is that making a distinction between a normal and abnormal mind has led to the drawing of an arbitrary line to help courts decide when expert evidence should be admitted. For example, in **R v Masih** [1968] Crim LR 395 the Court of Appeal held that the dividing line between the mentally normal and sub-normal should be drawn at an IQ level of 70, with those falling below 70 being designated as mentally sub-normal. However, this rule has itself been inconsistently followed and in **R v Henry** [2006] 1 Cr App R 118 (per Maurice Kay LJ) it was held that when considering the issue of the reliability of a confession it was not helpful to draw strict lines in relation to the admission of expert evidence that would help decide the question of reliability.

[8] Mentioning proposed reforms such as the Law Commission consultation paper and using academic opinion shows the examiner that your knowledge is up to date and that you have acquired a higher level of understanding through wider reading and this distinguishes the very good student from the average student.

The Law Commission in its Consultation Paper No. 190 (2009) 'The admissibility of expert evidence in criminal proceedings in England and Wales' proposes that the judge should have a 'gate-keeping' role in deciding the admissibility of expert evidence based on reliability. A. Roberts in his article, 'Rejecting general acceptance, confounding the gate-keeper: the Law Commission and expert evidence' [2009] Crim LR 551, suggests the test should be one of reliability based on whether the expert evidence has been tested and is based on sound scientific research and is accepted within the scientific community.[8]

[9] Reaching a final view as to the effectiveness of the rules in this area completes your answer and leaves the examiner with the impression of a well thought out and structured answer which in turn will earn you extra marks.

In the circumstances whilst a jury's fact-finding role should be protected wherever possible, it is clear that in order to ensure that the jury are provided with all the available facts assistance is sometimes needed either from a non-expert witness or indeed an expert witness. Whilst the rules relating to both can often seem inconsistent, it is also necessary that the rules remain flexible enough for judges to disregard them where necessary because the drawing of strict lines does not always ensure the proper administration of justice.[9]

Make your answer stand out

- When discussing the non-expert witness exception you can also mention cases such as *Wright* v *Tatham* (1838) 4 Bing NC 489, where the opinion of a person was accepted and *R* v *Beckett* (1913) 8 Cr App Rep 204, where condition of objects or their general value could be commented upon by a witness.

- When criticising the *Turner* rule mention cases such as *R* v *MacKenney* (1981) 76 Cr App Rep 271 and *R* v *G and H* [2005] EWCA Crim 1828 where, despite the *Turner* rule, medical evidence on witness reliability was admitted because it did more than show whether a witness was reliable it showed the witness had an 'abnormal' condition.

- Use comparative jurisdictions such as the US (r.701 Federal Rules of Evidence) and New Zealand (s.24 New Zealand's Evidence Act 2006), where similar exceptions relating to non-experts exist.

- When discussing the use of evidence of psychiatrists and psychologists refer to journal articles such as D. Faust and J. Ziskin 'The expert witness in psychology and psychiatry', (1988) *Science*, 24 July on criticisms of the ability of such experts to reach reliable or valid conclusions.

- When discussing proposed reforms to the admissibility of expert evidence also mention the report of Auld LJ *A Review of the Criminal Courts of England and Wales* (2001), which rejected calls for court appointed experts in criminal proceedings.

! Don't be tempted to...

- Simply discuss the role of the jury without tying this in to issues relating to opinion evidence.

- Fail to address the quotation in the question – you must examine the quotation in the context of the question.

- Discuss only the expert exception to the exclusionary rule without considering non-experts – you must discuss all the exceptions to the rule.

❓ Question 4

Consider the admissibility of the following evidence in the context of the rules relating to opinion evidence and previous judgments:

(a) Witness A in a criminal trial relating to dangerous driving who intends to give evidence that in her opinion the defendant's car was being driven at 100 mph and that the defendant was unfit to drive.

(b) In a criminal trial of defendant B for handling stolen goods (namely computer equipment) the prosecution wish to use details of the conviction of defendant B's friend for theft of the same computer equipment.

(c) In a civil action for defamation brought by claimant C the defence wish to produce evidence that claimant C has a conviction for perjury.

(d) In a criminal trial where defendant D confesses to murder his defence team wish to produce medical evidence that he suffers from schizophrenia and that this therefore makes the confession unreliable.

Answer plan

→ Discuss the exception of perceived facts when discussing witness A's ability to give opinion evidence.

→ Examine s.74 Police and Criminal Evidence Act 1984 in the context of defendant B.

→ Apply s.11 of the Civil Evidence Act 1968 in relation to claimant C.

→ Discuss the use of expert evidence in relation to the reliability of confession evidence for defendant D.

Diagram plan

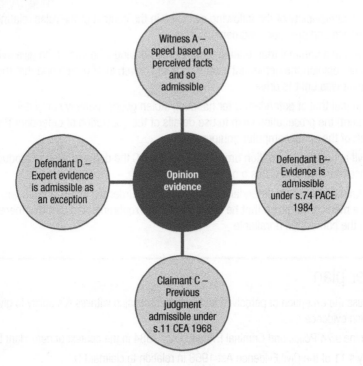

A printable version of this diagram plan is available from www.pearsoned.co.uk/lawexpressqa

Answer

In considering the admissibility of the various pieces of evidence it will be necessary to consider the exclusionary rule relating to opinion evidence and the use of previous judgments at trial.

[1] Briefly discussing the rationale for the exclusionary rule helps to give some background to your answer and in turn demonstrates to the examiner that you have a wider level of understanding of the origins of the rule.

Witness A

Opinion evidence is normally inadmissible on the basis that it is irrelevant to the facts in issue and usurps the jury's fact-finding role and their determination of the 'ultimate issue'.[1] However, witnesses should only testify to facts which are within their own personal knowledge rather than those based on opinion. Section 89 of the Road Traffic Regulation Act 1984 allows witnesses to give an estimate of speed. As long as witness A actually saw the car at the time and therefore is in a position to estimate the speed of the car, her evidence will be acceptable. It will still be open to the defence to challenge the estimate given and the jury can still decide how much weight to attach to A's evidence. However, witness A goes on to suggest that the defendant was unfit to drive. This is not based on anything witness A has seen or knows to be a fact. According to **R v Davies** [1962] 1 WLR 1111, where a witness gives opinion evidence they must also give details of the factual basis on which they formed that evidence.[2] As shown in the case of **Davies** the question of fitness to drive may well be an issue for an expert witness. This part of witness A's evidence would have to be excluded as opinion evidence which witness A is not qualified to give.

[2] Spotting additional clues in the question such as the fact that witness A's evidence goes beyond what she observed shows the examiner that you are perceptive and have command of the material and are able to recognise how to apply the correct law to the facts.

Defendant B

The admission of the previous conviction of defendant B's friend in defendant B's criminal trial would usually be inadmissible under the rule in **Hollington v Hewthorn** [1943] KB 587. Whilst this rule originates in civil proceedings it also has application in criminal proceedings. The rule prevented previous convictions and civil judgments being used in subsequent proceedings between different parties to prove the truth of the conviction or judgment. Section 74 of the Police and Criminal Evidence Act 1984 (as amended by s.331 of the Criminal Justice Act 2003) allows evidence of the friend's conviction to be admissible to show that the friend committed the offence of the theft of the computer equipment if it is also relevant to the issue of whether the defendant handled those same stolen goods. The admission of the friend's conviction raises a persuasive presumption that the friend committed the theft of the goods but this can be challenged by the friend. The judge still has a discretion to exclude such evidence under s.78 Police and Criminal Evidence Act on the basis that its admission would have such an adverse effect on the fairness in the proceedings it ought not to be admitted.[3] In the case of **R v Curry** [1988] Crim LR 527 it was held by the Court of Appeal that s.74 should be used sparingly, especially in cases such as conspiracy where the prejudicial effect of admitting the previous conviction was likely to be high.

[3] A discussion of admissibility always requires you to look at how the evidence could equally be excluded and therefore a discussion of s.78 PACE is relevant here. This will earn you marks for providing a full rather than a partial answer to the problem.

Claimant C

Evidence in the civil trial that claimant C has a previous conviction for perjury would previously have offended against the rule in **Hollington v Hewthorn**. However, s.11 of the Civil Evidence Act 1968 forms an exception to the rule. A criminal conviction from a UK court can be used in civil proceedings for the purpose of proving that the person was convicted. Under s.11(2)(a) a persuasive presumption is raised that claimant C committed the offence but it is open to claimant C to challenge this although cases such as **Hunter v Chief Constable of the West Midlands Police** [1981] 3 WLR 906 state that whilst this would only need to be shown on a balance of probabilities it would still be a difficult thing to prove.

However, as claimant C's civil action is for defamation, s.13 of the 1968 Act also applies which states that evidence that a person has been convicted of a criminal offence is conclusive proof that they committed the offence. In the circumstances there is an irrebutable presumption which claimant C could not challenge as far as the conviction is concerned.[4]

4 An ability to recognise more than one relevant issue within the scenario, namely the s.13 exception of the Civil Evidence Act 1968 as well as s.11, demonstrates a deeper level of thinking and awareness of the issues, which in turn will earn you additional marks.

Defendant D

Expert evidence forms an exception to the exclusionary rule relating to the admission of opinion evidence. However, according to the case of **R v Turner** [1975] 2 WLR 56 the evidence will only be admissible if it assists the judge and jury rather than taking over the jury's fact finding role. Expert medical evidence relating to whether or not defendant D suffers from schizophrenia is clearly admissible because it goes beyond what the jury could be expected to decide for themselves. However, the medical evidence is admissible for another purpose and that is to show that the schizophrenia makes defendant D's confession unreliable. In cases such as **R v Ward** [1993] 1 WLR 619 and **R v O'Brien** [2000] Crim LR 676 the Court of Appeal expressed the view that the evidence of a psychiatrist or a psychologist could be admitted to show that a defendant's confession is unreliable because they were suffering from the mental condition at the time. The condition must be categorised as a mental illness or condition and schizophrenia can be regarded as satisfying this. The case of **O'Brien** emphasised that the condition must be one that would make the confession unreliable and that

⁵ A summary of the issues in the conclusion helps the examiner to see at a glance that you have covered all the characters in the question as well as providing a good structure to your answer by summarising your final view/advice.

there must be independent evidence to show that the defendant suffered from it before the confession was made.

In the circumstances it is likely that the evidence of claimant C and defendant D will be admissible without any difficulties. However, only part of witness A's evidence will be admissible and this is the part relating to the estimation of speed. The previous conviction of defendant B's friend will depend on the view taken by the trial judge as to whether its admission would be too prejudicial.⁵

 Make your answer stand out

- When mentioning the fact that a witness cannot comment on the 'ultimate issue' in a trial, point out that whilst this has been removed in civil proceedings under s.3(3) Civil Evidence Act 1972, it has not yet been removed in criminal proceedings despite a recommendation in the Criminal Law Revision Committee's Eleventh Report (Cmnd 4991, para 270).
- When discussing s.74 PACE 1984 discuss further cases, criticising its use such as R v Robertson [1987] 3 All ER 231 and in particular Lord Lane's comments regarding the correct interpretation of 'issue in the proceedings'.
- When discussing s.74 PACE 1984 mention that the provisions of s.100 of the Criminal Justice Act 2003 could also apply on the facts.

! **Don't be tempted to...**

- Ignore the fact that witness A expresses two different opinions – you must examine each in turn.
- Go into great detail about s.100 Criminal Justice Act 2003 when discussing defendant B's friend – whilst this section is relevant the focus of the question is on its admission as proof of the conviction rather than issues of credibility as under s.100 and so your focus should be on s.74 of PACE 1984.
- Ignore the fact that both s.11 and s.13 of the 1968 Act are capable of applying to the circumstances of claimant C.

Character evidence

How this topic may come up in exams

This is a big topic because it includes the rules on both good and bad character. Character (together with hearsay, improperly obtained evidence, confessions, silence and competence and compellability) is rarely omitted from an examination paper because it is an important area. Character can appear in the form of either an essay or problem question and it is difficult to predict which form it will take. However, in whatever form it is examined it will be necessary to have a detailed understanding of the gateways under ss.100 and 101 Criminal Justice Act 2003. Judicial discretion is also very important in this area.

Attack the question

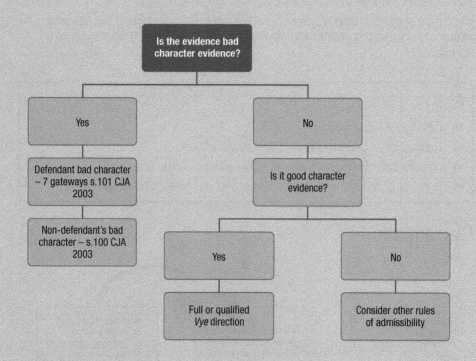

Question 1

'A person's character should not be regarded as invisible. If certain parts of it are sufficiently relevant to be revealed to fact-finders then so be it, but no more should be revealed than is necessary for the interests of justice to be served.' (Law Commission Report: *Evidence of Bad Character in Criminal Proceedings* (2001) No. 273, para. 1.8(6))

Discuss the above quotation in the context of the admissibility and use of bad character evidence in criminal proceedings and whether this prejudices the defendant's right to a fair trial.

Answer plan

→ Definition of bad character.

→ Discuss use for propensity and credibility under s.101.

→ Consideration of safeguards such as judicial warnings in this area.

→ Is the use of bad character evidence curtailed or can it lead to breaches of Art.6?

Diagram plan

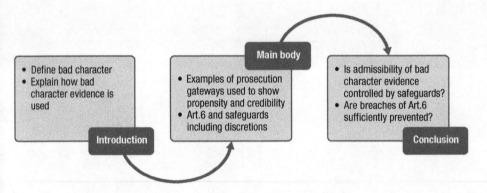

A printable version of this diagram plan is available from www.pearsoned.co.uk/lawexpressqa

Answer

¹ A definition in your introduction shows the examiner that you understand the meaning of the term that you have been asked to discuss and therefore that you have at least a basic level of understanding.

The Criminal Evidence Act 1898 did not contain a definition of bad character but it was widely accepted to mean both reputation and disposition. The Criminal Justice Act 2003 has given bad character evidence a wider definition under s.98 of the 2003 Act as misconduct, which means 'the commission of an offence or other reprehensible behaviour'.¹ Cases such as **R v Z (prior acquittal)** [2000] 3 WLR 117, HL show that it is immaterial whether the defendant was convicted of an offence or acquitted.²

² Using cases to explain the definition demonstrates wider reading on your part, takes you beyond a basic answer and shows application.

Due to the fact that bad character evidence is circumstantial evidence, it has greater potential to breach Art.6 of the ECtHR in relation to the defendant's right to a fair trial. Therefore, the use to which bad character evidence is put is very important.³

³ This ties your answer in to the question and shows that you are able to focus your answer on what is relevant.

The quotation of the Law Commission reflects the fact that character evidence should be treated with caution.⁴ Prior to the Criminal Justice Act (CJA) 2003, the Criminal Evidence Act 1898 gave the defendant a 'shield' (in certain circumstances) against bad character evidence being referred to during cross-examination.

⁴ It is important to refer to the quotation in your answer as this shows the examiner that your answer is focused and that you are attempting to address the question.

In addition, bad character evidence was confined largely to challenging a defendant's credibility (see **R v McLeod** [1994] 3 All ER 254) and such character could only be used towards propensity if its probative value outweighed its prejudicial effect such as in the case of similar fact evidence (see cases such as **DPP v Boardman** [1974] 3 WLR 673 as clarified in **DPP v P** [1991] 3 WLR 161, HL).⁵

⁵ A description of how the rules on bad character have evolved shows a command of the subject area as well as an ability to analyse.

⁶ This demonstrates to the examiner that you have an understanding of the gateways and avoids the need simply to provide a bare list of all the gateways but shows that you can instead discuss them in some context. A focused answer shows that you are in command of the material.

The Criminal Justice Act 2003 extended the ways in which bad character evidence could be admitted using seven gateways. In addition, once the evidence has been admitted under a gateway it potentially becomes relevant to both credibility and propensity. It is arguably the use of bad character evidence towards propensity which poses the greatest risk to the defendant's right to a fair trial under Art.6 of the European Convention on Human Rights. The gateways that pose the greatest problem for the defendant are those used by the prosecution (gateways (c), (d), (f) and (g) and the co-defendant (gateway (e)). All these gateways can be used towards credibility or propensity or both.⁶

[7] By explaining to the examiner where and why you intend to concentrate your arguments, you justify your structure and show an ability to sift and select relevant information.

[8] An understanding that gateway (d) is not restricted simply to offences of the same description and same category shows the examiner that you have more than a basic knowledge of this area of law.

[9] An ability to compare and contrast decisions in this way using cases such as R v Sully and R v Michael is a good example of analysis and will earn you extra marks.

The gateway which provides the most scope for using bad character evidence towards propensity is s.101(1)(d) as this gateway is concerned with propensity.[7] Section 103 provides that the question of whether the evidence has substantial probative value to a matter in issue between the prosecution and the defence is decided by showing the defendant has a propensity to commit offences of the kind for which he is charged or a propensity for untruthfulness.

Gateway (d) also allows in evidence which is not restricted to simply previous convictions of the same description or same category, as can be seen in cases such as **R v Isichei** [2006] EWCA Crim 1815,[8] where evidence of involvement in the importation of cocaine was admitted in a trial for robbery as it supported a witness's visual identification evidence. Section 144 of the Coroners and Justice Act 2009 has also extended this area to include convictions in foreign jurisdictions which increases the potential for prejudicial effect.

However, whilst the judge is entitled to take propensity into account under gateway (d), it is only one of the factors the judge will have to look at and safeguards have been built into gateway (d). Section 103(1)(a) provides that propensity to commit an offence is not relevant where the defendant having propensity 'makes it no more likely that he is guilty of the offence'. The case of **R v Hanson; R v Gilmore, R v P** [2005] 1 WLR 3169 suggests that a single conviction or one committed some time ago will have less probative value. Also under s.103(3) if the judge considers that due to the passage of time the previous convictions have less probative value he can exclude such evidence. However, what constitutes propensity is a matter of fact and this has led to inconsistent approaches, for example, in **R v Sully** [2007] All ER (D) 421 (Nov) two convictions for sexual assault on children which were over 30 years old were admitted, whereas in **R v Michael** [2007] Crim LR 637 a 20-year-old conviction for possessing a sawn off shotgun was held to have been wrongly admitted.[9]

The judge also has an exclusionary discretion under s.101(3) and can exclude such evidence if its admission would have an adverse

[10] It is important to mention this case to show the examiner that you understand that it is the judge who decides how the bad character evidence is to be used once it is admitted and directs the jury accordingly. This shows wider knowledge on your part.

[11] By continuing to compare and contrast the old and new law you give force to your arguments about the present rules on admissibility prejudice a defendant's right to a fair trial. You also continue to show analytical skills and a deeper understanding of the material.

effect on the fairness in the proceedings. In addition, cases such as **R v Highton** [2005] 1 WLR 3472 have confirmed that a distinction should be drawn between the basis for admitting bad character evidence and the use to be made of it.[10] As such the judge must give a clear warning to the jury in his summing-up against placing undue reliance on such evidence and explain why it has been admitted and the ways in which it is relevant.

However, this can be problematic in itself. For example, whilst the 1898 Act restricted the equivalent of gateway (g) (casting imputations on a prosecution witness under s.1(3)(ii) Criminal Evidence Act 1898) to going to credit, in **R v Highton** (above) the trial judge's decision to give a propensity direction for gateway (g) was upheld.[11] Additionally, creating a false impression under gateway (f) is technically capable of going towards propensity as well as credibility, although there is not a logical link with propensity.

However, for gateways (c) and (f) the judge can exercise judicial discretion under s.78 PACE to exclude bad character evidence and for gateway (d) and (g) the discretion under s.101(3) would apply. In addition, under s.105(3) for gateway (f) the defendant can withdraw or disassociate himself from the 'false impression' alleged to have been created.

Under the second part of gateway (d) relating to propensity to be untruthful the jury can only use such evidence towards credibility if it shows a propensity to be untruthful. However, s.103(1)(b) has limited effect as the Explanatory Notes to the 2003 Act make clear that it is to be limited to evidence such as convictions for perjury.

[12] A reasoned conclusion demonstrates that you are able to reach a view based on the material.

In conclusion,[12] whilst the circumstantial nature of bad character evidence makes it inherently prejudicial the 2003 Act imposes a number of safeguards such as a judicial discretion and warning to exclude such evidence taking into account the nature, seriousness and number of incidents of bad character. However, the fact that propensity is a question of fact still provides the potential for miscarriages of justice to occur in this area.

✓ Make your answer stand out

■ When discussing bad character definition compare with the previous more limited definition under the common law in *R* v *Rowton* (1865) 29 JP.

■ Refer to the Law Commission's Report, *Previous Misconduct of a Defendant* (1996) CP No.141 when talking about the prejudicial effect of bad character evidence – report identifies 'reasoning prejudice' and 'moral prejudice'.

■ Provide brief discussion of gateways (c), (g), (e) and (f) and point out that no discretion appears to apply to (e) and mention cases such as *R* v *Musone* [2007] 1 WLR 2467, where the Court of Appeal held it was possible for a judge to exclude evidence under gateway (e) where the notice requirements under the Criminal Procedure Rules 2011 had not been met.

■ Use of other cases to support inconsistencies in approach to propensity under gateway (d), e.g. *R* v *M* [2007] Crim LR 637, *R* v *Awaritefe* [2007] EWCA Crim 706, etc.

■ Refer to cases such as *R* v *Campbell* [2007] 1 WLR 2798 and *R* v *Ellis* [2010] EWCA Crim 163 when discussing s.103(1)(b).

■ Mention *R* v *Lafayette* [2008] EWCA Crim 3238 when discussing the direction to the jury on the use of the bad character evidence.

! Don't be tempted to...

■ Discuss or list all of the seven gateways under s.101 Criminal Justice Act 2003 – confine yourself to the gateways relevant to the prosecution on the issue of a fair trial.

■ Ignore how bad character is used – you must discuss the issue of credibility and propensity because the quotation and question require you to focus on the use of bad character evidence not only its potential to prejudice a fair trial.

■ Ignore the issue of judicial discretion as this effects the question of admissibility and therefore whether the evidence can be used towards credibility and propensity. It is also relevant to the issue of a fair trial.

? Question 2

Emilio and Badel, who are both security guards, are charged with robbery of a local bank. Emilio has no previous convictions but Badel has a previous conviction for theft in 2001. At trial Badel comes to court wearing his security guard uniform. Badel alleges in his defence that the money was stolen by Emilio. Emilio denies any involvement in the offence. The prosecution have a witness, Sereena, who was a passer-by at the time of the robbery and who is able to place both Emilio and Badel at the scene of the crime. Sereena has a previous conviction for perjury in 1990.

Advise the defence about the evidential issues arising from the above set of facts.

Answer plan

→ Discuss *Vye* direction in respect of Emilio.

→ Define bad character and discuss gateways (d) and (f) of s.101 Criminal Justice Act 2003 for Badel.

→ Discuss s.100 Criminal Justice Act 2003 for Sereena.

→ Consider judicial discretion in respect of bad character evidence.

→ Consider whether all the evidence goes to credibility or propensity.

Diagram plan

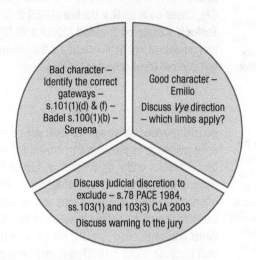

Bad character –
Identify the correct gateways –
s.101(1)(d) & (f) –
Badel s.100(1)(b) –
Sereena

Good character –
Emilio
Discuss *Vye* direction
– which limbs apply?

Discuss judicial discretion to
exclude – s.78 PACE 1984,
ss.103(1) and 103(3) CJA 2003
Discuss warning to the jury

A printable version of this diagram plan is available from www.pearsoned.co.uk/lawexpressqa

Answer

In order to advise Emilio and Badel's defence team it will be necessary to consider the evidential rules relating to good and bad character evidence.

Emilio

[1] Show the examiner that you understand the importance from the facts that Emilio has no convictions and that you understand the basis of the *Vye* direction and are able to apply it. This demonstrates that you have the necessary knowledge to lay the foundations for a good argument on the facts.

Emilio has no previous convictions and in those circumstances he may be entitled to a good character direction. According to cases such as **R v Aziz** [1995] 3 WLR 53 and **R v Vye** [1993] 1 WLR 471, a defendant's good character is relevant to credibility and propensity in the same way that bad character is relevant. According to the guidelines in **Vye**, the trial judge should give a direction to the jury about the relevance of Emilio's good character as seen by the lack of any previous convictions.[1] The first limb of the **Vye** direction relating to credibility should be given because Emilio has made a pre-trial statement, namely his police station interview. The second limb relating to propensity is nearly always given regardless of whether Emilio has made pre-trial statements or testifies at court.

[2] This shows the examiner that you understand that there is no particular form of wording for the *Vye* direction and that you understand that a *Vye* direction is normally mandatory. This gives depth to your answer.

The form of the direction is a matter for the judge as long as it covers the relevant limbs (see **R v Miah** [1997] 2 Cr App Rep 12, CA). Cases such as **R v Durbin** [1995] 2 Cr App Rep 84, CA and **Teeluck v State of Trinidad** [2005] 1 WLR 2421 have confirmed that an appeal will be successful if the failure to give a **Vye** direction affected the outcome of the trial.[2]

Badel

[3] This shows the examiner that you are able to use the facts to decide on a suitable gateway and that you have spotted the importance of the clue that Badel comes to court wearing a uniform. This shows good practical skills and will earn you marks for good application.

Badel's previous conviction for theft will be regarded as bad character evidence as previous convictions fall within the definition of bad character under s.98 Criminal Justice Act 2003, spent convictions will also fall within the definition. Therefore, although the offence occurred in 2001 it may still be admissible but only if it satisfies one of the criteria in s.101 of the 2003 Act. The fact that Badel comes to court wearing his security guard uniform is relevant because under s.101(1)(f) it may be regarded as evidence to correct a false impression given by Badel.[3] Under s.105(1)(a) the

⁴ You should deal with the fact that the defendant can stop gateway (f) from applying – if you do not cover this issue you will not have fully dealt with gateway (f).

⁵ Dealing with the issue of judicial discretion to exclude is important to ensure that you again fully apply gateway (f).

⁶ This shows the examiner that you have used the facts to help you decide the use to which the bad character evidence will be put. This is an example of good application and will earn you extra marks as it shows a deeper level of understanding.

⁷ You should use as many gateways as possible as long as the facts suggest admissibility under that gateway this ensures your answer is a full one.

⁸ Show the examiner that you are able to apply gateway (d) to the facts in the problem question.

⁹ This shows that you have understood that the age and number of convictions is important and that you have spotted and dealt with an important clue. This will continue to earn you the available marks.

¹⁰ Again, you should deal with judicial discretion otherwise you will not have fully applied gateway (d) and will not therefore obtain all the available marks for this part of the question.

false impression can be express or implied and can be by words or conduct (s.105(4)). Conduct under s.105(4) includes appearance or dress. The prosecution may therefore seek to admit Badel's previous convictions under gateway (f). However, Badel can withdraw or disassociate himself from the false impression (s.105(3))⁴ by no longer wearing his security guard uniform. The prosecution will then be prevented from relying on gateway (f).

If the convictions are admitted under gateway (f) the defence can ask the judge to exercise his discretion to exclude the convictions under s.78 Police and Criminal Evidence Act 1984 on the basis that its admission would have an adverse effect on the fairness of the proceedings (as confirmed in cases such as **R v Highton** [2005] 1 WLR 3472, HL⁵ and **R v Weir (Anthony Albert)** [2005] EWCA Crim 2866). Even if the evidence is admitted it will go to credibility rather than propensity.⁶

Alternatively, the prosecution may rely on gateway (d)⁷ and argue that the previous convictions are relevant to an important matter in issue between the defence and the prosecution. Section 103(1)(a) states that this includes a propensity to commit offences of the kind with which the defendant is charged or a propensity for untruthfulness. Theft cannot be said to be the same description as the present charge of robbery. Theft and the present charge of robbery, however, are within the same category of offences under the Theft Act (see the Criminal Justice Act 2003 (Categories of Offences) Order (SI 2004/3346)).⁸ However, cases such as **R v Hanson, Gilmore and Pickering** [2005] 1 WLR 3169 have confirmed that a single or small number of convictions will not necessarily show propensity and that old convictions could affect the fairness of the proceedings.⁹

The defence may ask the judge to exercise his discretion under s.101(3) to exclude the evidence of Badel's previous conviction on the basis that its admission would have an adverse effect on the fairness in the proceedings. Alternatively, the court can exercise its discretion under s.103(3) to exclude the evidence of the conviction due to the length of time since the conviction (see cases such as **R v M** [2007] Crim LR 637).¹⁰

[11] You could equally cite the case of *R* v *Hanson* here. It is OK to use different cases as long as the legal principle is the same but you should always cite important leading cases from which guidelines originate.

[12] This shows that you understand that the rules on bad character apply to non-defendants as well and is covered by a separate statutory provision and this is necessary for any basic understanding of bad character and is knowledge that you would be expected to have in order to obtain the available marks.

[13] This demonstrates your understanding that bad character evidence is not automatically admissible under s.100 and this in turn shows a good level of knowledge.

[14] It is important to identify the correct gateway because this shows application of the law to the facts.

[15] This shows the examiner that you understand what gateway (b) says and more importantly that you are able to apply it to the facts. This will earn you the available mark.

[16] This shows the examiner that you understand that, before applying gateway (b), the judge must consider certain factors.

The judge must give a clear direction to the jury as to how the bad character evidence is to be treated, that is whether it goes to credibility, propensity or both (see cases such as **R v Edwards** [2005] EWCA Crim 1813)[11] and that they should not place 'undue reliance' on the evidence.

Sereena

Sereena is an important prosecution witness because she is able to give identification evidence that places Emilio and Badel at the scene. However, the defence could challenge her credibility by seeking to admit bad character evidence on the basis of her previous conviction for perjury. Under s.100 of the 2003 Act[12] a non-defendant's bad character is admissible if it falls into one of three gateways. However, leave of the court is required.[13] Gateway (b) is relevant here.[14] The defence may argue that the evidence of Sereena's bad character has substantial probative value in relation to a matter in issue in the proceedings (i.e. whether or not Emilio and Badel committed the offence). They would also have to show that it is of substantial importance in the context of the case as a whole. If the prosecution evidence rests solely or mainly on Sereena's identification evidence then her credibility can be said to be of substantial importance and if the defence's case is that Sereena is lying then her previous conviction becomes relevant.[15]

In order to decide the probative value the court will consider the factors in s.100(3).[16] Therefore, the fact that the evidence relates to only one conviction is important because the court will consider the nature and number of the events in question and one conviction

[17] This again shows that you understand from the facts that the age of the conviction is relevant.

does not suggest persistent dishonesty. The fact that the conviction was in 1990[17] is also of importance as the court will have to consider when the events are alleged to have occurred. A conviction in 1990 does not suggest the witness cannot be trusted now.

The defence should be advised that Emilio will be entitled to both limbs of the **Vye** direction. However, Badel's previous convictions could be used as evidence against him by the prosecution who may rely on either gateway (d) or (f) of s.101. The defence should object to the admission of the bad character evidence and ask the court to use its discretion to exclude the evidence. The defence will have some difficulties relying on Sereena's conviction for perjury. Whilst it suggests a propensity for untruthfulness, it may be excluded by the judge when applying the s.100(3) factors.

 Make your answer stand out

- Briefly discuss the difference between the s.101(3) discretion under the Criminal Justice Act 2003 and s.78 PACE 1984 namely that the case of *Hanson* suggests that, whilst the wording under s.78 is 'may' and the wording under s.101(3) is 'must', they are both discretions.

- When discussing the possibility that Badel's convictions might be spent mention the Rehabilitation of Offenders Act 1974 and the fact that whilst the Act applies to criminal proceedings the Practice Direction (Criminal Proceedings: Consolidation) [2002] 1 WLR 2870 provides that references to spent convictions in criminal proceedings should not be made without leave of the court.

- Briefly discuss the fact that s.100 and s.101 provide an exception to the rule of finality.

- Discuss how the use of good and bad character in joint trials can prejudice a co-defendant by discussing cases such as *R* v *Cain* (1993) 99 Cr App R 208.

Don't be tempted to...

- Discuss all the gateways for s.100 and s.101 of the 2003 Act – only discuss the gateways that apply on the facts.

- ignore the operation of judicial discretion in this area – even if a gateway is satisfied the bad character evidence may still be excluded.

- Discuss the character provisions in the Criminal Evidence Act 1898 or the Youth Justice and Criminal Evidence Act 1999 – you must apply the current law to a problem question and the correct statute is the Criminal Justice Act 2003.

- Do not be side tracked in to discussing the *Turnbull* warning in respect of Sereena simply because identification is mentioned – the main issue is the admissibility of her previous conviction for perjury.

Question 3

'The fact that a man has an unblemished reputation leads to the presumption that he is incapable of committing the crime for which he is being charged.' (Cockburn CJ in *R v Rowton* (1865) 29 JP)

Analyse the above quotation with regard to the modern day approach to extent to the admissibility of good character evidence.

Answer plan

→ Consider the definition of good character.

→ Discuss how good character was historically used and explain the present day position.

→ Evaluate whether there are any advantages and disadvantages to the current use of *Vye* directions using cases to analyse the court's approach.

→ Reach a view as to whether the current system is effective.

Diagram plan

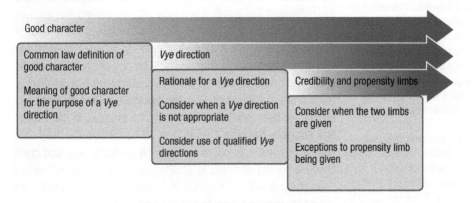

A printable version of this diagram plan is available from www.pearsoned.co.uk/lawexpressqa

Answer

[1] A definition which also includes the case mentioned in the quotation is a good way to show the examiner that you are tackling the issues in the question at an early stage and therefore that you are able to keep your answer focused.

Good character evidence has historically been restricted to the general reputation of the defendant as known in his neighbourhood rather than the personal views held of him by a witness. This rule came from the case **R v Rowton** (1865) 29 JP.[1] However, the admissibility of such evidence was primarily restricted to the credibility of the defendant rather than the defendant's propensity to commit the offence charged. Whilst Cockburn CJ in **Rowton** accepted that good character raised a presumption of innocence there was a reluctance to change the law as it stood at the time.

[2] A brief historical mention of the emergence of the current rules gives some depth to your answer and in turn gives the examiner the impression that you have a wider understanding of the topic area and this in turn will earn you extra marks.

The **Rowton** rule emerged at a time when the defendant was neither competent nor compellable to testify on his own behalf. However, following s.1 of the Criminal Evidence Act 1898 the rule appeared less logical as the defendant could now give evidence of his own good character without relying on others. It seemed unfair that bad character evidence could go to both credibility and also propensity in some circumstances under the 1898 Act but that good character could not go to both.[2]

The position was settled in the cases of **R v Vye** [1993] 1 WLR 471. In **R v Vye** Lord Chief Justice Taylor laid down clear guidelines which confirmed that a defendant with good character would be entitled to a judicial direction that good character went to credibility and/or propensity. Good character in this sense meant the absence

³ This shows the examiner that you understand that there is a difference between good character evidence generally and the meaning of good character for the purposes of a *Vye* direction. This shows a good understanding of the topic and will earn you the available marks.

⁴ It is important to explain the two limbs of the *Vye* direction to show the examiner that you understand that the direction will vary. This is necessary to any basic understanding of the topic area and will earn you marks.

⁵ This begins your attempt at analysing the issues which is important in order to move your answer away from a purely descriptive one of the law to one where you are able to discuss the strengths and weaknesses of the rules relating to good character evidence. Good analysis will earn you extra marks.

⁶ Discussion of a qualified *Vye* direction is important to a good understanding of the practical implications of *Vye* directions and their limitations and reference to the use of such directions would be expected in order to earn you the available marks.

of any or any relevant previous convictions.³ There are two limbs to the direction and a defendant is entitled to the credibility limb where the defendant has testified or made pre-trial statements such as at a police station interview. However, as confirmed in the case of **R v Aziz** [1995] 3 WLR 52 such statements did not include wholly exculpatory (blameless) statements.⁴ The propensity limb must be given regardless of whether or not the defendant has testified or made pre-trial statements. However, the application of the limbs has sometimes been applied inconsistently, for example, in the case of **R v Zoppola-Barraza** [1994] Crim LR 833 where the defendant had no previous convictions but only the credibility limb was given because he had admitted to another offence although he had not been charged with it. The Court of Appeal held that it would be 'an affront to common sense' to give the propensity limb.⁵

Whilst a judge does not have to use any particular words as long as the correct limb(s) are given, cases such as **R v Durbin** [1995] 2 Cr App R 84 confirm that failure to give a **Vye** direction would be grounds for appeal. Giving the **Vye** direction in the form of a series of rhetorical questions was also held to be unacceptable in the case of **R v Lloyd** [2000] 2 Cr App Rep 355 and judges are expected to adhere closely to the relevant direction in the *Crown Court Bench Book*.

In **R v Aziz** the House of Lords held that even if the defendant had no previous convictions but there was evidence of criminal conduct then the judge would have to consider giving a qualified **Vye** direction. The judge's power to give a qualified **Vye** direction is a discretionary one and cases such as **R v S** [2000] All ER (D) 1482 have indicated that the appeal courts will not interfere with this decision. This is problematic because different outcomes can be reached by different judges.⁶

For example, the discretion of the judge to give a qualified **Vye** direction is also extended to situations where the defendant has a previous conviction but it is spent under the Rehabilitation of Offenders Act 1974. The judge has a discretion to take the 1974 Act into account in criminal proceedings although it was enacted largely for civil proceedings. The case of **R v Nye** (1982) 75 Cr App Rep 247 provides that the defendant can still be given a qualified

Vye direction where he or she has spent convictions. The discretion also extends to minor convictions, as can be seen in the cases such as **R v Gray** [2004] EWCA Crim 1074, where the Court of Appeal held that if the convictions were irrelevant in nature or old a defendant could still be entitled to a qualified **Vye** direction. Roderick Munday in his article 'What constitutes a good character?' [1997] Crim LR 247 argues that the good character direction has now become 'complex' and 'stylised'.

Further inconsistency of approach can be seen in the case of **R v Teasdale** [1993] 4 All ER 290, where there is an alternative lesser charge on the indictment to which the defendant pleads guilty so that if the defendant is found guilty of the greater charge, the lesser charge will be dropped and he is still entitled to a qualified **Vye** direction which is worded to take into account the guilty plea. However, in **R v Challenger** [1994] Crim LR 202 it was held that this did not apply to other circumstances in which a defendant pleads guilty to another charge on the indictment.[7]

[7] An ability to compare and contrast cases in this way demonstrates wider reading and a deeper level of understanding. It is a good example of an analytical approach to the question and will earn you extra marks.

Whilst the ability of good character to go towards propensity is seen as a welcome change made by the cases of **Vye** and **Aziz**, it does have the potential to cause unfairness in a situation where there is a co-accused who has bad character. The jury may place too much weight on the propensity direction given to a defendant who has good character and may be more likely to consider that a co-accused with bad character is guilty of the offence. In **R v Cain** (1993) 99 Cr App R 208 it was held that in such situations, to avoid disadvantage to the co-accused, the judge should direct the jury that the co-accused's previous convictions are only relevant to credibility.

In conclusion, the present law on good character evidence entitles a defendant to a direction that lack of previous convictions can go to both credibility and or propensity but that this is not an absolute rule and the trial judge is given a discretion to give a qualified **Vye** direction or no **Vye** direction in cases where the defendant's criminal conduct cannot be said to suggest he is of unblemished character or where the presence of previous convictions are of minor relevance due to their nature or age.

Make your answer stand out

- Use comparative jurisdictions such as New Zealand to highlight that not all countries consider that a rule of practice on good character evidence is necessary and that a good character direction can be left to the discretion of the trial judge.
- When discussing the *Rowton* rule, use cases such as *R* v *Samuel* (1956) 40 Cr App Rep 8 and *R* v *Redgrave* (1981) 74 Cr App R 10 to show the inconsistent approach taken by the courts in applying the definition of 'reputation'.
- When discussing the inconsistent approach to the use of the qualified *Vye* direction, mention further cases such as *R* v *Durbin* [1995] 2 Cr App Rep 84 to compare with *R* v *Nye* (above) and also cases such as *R* v *Payton* [2006] EWCA Crim 1226 and *R* v *Kebell* [2004] EWCA Crim 1299.

! Don't be tempted to...

- Discuss issues of bad character – the question requires you to focus only on good character.
- Discuss the general use of good character evidence towards credibility without discussing the effect of the *Vye* direction.
- Confuse the use of the *Vye* direction with general evidence of reputation.

? Question 4

Stefan is arrested for arson and insurance fraud in relation to his business premises. It is alleged that he deliberately set the premises on fire to claim from the insurance because the business was due to go into liquidation. The main prosecution witness is an off-duty police officer, PC Willets, who saw Stefan leave the premises at the time the fire was started and although the flames were clearly visible Stefan 'appeared unconcerned'. Stefan has a previous conviction for burglary in 2003 and arson in 2009. Stefan alleges that one of the investigating police officers in his case, PC Willets, has recently been disciplined for withholding vital documents in the case and that the evidence of PC Willets cannot be trusted. The prosecution also wish to use evidence at trial of an allegation that Stefan attempted to set the same shop premises alight five years ago but that the fire was successfully put out by the owner of the shop next door, who spotted the fire in time.

Advise the prosecution on the admissibility of the character evidence at the trial.

Answer plan

→ Consider whether Stefan's previous convictions and previous conduct meet the definition of bad character and also fall into one of the gateways under s.101 Criminal Justice Act 2003.

→ In particular, discuss gateways (d) and (g) and the exclusionary discretion under s.101(3).

→ Discuss whether PC Willets' misconduct meets the definition of bad character under s.98 or whether it is excluded.

Diagram plan

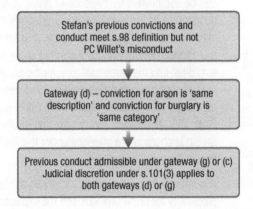

Stefan's previous convictions and conduct meet s.98 definition but not PC Willet's misconduct

↓

Gateway (d) – conviction for arson is 'same description' and conviction for burglary is 'same category'

↓

Previous conduct admissible under gateway (g) or (c) Judicial discretion under s.101(3) applies to both gateways (d) or (g)

A printable version of this diagram plan is available from www.pearsoned.co.uk/lawexpressqa

Answer

[1] Including a definition of bad character at an early stage is important to show the examiner that you at least have a basic understanding of the subject area and this will earn you any available marks.

In order to advise the prosecution as to the admissibility of character evidence at the trial of Stefan it is necessary to consider whether each piece of evidence meets the definition of bad character evidence. Bad character is defined in s.98 of the Criminal Justice Act 2003 as evidence of a disposition towards misconduct. Misconduct is further defined in s.112 as the commission of an offence or other reprehensible behaviour.[1]

Stefan's previous convictions

[2] It is important to explain under which gateway the bad character evidence is admissible and why in order to show application of the law to the facts. The more relevant gateways you can identify, the more marks you will obtain. However, you must satisfy the examiner that the gateways selected meet the criteria set out in s.101.

[3] Application of the relevant law to the facts is what the examiner is looking for in a problem question and this will earn you extra marks as it shows an ability to be selective with the material and to apply only the relevant law. By illustrating how Stefan's previous convictions meet the requirement of s.101(1)(d) you demonstrate a good knowledge of the relevant law as well as good command of the material.

[4] This shows the examiner that you have recognised a potential route of admissibility but have ruled it out based on case law. This again shows familiarity with the subject area and a good level of understanding and will earn you additional marks.

Previous convictions come within the definition of bad character under s.98 and therefore would be admissible under one of the gateways in s.101 of the 2003 Act. Stefan has a previous conviction for burglary and arson. These may be admissible under s.101(1)(d) on the basis that they are relevant to an important matter in issue between the prosecution and the defendant.[2] Section 103 defines 'an important matter in issue' as the question of whether the defendant has a propensity to commit offences of the kind with which he is charged or a propensity for untruthfulness. Section 103(2) goes on to state that an important matter in issue can be established by evidence of previous convictions of the same description or the same category. Stefan's previous conviction for arson is the same description as the present charge. With regard to the offence of burglary this is not the same description. However, it would fall into the same category, as the Secretary of State has prescribed that the categories are Theft Act cases and sexual offences on minors (see Criminal Justice Act 2003 (Categories of Offences) Order 2004). Both burglary and the insurance fraud with which Stefan is charged are offences under the Theft Act 1968 and therefore in the same category.[3]

It is unlikely that the burglary conviction can also be used to show a propensity for untruthfulness and the explanatory notes to the 2003 Act, together with the decision in **R v Hanson** [2005] 1 WLR 3169, clearly state that propensity for untruthfulness is not the same as dishonesty. However, in the case of **R v Ellis** [2010] EWCA Crim 163 it was accepted that deception offences could be relevant in showing the defendant's willingness to be untruthful in certain circumstances but, given the possible prejudicial effect, a warning should be given to the jury that the deception offences do not prove that the defendant is being untruthful in his current testimony.[4]

The prosecution should be advised that the defence may ask the judge to exercise his discretion to exclude the previous convictions under s.101(3) of the 2003 Act on the basis that the admission of such evidence would have an adverse effect on the fairness of the proceedings. The trial judge will have to consider issues such as the length of time that has elapsed between the previous conviction and the current offence. The judge also has discretion to exclude the evidence under s.103(3) if, by reason of the length of time since the conviction, it would be unjust to apply it to the defendant's case.[5] On this basis, the burglary conviction in 2003 may be considered too old to have any probative value. In addition, the case of **R v Hanson** (above) held that the fewer the number of previous convictions, the less likely their probative value.

Stefan's previous conduct

An allegation has been made that Stefan attempted to set fire to his business premises five years ago. No charges appear to have been brought. However, because the definition of bad character under s.98 includes 'other reprehensible behaviour' then it is still possible that this allegation could be introduced as evidence of bad character. It is for the trial judge to decide whether the definition has been met and this will involve the judge looking objectively at whether most reasonable people would disapprove of the behaviour. Even non-criminal behaviour has been held to amount to reprehensible behaviour, as can be seen in the case of **R v Saleem** [2007] EWCA Crim 1923. In addition, the allegations do not have to have been proved to be true, as can be seen from cases such as **R v Ngyeun** [2008] EWCA Crim 585.[6]

[6] The use of cases to illustrate the different approaches taken by the courts on the interpretation of s.98 gives more depth and authority to your answer and will earn you additional marks.

The prosecution would still have to find a gateway to admit such evidence. A possible gateway is under s.101(1)(g) on the basis that Stefan has made an attack on another person's character. He has made allegations regarding the dishonesty of the investigating officer PC Willets. However, the defence can still ask the trial judge to exercise judicial discretion under s.101(3) to exclude the evidence on the issue of fairness.

[7] Recognising and discussing additional relevant gateways will show the examiner that you have a wider knowledge of the subject area and are able to consider all possible solutions to the problem question. This in turn will earn you additional marks.

The prosecution should also be advised that they could attempt to admit the allegations of Stefan's previous conduct under s.101(1)(c) on the basis that it is important explanatory evidence.[7] Section 102 defines this as evidence without which the court or jury would find it impossible or difficult properly to understand other evidence in the case. It must also have substantial value for understanding the case as a whole. It must therefore be more than merely background evidence. The prosecution may argue that evidence that Stefan has attempted to set fire to his business premises before shows intent and therefore amounts to important explanatory evidence. It also helps to dispel any suggestion by Stefan that he is of good character and that the jury should therefore believe him. In the case of **R v Haigh** [2010] EWCA Crim 90 the prosecution were permitted to use allegations of bad character under gateway (c) to prevent the jury being misled by an incomplete picture of the defendant.

Allegations of misconduct by PC Willets

[8] This shows the examiner that you truly understand the definition of bad character and recognise what is excluded from the definition. This in turn will make you stand apart from a weaker student, who might fall into the trap laid by the question and assume that bad character includes character relating to the current offence. This gives the impression that you are in command of the material and will earn you the available marks.

The allegations of misconduct by PC Willets do not fall into the definition of bad character evidence because it is evidence which has to do with misconduct in connection with the investigation or prosecution of the offence and this is expressly excluded from the definition of bad character under s.98(b) of the 2003 Act.[8] However, such evidence would still be admissible as circumstantial evidence during the course of the trial on the basis that it is to do with the facts of the offence and points to Stefan's innocence, as can be seen in cases such as **R v Watson** [2006] EWCA Crim 2308. The issue will depend on whether the allegations of misconduct were sufficiently connected in time with the offence (see **R v Tirnaveanu** [2007] 2 Cr App Rep 295).

In respect of any admissible bad character evidence the judge must give a direction to the jury as to whether the evidence is to be used towards credibility and or propensity (see **R v Highton** [2005] 1 WLR 3472) and this direction is considered essential. According to **R v Davis** [2008] 3 All ER 461, evidence admitted under gateway (c) should be used towards credibility rather than propensity. Evidence admitted under gateway (g) is also likely to be used for credibility only. However, admission under gateway (d) can be used for propensity.

Make your answer stand out

- When discussing the case of *R* v *Ellis* [2010] EWCA Crim 163, go on to mention that whilst a single conviction for deception can show propensity for untruthfulness (unlike propensity to commit an offence), only offences such as perjury can be strong enough to show that the defendant is actually lying in his testimony.
- Mention s.110 of the Criminal Justice Act 2003, that the judge must give reasons for any decision to admit bad character evidence.
- When discussing cases such as *R* v *Highton* (above) and the direction to be given to the jury as to the use to be made of the bad character evidence, also discuss cases such as *R* v *Campbell* [2007] 1 WLR 2798 and the dissenting speech of Lord Phillips CJ.

! Don't be tempted to...

- Discuss bad character evidence under s.100 in respect of PC Willets – his misconduct must be previous misconduct rather than related to the actual offence.
- Focus only on the previous conviction for arson when discussing Stefan's previous convictions simply because he is charged with arson – you must also consider how the burglary conviction can be admitted.
- Ignore the facts relating to the allegation of Stefan's previous misconduct – you must consider whether this misconduct meets the definition of bad character under s.98.
- Be distracted by potential issues of hearsay simply because you are told that there is an allegation that Stefan previously set his shop premises alight five years ago – the question specifically asks you to focus on the admissibility of character evidence.

Improperly obtained evidence and confessions

How this topic may come up in exams

Improperly obtained evidence and confessions are often linked together because the judicial discretion found in s.78 and s.82(3) of the Police and Criminal Evidence Act 1984 is important to both topics. Cell confessions are also regarded as a type of improperly obtained evidence. Both these areas are favourites in problem questions and appear regularly in examination papers. Confessions in particular can appear as part of a multi-issue problem question but some institutions prefer to examine confessions in isolation because it is a very full topic in itself.

■ Attack the question

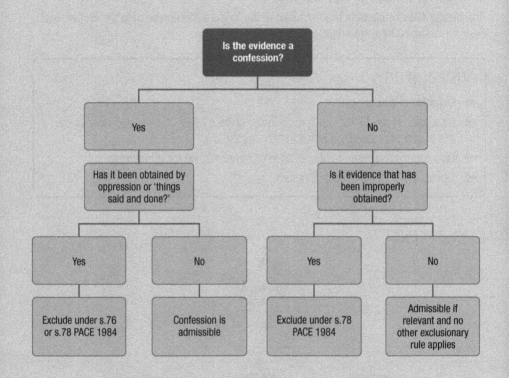

Question 1

'It is simply not acceptable that the State through its agents should lure its citizens into committing acts forbidden by the law and then seek to prosecute them for doing so.' (Lord Nicholls in *R v Looseley* [2001] 1 WLR 2060)

Analyse the above statement in the context of the modern day approach to the exclusion of evidence obtained by entrapment.

Answer plan

→ Definition of entrapment.

→ Discussion of function of statutory discretion under s.78 PACE 1984 and when to use this or stay of proceedings with reference to case law.

→ Discussion using case of *Looseley* as to preferred method for entrapment.

→ Discussion of merits of each approach.

Diagram plan

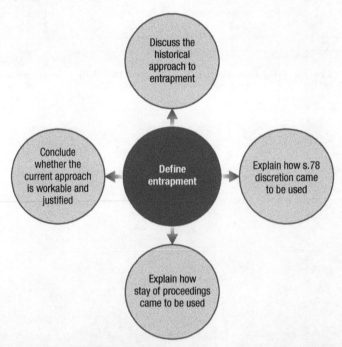

Answer

Entrapment is defined as a situation where agents of the State act as agents provocateurs to entice or instigate the commission of an offence. Lord Nicholls' comments reflect the fact that entrapment is regarded as offensive to notions of fairness, particularly as it will be a breach of the defendant's right to a fair trial under Art.6 of the European Convention on Human Rights. The case of **Teixeira de Castro v Portugal** (1998) 28 EHRR 101 supported the view that to incite an accused to commit an offence he would not otherwise commit would be a violation of Art.6 of the European Convention on Human Rights.[1]

Prior to PACE, the accepted view, following the decision in **R v Sang** [1979] 3 WLR 263, HL, was that there was no common law discretion to exclude prosecution evidence obtained by entrapment, this was because excluding evidence would give the false impression that there is a defence of entrapment in English law.[2]

The appeal cases of **R v Smurthwaite, R v Gill** (1993) Cr App R 437 confirmed that it was possible for the judge to use the s.78 discretion to exclude evidence obtained by entrapment. The Court of Appeal listed factors that the trial judge should consider in deciding whether to exercise the s.78 discretion. These included considerations as to whether the officer was acting as an agent provocateur in the sense that the accused was enticed to commit an offence he would not otherwise have committed as well as considering how active or passive the police officer's role was in obtaining the evidence.

In the case of **R v Latif** [1996] 1 WLR 104 Lord Steyn indicated that, in deciding whether to exercise discretion under s.78 or stay proceedings, a judge has to balance the 'countervailing considerations of policy and justice'. Evidence obtained by entrapment would be excluded under s.78 if its admission would have such an adverse effect on the fairness in the proceedings that it ought not to be admitted.

[3] Using cases to illustrate the difference between police trickery and entrapment and the view taken of unfairness for the purposes of s.78 adds depth to your answer and helps to show that you have a wider understanding of the subject area.

[4] This shows the examiner that you are familiar with the leading case in this area of law which is necessary to demonstrate a sufficient level of knowledge. It also moves your answer from a historical summary to an assessment of the current law which is the focus of the question.

[5] Use of judicial commentary as well as reference to comparative jurisdiction such as the United States marks you out as a good student who has read widely on the topic and has a greater level of knowledge. This in turn will separate you from weaker candidates and help you to obtain additional marks.

The predisposition of the accused to commit an offence was regarded as an important factor in determining whether or not the police actions were fair. For example, in the case of **R v Christou** [1992] 3 WLR 228 it was held that 'it is not every trick producing evidence against an accused which results in unfairness'.[3] In **Williams v DPP** [1993] 3 All ER 365, leaving a van unattended with bogus cartons of cigarettes was not regarded as entrapment by the police as they had not applied pressure on the defendants by words or conduct and their actions were merely passive. It is worth noting, however, that these cases were heard before the passing of the Human Rights Act 1998. The real issue was whether the crime had been artificially created (see **Attorney-General's Reference (No. 3 of 2000)** [2001] 1 WLR 2061).

A turnaround both in the approach of considering whether the police's trick merely provided the accused with an opportunity to commit the offence and whether to use s.78 or a stay of proceedings occurred as a result of the decision in **R v Looseley** [2001] 1 WLR 2060 which paid greater consideration to Art.6 rights and cited the case of **Teixeira de Castro v Portugal** (1998) 28 EHRR 101.[4]

Lord Nicholls held that the existence or absence of the accused's predisposition to commit the crime was irrelevant and rejected this approach even though it was favoured in the United States.[5] The question of whether the police had been 'active' or 'passive' was also regarded as too simplistic. Lord Hutton also re-affirmed the balancing test of Lord Steyn in **R v Latif**. The House of Lords held that in the case of entrapment the appropriate remedy in most cases would be to stay the proceedings as an abuse of process. However, in certain situations it might be appropriate to exclude the evidence under s.78 and this could include all prosecution evidence so that the end result would be the same as a stay. This would be useful where an application for a stay of proceedings has been made at a late stage. Lord Steyn's balancing test was expanded to include considerations such as whether the conduct of the police was so improper that it brought the administration of justice into disrepute.

In the case of **R v Shannon** [2001] 1 WLR 51 Potter LJ held that a stay of proceedings applied to abuse of process on the part of the police or prosecuting authority and rejected its application to entrapment by a journalist. This approach was approved in **Loosely**. However, as Kate Hofmeyr points out in her article 'The problem of private entrapment' [2006] Crim LR 319, the lower courts have adopted a contradictory approach to this principle which is sometimes overlooked or ignored altogether and this area continues to be problematic.[6]

[6] Reference to academic opinion from journal articles demonstrates wider reading and wider knowledge on your part. This gives depth and quality to your answer and will earn you additional marks.

In conclusion, entrapment is an example of when the general principle that relevant evidence, however obtained, is admissible will not be applied. The court will be prepared to stay proceedings or exclude such evidence if obtained by agents of the State and its admission would bring the administration of justice into disrepute.

✓ **Make your answer stand out**

- Include a discussion of *R v Horseferry Magistrates Court, ex parte Bennett* [1993] 3 WLR 90, which confirms the court's inherent powers to order a stay of proceedings where there is an abuse of process.
- When discussing the effectiveness of the current rules on entrapment you might mention journal articles such as D. Squires 'The problem with entrapment' (2006) 26 OJLS 351 or D. Ormerod and D. Birch 'Evolution of the discretionary exclusion of evidence' [2004] Crim LR 138.
- Discuss in greater detail Lord Hoffmann's views in *R v Looseley* when active instigation by an agent provocateur might be acceptable.
- Discuss the opposing views on whether entrapment is a breach of Art.6 as seen in *Teixeira de Castro v Portugal* (above) and *Ludi v Switzerland* (1992) 15 EHRR 173 and distinguish these cases.
- Discuss the factors identified in the case of *Smurthwaite* in greater detail.

> **!** Don't be tempted to...

- Ignore the historical development of the approach to entrapment – you need to explain how the judge's statutory discretion to exclude in entrapment cases emerged.
- Ignore the operation of the remedy of stay of proceedings and the case of *R* v *Looseley* – this challenges the notion that s.78 discretion is the primary remedy for entrapment.
- Ignore Lord Steyn's balancing test in *R* v *Latif* – this is still relevant to the modern day approach to entrapment.

? Question 2

Francis, aged 42, and Noel, aged 50, are arrested for rape. Francis has an IQ of 68. Both men are taken to the local police station where they are placed in separate cells. Both men are interviewed. Francis is distraught about being arrested. He talks to his cellmate Tim. Francis is unaware that Tim is an undercover police officer and the police have installed listening devices in the cell to record Tim's conversation with Francis. During the conversation Francis admits to knowing the complainant. Francis is interviewed afterwards. No solicitor is present. The interviewing police officers shout at Francis repeatedly. Francis repeatedly denies involvement in the crime but is heckled and bullied until he breaks down and confesses.

Noel insists on seeing a solicitor. He is told that his solicitor is on the way and will take some time to arrive but that, in the meantime, the police have interviewed Francis who has confessed and implicated Noel. This is in fact a lie. Noel, who is unaware that the police officers are lying, breaks down and admits involvement in the rape. When his solicitor arrives the police repeat the same information to the solicitor but do not tell the solicitor that Noel has already been interviewed. A second interview is held and Noel confesses to the rape and is charged.

Advise the defence as to the admissibility of the prosecution evidence against Francis and Noel.

Answer plan

→ For Francis consider issues relating to breaches of s.58 and s.77 PACE and whether oppressive questioning amounts to a breach of s.76(2)(a) and (b) and whether the conversation with Tim amounts to improperly obtained evidence justifying the exercise of s.78 discretion.

→ For Noel discuss whether there has been a breach of s.58 and s.76(2)(b) and whether the police lie justifies use of the s.78 discretion.

→ Discuss all relevant cases relating to breaches of s.76 and s.78.

→ Reach a conclusion as to whether the various pieces of evidence are admissible.

Diagram plan

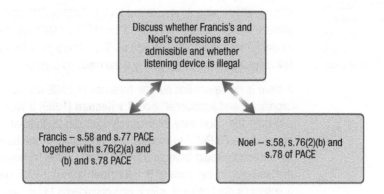

A printable version of this diagram plan is available from www.pearsoned.co.uk/lawexpressqa

Answer

[1] An introduction which summarises the issues to be addressed shows the examiner that you are able to identify the evidential issues and this in turn shows the skill of application of the law to the facts at the very beginning of your answer.

In order to advise the defence as to the admissibility of the prosecution evidence against Francis and Noel it is necessary to consider whether the evidence has been improperly obtained and whether it can be excluded by a rule of law or using judicial discretion.[1]

Francis

The first issue that arises relating to Francis is the confession that he makes to Tim the undercover police officer. A confession is defined by s.82(1) of the Police and Criminal Evidence Act 1984 (PACE) as including 'any statement wholly or partly adverse to the person who made it ...' Therefore, Francis's admission that he knew the complainant can be regarded as a confession.[2] Francis makes a further confession following interview. The defence can seek to have the confession at the interview ruled inadmissible if they are able to establish that under s.76(2)(a) the confession was obtained by oppression or that under s.76(2)(b) the confession has been rendered unreliable due to 'things said and done'.

[2] Show the examiner that you have understood the wide definition of confession by illustrating that it can apply to admitting to knowing the complainant and that you are able to apply it, as this will show a familiarity with the material.

Francis did not have a solicitor present at his interview. Under s.58 of PACE a suspect in custody has a right to access to legal advice. Francis should therefore have been asked whether he wanted a solicitor to be present. Francis also has an IQ of 68. Cases such as **R v Masih** [1986] Crim LR 395, CA have suggested that IQ

135

[3] This shows application
of the law to the facts as
you have recognised the
importance of clues such as
the lack of access to legal
advice and Francis's low IQ.

levels below 70 would suggest that a person is of low intelligence and mentally defective. In accordance with s.77 of PACE the police officers should also have ensured that an 'appropriate adult' was present. The breaches of s.77 and s.58 of PACE may make the confession unreliable under s.76(2)(b) of PACE. There must be a causal link between the police conduct and the resulting confession.[3]

If there is no causal link but the breaches of PACE are considered 'significant and substantial' (see **R v Keenan** [1989] 3 WLR 1193, CA) then the court may alternatively exercise its judicial discretion under s.78 PACE to exclude the confession on the basis that its admission would have an adverse effect on the fairness of the proceedings. In the case of **R v Samuel** [1988] 2 WLR 920, CA a suspect's right to legal advice was considered to be 'one of the most important and fundamental rights of a citizen'. The court was therefore prepared to exercise its judicial discretion under s.78 PACE to exclude the confession. In **R v Aspinall** [1999] 2 Cr App Rep 115, CA the breach of s.77 was also enough for the judge to exclude the confession under s.78 PACE. The defence could therefore ask the trial judge to use s.78 to exclude Francis's confession given the breaches of s.58 and s.77.

[4] Show the examiner that
you are able to take your
advice further by considering
the need for judicial
warnings if the confession
is admitted in the case of
s.77. This demonstrates
wider knowledge on your
part which is not restricted to
simply the provisions of s.76
and s.78. This will help you
to obtain additional marks
and will separate you from
the weaker student.

Even if the confession is admitted then the s.77 breach means that if the prosecution case depends substantially on the confession the judge must warn the jury of the 'special need for caution' before convicting on Francis's confession and explain why.[4]

Francis was also subjected to some intensive questioning by the police and it is necessary to consider whether the style of the questioning was oppressive. Section 76(8) PACE provides a partial definition of oppression as including 'torture, inhuman or degrading treatment and the use or threat of violence'. Oppression was given its dictionary meaning in the case of **R v Fulling** [1987] 2 WLR 923 and Lord Lane CJ concluded that it connotes 'detestable wickedness'. The behaviour of the police officers does not appear to meet the definition in s.76(8) or the definition taken in **R v Fulling**. However, in the case of **R v Paris; R v Abdullahi; R v Miller** (1992) 97 Cr App Rep 99, CA it was held that the psychological effect of the questioning on the suspect can be regarded as oppressive and it was not necessary for physical violence to take place.[5] In this case the defendant, Miller, was bullied and heckled by police officers over a 13-hour period with questions being repeated up to

[5] This demonstrates your
knowledge that the definition
of oppression is wide and
shows your ability to use case
law to help apply the definition.

300 times. As Francis was also heckled and bullied there is a possibility that the questioning could be regarded as oppressive.

The final issue relates to the use of an undercover police officer to obtain information from Francis. The issue is whether this can be regarded as police trickery and whether it is capable of making the confession unreliable. As highlighted in **R v Christou** [1992] 3 WLR 228, not every trick which produces evidence will be regarded as unfair. However, if the police use trickery to circumvent the Codes of PACE then this could make the resulting evidence unfair. The fact that the police install listening devices in the cell does not automatically render the confession inadmissible, as can be seen by the decision in **R v Mason** [2002] EWCA Crim 385. However, Francis confesses in the cell rather than during a formal interview which would have to be conducted under Code C and E of PACE. Therefore, it is arguable that the police have circumvented the Codes of PACE and the pre-interview admission will not be admissible. This is in line with **R v Allan** [2004] EWCA Crim 2236.[6]

[6] This shows the examiner that you have the skill of sifting through material and applying only relevant aspects by distinguishing case law such as *R* v *Christou* and *R* v *Allan*. This demonstrates a good analytical approach and will earn you extra marks.

Noel

Noel is given access to legal advice but is interviewed before his solicitor arrives and confesses. This means that this first interview is in breach of Code C of PACE which requires police officers to wait for the solicitor if one has been called. When the solicitor arrives a second interview is held. This is similar to the facts of the case of **R v McGovern** (1990) 92 Cr App Rep 228,[7] where the first interview was held to have tainted the second interview because the solicitor had not been aware that the first interview had taken place. In the circumstances the defence could argue that the confession should be excluded under s.76(2)(b) PACE due to the conduct of the police officers and that there is sufficient causation. The court should still be invited to exercise its discretion under s.78 on the fairness principle in relation to the lie told to Noel (see **R v Mason** [1988] 1 WLR 139).

[7] Show the examiner that you have familiarity with the facts of important cases and are able to recognise when the facts are similar to the question.

[8] As the outcomes for Francis and Noel are different, a summary in your conclusion shows the examiner that you have grasped the issues that are important to your advice.

In conclusion,[8] the defence should be advised that Francis's pre-interview confession is likely to be excluded under s.78 as a police trick. It is also possible to apply to have Francis's confession at interview ruled inadmissible under s.76(2)(a) and (b) or s.78 of PACE. In addition, Noel's confession will be inadmissible under s.76(2)(b) if there is sufficient causation.

Make your answer stand out

- Mention that issues of the admissibility of the confession will be decided at a *voir dire*.
- When discussing s.76(2)(a) mention that even if the confession is ruled inadmissible this does not prevent the defence calling evidence before the jury about the way in which the evidence was obtained. Mention the case of *R* v *Mushtaq* [2005] 1 WLR 1513 – the judge must still direct the jury that they can diregard the confession if they accept the defence's evidence that it was obtained by oppression.
- In relation to the exercise of the s.78 you might briefly discuss the four principles of reliability, disciplinary, protective and integrity.
- Mention the use of the alternative exclusionary discretion under s.82(3) PACE 1984 when discussing the use of s.78.

 Don't be tempted to...

- Ignore s.78 – this applies equally to confessions as it does to other improperly obtained evidence.
- Discuss entrapment with regard to the confession to the undercover police officer – the definition of entrapment has not been met because the offence has already been committed.
- Fail to differentiate between s.76(2)(a) and (b) issues – you must make it clear which provision you are relying on and why.

🖎 Question 3

'In their Lordships' opinion the test to be applied in considering whether evidence is admissible is whether it is relevant to the matters in issue. If it is, it is admissible and the court is not concerned with how the evidence was obtained ...' (Lord Goddard CJ in *Kuruma* v *R* [1955] 2 WLR 223)

Analyse the above quotation with reference to the modern day approach to the admissibility of improperly obtained evidence.

Answer plan

→ Consider the importance of the principle of relevance to admissibility.

→ Mention that there are other considerations such as issues of fairness.

→ Discuss the judicial discretions that operate in this area.

→ Discuss strengths and weaknesses of discretions such as s.78 and s.82(3) PACE 1984 and r. 32 Civil Procedure Rules 1998.

→ Reach a final view as to whether the quotation is a correct representation of the current approach.

Diagram plan

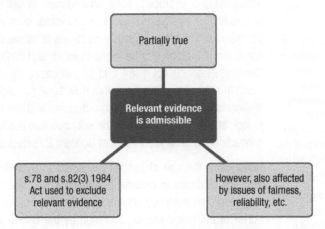

A printable version of this diagram plan is available from www.pearsoned.co.uk/lawexpressqa

Answer

Relevance has been described in **DPP v Kilbourne** [1973] AC 729 as 'logically probative or disprobative of some matter which requires proof'. Therefore, evidence is relevant if it is capable of proving or disproving a fact in issue. The issue of probity was considered so important in the case of **R v Leatham** (1861) 25 JP 468 that Crompton J set out the principle that 'it matters not how you get it, if you steal it even, it would be admissible in evidence'.[1] Thus in cases such as **Kuruma v R** [1955] 2 WLR 223 evidence obtained through an illegal search was not excluded and was admitted as evidence at the trial.

[1] An ability to quote directly from cases shows a wider knowledge of the case and gives depth to your answer.

[2] Addressing the quotation at an early stage shows the examiner that you are tackling the question. This gives the examiner a good first impression of your answer.

[3] By going on to discuss the ways in which the quotation does not represent the sole approach you demonstrate to the examiner that you have an insight into what is required by the question and that you are attempting some analysis. This will earn you the available marks.

[4] Being able to discuss both civil and criminal jurisdictions shows the examiner that you realise the question is not confined to discussing one jurisdiction and this also demonstrates that you have wider knowledge of the subject matter which will earn you additional marks.

[5] Being able to recognise and then go on to discuss other issues that impact on the admissibility of improperly obtained evidence in this way demonstrates a considered and reasoned approach to the question which will impress the examiner and earn you extra marks. Continued reference to the quotation also shows that you are able to keep your answer focused and relevant.

The modern day approach to the admissibility of improperly obtained evidence is to focus on whether the evidence is relevant and the quotation of Lord Goddard is correct in this respect.[2] However, the quotation does not reflect the true position with regard to all improperly obtained evidence. With regard to confessions, relevance becomes less of an issue because under s.76 Police and Criminal Evidence Act 1984 (PACE) confessions must be excluded if obtained by oppression (s.76(2)(a)) or 'things said and done' which would make the confession unreliable (s.76(2)(b)) regardless of whether the confession is relevant or true (see s.76(2) of the 1984 Act).[3] This is a rule of law and exclusion is mandatory rather than discretionary.

Relevance is not the only consideration when considering the admissibility of improperly obtained evidence. In civil and criminal proceedings the judge has discretion to exclude such evidence and the discretions are based largely on issues of fairness. In criminal cases the discretion can be found in ss.78 and 82(3) Police and Criminal Evidence Act 1984 and in civil cases the discretion is found in r. 32 of the Civil Procedure Rule 1998.[4] Judicial discretion is therefore also an important consideration and the court is able to look at the method in which the evidence was obtained and this contradicts the second part of Lord Goddard CJ's quotation.[5]

Historically, the use of judicial discretion to exclude improperly obtained evidence in criminal proceedings was not the accepted approach. The evidence scholar John Bradley Thayer was a supporter of increased use of discretion by the courts generally, as seen in his work *A Preliminary Treatise on Evidence at the Common Law* (Boston: Little, Brown, 1898). However, In cases such as **Jeffrey v Black** [1977] QB 490 the courts had been adamant that there was no general discretion to exclude the evidence. The position was clarified by the House of Lords in **R v Sang** [1979] 3 WLR 263 where the court held that a judge has a discretion to exclude prosecution evidence if its admission would prevent the defendant receiving a fair trial. Thus it was recognised that the judge has a discretion to exclude relevant evidence if its prejudicial effect would outweigh its probative outcome. This would effectively involve issues of fairness. This discretion has since been preserved by s.82(3) Police and Evidence Act 1984 (PACE).

PACE also introduced a further discretion under s.78 which operates on the sole principle of fairness. A judge may exclude a piece of relevant evidence if its admission 'would have such an adverse effect on the fairness of the proceedings it ought not to be admitted'.

[6] Discussing the four principles relating to the use of s.78 shows the examiner that you have undertaken wider reading in this area and that you have more than just a basic understanding of s.78 and this will earn you extra marks.

When using s.78 to exclude evidence as a result of police impropriety the courts are guided by a number of principles.[6] The reliability principle looks at whether the method of obtaining the evidence has affected its reliability and this is the main principle (see **R v Chalkley** [1998] 3 WLR 146). The aim is to ensure 'forensic fairness' and exclude evidence in line with the **R v Sang** principle. The disciplinary principle is given less weight as cases such as **R v Sang** (above) have suggested that it is not the role of the court to discipline police officers. Any breaches of the Codes of PACE must be 'significant and substantial' before s.78 is used (see **R v Keenan** [1989] 3 WLR 1193).[7] The protective principle, which requires a suspect's fundamental human rights to be considered, also appears to influence the courts less, unless the breach relates to Art.6 (see **R v Loveridge** [2001] EWCA Crim 734). The integrity principle is given due weight particularly in entrapments cases (see **R v Latif** [1996] 1 WLR 104 where the court will consider whether the admission of the evidence would bring the criminal justice system into disrepute).

[7] You can equally use the case of *R* v *Walsh* (1989) 91 Cr App Rep 161 here, as long as the legal principle is the same then this is acceptable and you have some flexibility in the cases you use to illustrate the principles. However, you will be expected to know the key leading cases.

One difficulty with judicial discretions as a whole is that they are difficult to appeal. Cases such as **R v O'Leary** (1988) 87 Cr App Rep 387 indicate that in order to appeal the use by the trial judge of a s.78 discretion it would be necessary to show that the trial judge acted in a way which could be regarded as '**Wednesbury** unreasonable', in that no reasonable judge could have reached the same decision.

[8] It is important to balance your answer by looking at the treatment of improperly obtained evidence in civil proceedings, as the question does not require you to confine your discussion to the criminal jurisdiction. This allows you to undertake some comparative discussion supported by case law, which in turn gives depth to your answer and will earn you additional marks.

With regard to the civil exclusionary discretion under r. 32 of the Civil Procedure Rules this is used far more sparingly than the judicial discretions in criminal proceedings. In **Jones v University of Warwick** [2003] 1 WLR 954, for example, evidence which had been secretly recorded was not excluded.[8] The Court of Appeal upheld the decision on the basis that it is often hard to reconcile the two competing public interests of revealing the truth in litigation and discouraging the use of unlawfully obtained evidence. In civil cases improper conduct is more commonly dissuaded by the use of cost orders.

[9] Offering a final analysis in your conclusion completes your answer and gives the impression of a good structured answer which in turn will earn you the available marks, as good structure is one of the considerations that the examiner will take into account as well as content.

In conclusion, the quotation partly summarises the position with regard to the importance of relevance when considering the admissibility of improperly obtained evidence. Relevance can be viewed as a starting point but it is not the only factor that determines admissibility. Admissibility is also affected by issues of fairness and judicial discretion is used to ensure fairness in both civil and criminal proceedings.[9]

 Make your answer stand out

- Mention journal articles such as E. Swift, 'One hundred years of evidence law reform: Thayer's triumph' (2000) *California Law Review* 88, which discusses views of legal academics such as John Henry Wigmore and James Bradley Thayer, who both supported the use of judicial discretion and how the excess use of discretion in over 40 States in America has now become problematic.

- When discussing the fact that relevance is not an issue in considering the admissibility of a confession under s.76, you might mention that truth of a confession is irrelevant (s.76(2) and also mention cases such as *Wong Kam-Ming* v *R* [1979] 2 WLR 81, where the Privy Council held that a defendant should not be asked during the *voir dire* whether his confession is true.

- When mentioning s.78 and s.82(3) you could carry out a comparison of the two discretions and mention that whilst the case of *R* v *Mason* (above) suggested that s.78 did no more than 'restate the power that judges had at common law', it can be seen from the way s.78 has been used that in fact s.78 is wider than the original discretion found in the case of *R* v *Sang* (above). For example, it was accepted in *R* v *Smurthwaite* [1994] 3 Cr App R 437 that s.78 could be used to exclude evidence obtained by entrapment whilst in the earlier case of *R* v *Sang* it was argued that the common law discretion could not be used in entrapment cases. Conversely, it could be argued that s.82(3) is wider, as it can be used to exclude evidence that has already been admitted as it is not restricted in use to the point at which admissibility is in issue (unlike s.78).

- When discussing the protective principle mention cases such as *R* v *Loveridge* [2001] EWCA Crim 734 where, although the court accepted there was a breach of Art.8, they admitted the evidence because a breach of Art.8 did not also lead to a breach of Art.6.

- Examine in greater detail the debate about whether s.78 is wider than s.82(3) using cases such as *R* v *Christou* [1992] 3 WLR 228 (per Lord Taylor CJ) and *R* v *Horseferry Road Magistrates' Court, ex parte Bennett* [1993] 3 WLR 90 (per Lord Griffiths).

- Mention that, even if improperly obtained evidence is admitted, the judge or jury can decide how much weight to attach to such evidence.

! Don't be tempted to...

- Discuss relevance in the context of evidence outside that of improperly obtained evidence – for example, do not discuss relevance in the context of exclusionary rules.
- Discuss only entrapment as an example of improperly obtained evidence – other examples include confessions, illegal searches and incorrect identification procedures.
- Discuss only s.78 – you must recognise that other judicial discretions operate in this area such as s.82(3) of Police and Criminal Evidence Act 1984 and r.32 of the Civil Procedure Rules 1998.

? Question 4

Isaac and Christian are defendants in a trial for burglary. It is alleged that they broke into a local university and stole £30,000 of computer equipment from the library. Advise the prosecution about the admissibility of the following pieces of evidence:

(a) During police questioning Isaac admits that he carried out the burglary on his own. Christian wishes to use Isaac's confession to prove that he (Christian) is innocent.

(b) The police carried out an illegal search of Isaac's flat and found a crowbar, which, they say, was used to enter the university library.

(c) Evidence comes to light that there had been a series of previous burglaries at the university and that the police had launched a 'sting' operation to find the culprits and had deliberately asked the university to leave the computer equipment unsecured so that it could be stolen. Isaac says in his confession that he only set out to steal the computers because a friend of his who is a student at the university had told him the computers were no longer secured to tables. Both he and Christian are shown on CCTV camera entering the library.

Answer plan

→ Consider s.76A Police and Criminal Evidence Act 1984 in relation to the use of Isaac's confession by Christian.

→ Discuss whether evidence of crowbar can be excluded under s.78 and s.82(3).

→ Discuss whether police actions amount to entrapment or police trickery.

Diagram plan

Isaac	Crowbar and CCTV	Police operation
Co-accused can use confession of defendant under s.76A	Crowbar obtained during illegal search can be excluded under s.78 or s.82(3) 1984 Act	Did the police act as agent provacateur to incite the offence
Must show it has not been obtained by oppression or things said and done	CCTV evidence may be admissible depending on nature of police operation	Are the tactics merely police trickery?

A printable version of this diagram plan is available from www.pearsoned.co.uk/lawexpressqa

Answer

In order to advise the prosecution as to the admissibility of the various pieces of evidence it will be necessary to consider the evidential rules relating to confessions and improperly obtained evidence.

[1] An ability to spot clues in the question and apply sections of the relevant statute such as s.76A shows that you are in command of the material and have good knowledge of the subject area which will earn you the available marks.

[2] As the question is silent on breaches of PACE, it is legitimate to consider what the position would be if there were breaches as well as if there were none. This shows the examiner that you have considered all possible issues and also ensures that your answer is a full one. This in turn will earn you any available marks.

Use of Isaac's confession by Christian

It is possible for Christian to use Isaac's confession to assist with his own defence. Under s.76A of the Police and Criminal Evidence Act 1984 a co-accused may use the confession of another co-accused as long as it is relevant to his defence.[1] Clearly Isaac's admission that only he carried out the burglary is important to the question of whether Christian was present at the time and also involved in the offence. However, the confession must not be capable of being excluded under s.76 of the 1984 Act.

There is nothing to suggest on the facts that Isaac's confession has been obtained by oppression (s.76(2)(a)) or 'things said and done' (s.76(2)(b)), which would make the confession unreliable. However, if for example Isaac was not offered access to a solicitor in accordance with s.58 of the 1984 Act or there were other breaches of the 1984 Act or Code C then the confession would potentially be inadmissible.[2] In those circumstances it would be for Christian to show on a balance of probabilities that the confession was not obtained in breach of s.76. This is irrespective of whether the confession is true.

In the case of **R v Myers** [1997] 3 WLR 552 the Court of Appeal held that a co-accused can still rely on a confession even if it would have been ruled inadmissible under the exclusionary discretion under s.78 of PACE if it had been used by the prosecution. This is because s.78 only applies to the exclusion of prosecution evidence; as such Christian would not also have to prove that the confession would not be excluded under s.78.[3]

[3] By going further and considering how s.78 impacts on s.76A this demonstrates to the examiner that you are able to take your answer beyond a basic one. This will show the examiner that you have a deeper level of knowledge and understanding which will earn you additional marks.

Crowbar found during an illegal search

The general principle with regard to improperly obtained evidence is that such evidence will still be admissible if it is relevant (see cases such as **Jeffrey v Black** [1977] QB 490). However, the trial judge still has discretion to exclude the evidence regardless of relevance. The trial judge can exclude the evidence of the crowbar under s.78 of the 1984 Act. This will apply where the admission of the evidence will have an adverse affect on the fairness in the proceedings it ought to be excluded.

[4] A mention of the reliability principle supported by case law alerts the examiner to the fact that you have a deeper understanding of s.78 and this takes your answer beyond a basic one and distinguishes you from an average student.

The judge will have to consider issues such as whether Isaac will be given the opportunity to challenge the reliability of the evidence if it is admitted. This is known as the reliability principle (see **R v Chalkley** [1998] 3 WLR 146).[4] Whilst the trial judge will have to consider the method by which the evidence was obtained this will not necessarily prevent its admission. Isaac's legal advisers will be given the opportunity to cross-examine the police officers about the nature of the search. Isaac can also give evidence as to whether the crowbar belongs to him and what he normally used it for.

[5] By considering all available judicial discretions you ensure that your answer is a full one and that you earn all the available marks.

Alternatively, the judge can use the discretion under s.82(3) of the 1984 Act and exclude the evidence on the basis that its prejudicial effect outweighs its probative value. However, the prejudicial effect of admitting the crowbar may be lessened if Isaac is given an opportunity to explain why it was in his possession.[5]

Even if the evidence is admitted the jury can decide how much weight to attach to the evidence and in the circumstances the judge may take the view that it should be admitted.

The police sting operation

The issue here is whether the police's action amounts to police trickery or entrapment. Entrapment occurs where the police act as an agent provocateur to encourage or incite the commission of a crime.[6] This will be regarded as an abuse of process or as Lord Hoffmann stated in the case of **R v Looseley, Attorney General's Reference (No. 3 of 2000)** [2001] 1 WLR 2061 an 'abuse of executive power' the only remedy should be a stay of proceedings. However, if the police have merely provided an opportunity for the offence to be committed but have not actually encouraged Isaac to commit the offence then it will merely be police trickery and the issue will be whether evidence of the CCTV footage should be excluded.[7]

In the case of **R v Smurthwaite, R v Gill** (1993) 98 Cr App R 437 the Court of Appeal listed a number of factors that a trial judge should take into consideration when deciding whether or not the police actions amount to entrapment. These include looking at whether the police's actions enticed a defendant to commit an offence he would not otherwise have committed.

However, in the case of **Williams v DPP** [1993] 3 All ER 365 it was held that a police operation involving parking an unattended van full of contraband cigarettes in a busy high street did not amount to entrapment as the police had not done anything to force passers-by to steal the cigarettes.[8] Isaac would therefore have difficulty arguing that the police sting operation actively involved efforts to force him to steal the computer. The **Smurthwaite** factors would also require the judge to consider the nature of the entrapment. The police provided an opportunity but they did not become involved in the sense of asking Isaac's friend to tell him about the unsecured computers. The police officer's role would appear passive rather than active in those circumstances and therefore unlikely to amount to entrapment.[9] However, Isaac's defence team could still argue that the evidence (namely the CCTV footage) should be excluded under s.78 PACE due to police trickery. According to cases such as **R v Chalkley** [1998] 3 WLR 146 the primary consideration when deciding fairness for the purposes of s.78 is the issue of the reliability of the evidence. There is nothing to suggest the evidence of the CCTV footage is not reliable.

[6] Including a definition of entrapment alerts the examiner to the fact that you are able to distinguish the difference between entrapment and police trickery which will earn you any available marks.

[7] A definition of police trickery also alerts the examiner to the fact that you understand how it differs from entrapment and that you are able to correctly apply this to the facts. This will separate you from the weaker student.

[8] Finding and applying cases with comparable facts shows the examiner that you understand the issues involved and this will earn you additional marks because it demonstrates a deeper level of understanding.

[9] An ability to apply the *Smurthwaite* guidelines to the facts shows good problem-solving skills on your part and this will again earn you extra marks.

The prosecution should therefore be advised that Christian is likely to be able to use Isaac's confession and the evidence of the crowbar and CCTV footage are likely to be admitted.

 Make your answer stand out

- When discussing the police sting operation, mention cases such as *R* v *Christou* [1992] 3 WLR 228 that 'it is not every trick producing evidence against an accused which results in unfairness'.
- Mention, when discussing police trickery, judicial comments such as those of McHugh J in *Ridgeway* v *The Queen* (1995) 184 CLR 19 that an opportunity to commit a crime can in itself be intrusive and the courts will scrutinise the degree of intrusiveness and the reasons of the police for using this method.
- Examine the view taken by the House of Lords in *Looseley* of the decision in *Teixeira de Castro* v *Portugal* (1998) 28 EHRR 101 – namely that nothing in that decision or Art.6 alters the English law approach to entrapment.

! Don't be tempted to...

- Discuss the use of the confession by the prosecution and therefore discuss s.76 – the facts clearly state that Christian wants to use the confession.
- Assume that entrapment has occurred – you must examine whether the facts fall into the definition of entrapment.
- Ignore other possible discretions to exclude improperly obtained evidence, such as s.82(3) PACE 1984.

Identification evidence

8

How this topic may come up in exams

Identification evidence also links into improperly obtained evidence (Chapter 7) because the judicial discretion under s.78 PACE 1984 is also relevant here. It is often examined as part of a problem question but is also an essay favourite when looking at whether the *Turnbull* guidelines sufficiently protect against miscarriages of justice.

■ Attack the question

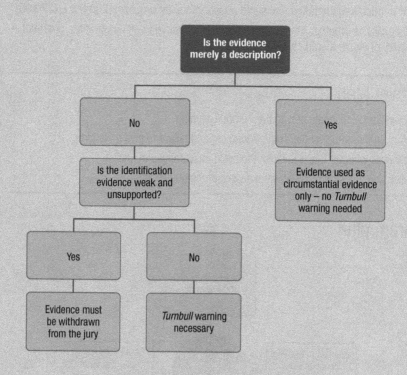

📝 Question 1

'There is a consensus among psychologists that the mind does not operate like a video recording, whereby once events are stored in the memory they can be recollected by accessing the discrete "part" of the memory in which they are stored.' (A. Roberts 'The problem of mistaken identification: some observations on process' (2004) 8 E & P 100)

Critically evaluate whether the law of evidence is effective in eliminating the potential unreliability of visual identification evidence.

Answer plan

→ Discuss the rationale behind the *Turnbull* warning.

→ Explain the nature of the *Turnbull* warning and failure to give a warning.

→ Discuss whether this is sufficient to avoid miscarriages of justice.

→ Examine any strengths and weaknesses of the guidelines.

Diagram plan

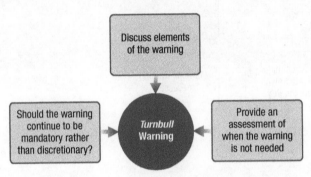

A printable version of this diagram plan is available from www.pearsoned.co.uk/lawexpressqa

Answer

Visual identification evidence has been described by the Criminal Law Revision Committee in its Eleventh Report (Cmnd 4991, 1972)[1] as 'the greatest cause of actual or possible wrongful convictions'. Andrew Roberts' quotation reflects the fact that visual identification evidence is inherently unreliable as it depends on the mind recollecting the first image it sees.[2]

As a result of the number of miscarriages of justice which came to light, a departmental committee chaired by Lord Devlin was set up to report on identification evidence (the Devlin Report (1976) Cmnd 338).[3] However, before Parliament had a chance to consider the recommendations made in the Devlin Report the Court of Appeal issued guidelines on identification evidence in the case of **R v Turnbull** [1976] 3 WLR 445, CA.

The **Turnbull** warning was designed to counter the unreliability of visual identification evidence by the judge warning the jury of the special need for caution. The **Turnbull** guidelines also require the judge to explain the reason for the need for a warning, examine closely the circumstances in which the identification came to be made and remind the jury of any specific weaknesses in the identification evidence. Failure to give a **Turnbull** warning can lead to a conviction being quashed (see **Reid v The Queen** [1990] Cr App R 121).[4]

One of the criticisms of the **Turnbull** guidelines is that it did not go as far as the proposals made in the Devlin Report. The Devlin Committee considered that there should be no conviction based solely or mainly on identification evidence and that corroboration should be a requirement. However, the **Turnbull** guidelines provide for the admission of uncorroborated identification evidence.[5] Lord Widgery said in **Turnbull** that to require corroboration would be an 'affront to justice'. However, a concession was made that where the identification evidence is weak then the evidence should be corroborated otherwise it must be withdrawn from the jury. The guidelines do not, however, define 'weak 'evidence other than to give an

---

[1] Reference to an important committee report such as the Law Revision Committee's Eleventh Report shows the examiner you have carried out wider reading and understand the historical context in which identification evidence and miscarriages of justice was examined.

[2] Early reference to the quotation puts your answer in context and shows that you are focused on the issues and this creates an overall impression of a good structure to your answer.

[3] Reference to reasons for the change in law by referring to the Devlin Report shows the examiner that you have a deeper understanding of the subject matter and its historical context. This can gain you higher marks.

[4] You can also refer to other cases such as *Scott v The Queen* [1989] 2 WLR 924, as long as the legal principles are the same this is permissible. However, you would always be expected to use the key leading cases.

[5] This shows the examiner that you have an ability to compare and contrast the recommendations in the Devlin Report and the *Turnbull* guidelines and shows analytical skills and a wider understanding of the subject matter. This will help to earn you extra marks.

[6] Balancing arguments about weaknesses with possible strengths and solutions shows that you are carrying out a proper evaluation as required by the question.

[7] This demonstrates familiarity with the Privy Council cases that suggest that, in exceptional cases, it may be acceptable not to give a *Turnbull* warning and this demonstrates a good understanding of the case law surrounding this area, which will mark you out as a good student and help in your formulation of arguments regarding the effectiveness of the guidelines.

[8] Show the examiner that you have an ability to compare and contrast cases such as *Courtnell* and the Privy Council decision in *Beckford* as this shows analytical skills and gives an impression of a solid and detailed answer.

[9] Your ability to distinguish cases in this way by explaining the opposing decisions in *Slater* and *Thornton* shows the examiner that you are able to conduct a critical analysis.

example of 'a fleeting glimpse'. In the Privy Council case of **Reid v The Queen** [1990] (above) it was suggested that weak identification might involve identification made in difficult circumstances such as where the view is obstructed or made in poor light or by someone with poor eyesight.[6] Cases such as **Edwards v R** [2006] UKPC 23 also reconfirm that the judge should ensure that the summing-up includes a proper assessment of the strengths and weaknesses of the identification evidence.

Another weakness is the fact that the **Turnbull** guidelines stipulate that a warning is necessary even for recognition identification evidence which is regarded as the best kind of identification evidence. However, cases such as **Freemantle v R** [1994] 1 WLR 1437, PC have shown that where a **Turnbull** warning has not been given but the evidence is recognition evidence and the suggestion is that the jury would have convicted anyway, the conviction will not be quashed.[7]

There is also some confusion as to when a **Turnbull** warning is necessary. In accordance with cases such as **R v Courtnell** [1990] Crim LR 115, CA a **Turnbull** warning is not needed if the issue is one of the witness's veracity. However, the case of **Beckford v R** (1993) 97 Cr App R 409 suggests that a warning may still be necessary as once the jury have decided the issue of veracity they still need to go on to consider the reliability of the identification evidence.[8]

Another area of confusion is in relation to the application of the **Turnbull** warning when the accused admits being present at the scene of the crime but denies committing the offence. In the case of **R v Thornton** [1995] 1 Cr App R 578 the Court of Appeal quashed the accused's conviction on the basis that a **Turnbull** warning should have been given. However, in the case of **R v Slater** [1995] 1 Cr App Rep 584 the Court of Appeal held that whether a full **Turnbull** warning is necessary depends on all the circumstances of the case. However, these cases can be distinguished on the facts. In a situation where there is a possibility of the accused having been mistaken for someone else, a **Turnbull** warning would be needed but where there is no risk of mistaken identification, a **Turnbull** warning may not be needed.[9]

[10] By showing the examiner that you are aware that identification evidence is regulated by Code D and that visual evidence does not just rely on the *Turnbull* guidelines, you show that you are able to take your arguments about the need for a *Turnbull* warning further and this will earn you additional marks.

The **Turnbull** warning is only one way in which the unreliability of identification evidence is countered. Code D of PACE 1984[10] provides a formal procedure whereby the correctness of identification evidence is tested. The procedure should be used wherever a suspect disputes the identification. Breaches of Code D can lead to the identification evidence being excluded by the judge using the discretion under s.78 PACE 1984. The case of **R v Forbes** [2001] 1 AC 473, HL confirms that wherever there has been a breach of Code D but the judge has still permitted the evidence to be used the jury should be given a direction explaining the breach and its possible consequences.

[11] By emphasising the safeguards you make your final view clear to the examiner.

In conclusion, the use of both the Code D procedure and a **Turnbull** warning together provide sufficient safeguards to counteract the potential unreliability of identification evidence.[11] The **Turnbull** warning in particular provides the judge with an opportunity to examine the strengths and weaknesses of the identification evidence when summing-up to the jury. Whilst it remains true that the mind is not always a reliable source of evidence, if properly directed the jury will be left in no doubt as to why such evidence should be treated with caution.

 Make your answer stand out

■ Use academic articles such as G. Williams 'Evidence of identification: 'The Devlin Report' [1976] Crim LR 407 and P. Jackson 'The insufficiency of identification evidence' [1986] Crim LR 203 when discussing problems with identification evidence.

■ Advance an argument that the fact that no mandatory words are to be used for a *Turnbull* warning is in itself a weakness as different judges may place different emphasis on each part of the warning and mention the case of *R* v *Nash* [2004] EWCA Crim 2696, which held that the 'full force 'of the warning should always be given.

■ Discuss the potential conflict between the power to withdraw weak and unsupported evidence and the *Galbraith* test in *R* v *Galbraith* [1981] 2 All ER 1060, which applies to an application of 'no case to answer'.

■ Discuss cases such as *R* v *Akaidere* [1990] Crim LR 808 and the judge directing the jury on supporting evidence for weak ID.

! **Don't be tempted to...**

- Simply list the elements of the *Turnbull* guideline without attempting to evaluate the strengths and weaknesses of each aspect of the warning.
- Ignore Code D and focus only on the *Turnbull* warning.
- Ignore the consequences of failure to give a warning – the *Turnbull* warning is considered mandatory yet is not always applied and therefore this is a good area to discuss when examining the effectiveness of the guidelines.
- Discuss other forms of identification evidence – the question requires you to focus on visual identification evidence.

？ Question 2

Iona Mathews is charged with assault. The police allege that she assaulted her former employer Douglas in a quiet alleyway a few minutes from where he worked. The police have witnesses to the alleged assault as follows:

(a) Meghan, who lives in a flat opposite the alleyway, who says that she saw a white woman aged approximately 25 with brown hair pushing a man into the alleyway. Meghan is 81 with poor eyesight. Iona in fact has blonde hair. Meghan was unable to pick Iona out in a video identification.

(b) Catherine, who was standing on the opposite side of the road, saw the assault. Her view was impeded every few seconds by cars passing in the road. Catherine accompanied police officers in a police car, where she was able to point Iona out in a crowded market some 40 minutes after the alleged assault when a police officer asked her if that is the person she saw.

(c) Siobhan works with Iona and was smoking outside the offices when she saw Iona emerge from the alleyway. She did not, however, see Douglas. The police did not ask Siobhan to take part in an identification procedure. Iona alleges that Siobhan is 'stitching me up' and denies being anywhere near the alleyway at the time.

(d) An audio recording of Iona's voice which was accidentally picked up on a dictaphone machine in the office. Iona is heard saying to Douglas that 'he deserves a good smack'. Iona denies that it is her voice.

Advise the prosecution as to the admissibility of the above evidence.

Answer plan

→ For Meghan discuss whether a *Turnbull* warning is necessary and the form the warning should take.

→ In the case of Catherine discuss the quality of her identification evidence and whether the correct procedure was followed under Code D PACE 1984.

→ For Siobhan discuss whether a *Turnbull* warning is needed – is the issue one of identification or whether a witness is telling the truth?

→ Discuss whether a qualified *Turnbull* warning should be given in the case of voice identification.

Diagram plan

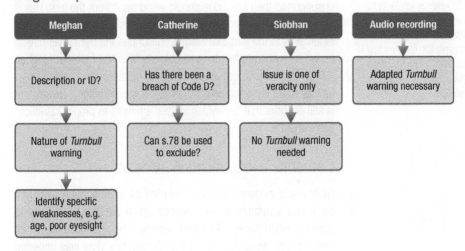

A printable version of this diagram plan is available from www.pearsoned.co.uk/lawexpressqa

Answer

¹ A short summary of the issues raised by the problem question shows the examiner that you are able to recognise the relevant evidential issues from the outset and therefore that you have an understanding of the question.

Visual identification evidence has the potential to be unreliable given that witnesses can often be mistaken. As such its admissibility is governed by guidelines set out in the case of **R v Turnbull** [1976] 3 WLR 445, CA. In advising the prosecution it will be necessary to consider the nature of the warning the judge will need to give at trial in relation to the various forms of identification evidence and also to consider whether the police have used the correct identification procedure under Code D Police and Criminal Evidence Act 1984.¹

Meghan's identification evidence

[2] This shows the examiner that you are able to distinguish between description and ID and that therefore you have a command of the relevant cases and legal principles in this area such as the case of *Gayle* and that your knowledge is good. This will earn you the available marks.

The first issue to consider is whether Meghan's evidence amounts to identification at all or whether it is merely a description. She is only able to describe the person she saw as white, aged approximately 25 with brown hair and this description could fit a large section of the population. In the case of **R v Gayle** [1999] 2 Cr App Rep 130, CA the court held that a **Turnbull** warning is not required if the description is merely of a type of person or their clothing rather than particular facial features. The evidence can be no more than circumstantial in this case.[2]

[3] By relating the facts to the legal test you show the examiner that you are able to apply the relevant law to the facts using the clues given such as Meghan's poor eyesight.

Even if the evidence could be regarded as sufficient to identify Iona, the case of **Turnbull** states that if the evidence is weak and unsupported then the judge should withdraw it from the jury. This is where the age of Meghan and her poor eyesight may be important together with the fact that Meghan describes the person as having brown hair when in fact Iona has blonde hair. The fact that Meghan was unable to pick out Iona in a video identification is also important as there is no support for her visual identification.[3] However, it is still doubtful that the evidence itself amounts to proper identification evidence.

Catherine's identification evidence

Catherine's evidence can be regarded as identification evidence but it has a number of weaknesses which the judge will have to point out when giving a **Turnbull** warning. The circumstances of the identification were poor given that Catherine's view was impeded and she was standing on the opposite side of the road.

[4] This demonstrates a wider knowledge on your part of the provisions of Code D and will separate you from the weaker student who may not appreciate the implication of the clue given in the question that Catherine's identification was prompted by a police officer.

There is also an issue here about the admissibility of the identification Catherine made when she was able to point Iona out in a crowd. There would appear to be a breach of Code D here as the Code prescribes video identification as the first method to be used unless it is not reasonably practicable. It is possible to use crowd identification where a person has been seen participating in an offence and is believed to still be in the area. However, the police officers must not direct the witness's attention to a particular individual.[4] The fact that the police officers drew Catherine's attention

5 Discussion of the
exclusionary discretion takes
your point through to its logical
conclusion and shows that you
have covered all eventualities
when discussing admissibility.

to Iona may make the identification unreliable. This may provide
grounds for the defence to ask the judge to exercise his discretion
under s.78 PACE to exclude the identification evidence on the basis
that its admission would have such an adverse effect on the fairness in the proceedings it ought not to be admitted.[5]

Siobhan's identification evidence

6 Summarising the various
elements of the *Turnbull*
warning in this way is
necessary at some point in
your answer to show that you
understand the subject matter
and have the requisite level
of knowledge. There will be
marks specifically awarded
for knowing the elements
of the *Turnbull* warning and
being able to apply them to
the facts in the question.

7 You could equally use cases
such as *Reid* v *The Queen*
[1990] Cr App R 121, as long
as the legal principles are the
same this is acceptable.

8 This shows an ability to
analyse and compare and
contrast cases critically. This
skill will be awarded with
additional marks.

9 Identifying exceptions to the
requirement for a *Turnbull*
warning demonstrates a
deeper understanding of the
subject matter and will gain
you higher marks where it is
applied correctly.

With regard to Siobhan's evidence it is likely that a **Turnbull** warning is needed here. Although it is based on recognition, a **Turnbull**
warning is still necessary. The judge should tell the jury of the special need for caution and explain why caution is needed, namely
that a convincing witness can be a mistaken one and that a number
of witnesses can all be mistaken. The judge should then direct the
jury to look at the circumstances in which the identification evidence was made and this would involve considering, for example,
how long Meghan had Iona in her sight and from what distance.
The judge should then remind the jury of any specific weaknesses
which have appeared in the identification evidence.[6] The judge
should point out to the jury the additional evidence that is capable
of supporting Siobhan's evidence, namely the evidence of Catherine
if it is admissible. A failure to follow these guidelines can result
in a conviction being quashed, as seen in the case of **Scott v The
Queen** [1989] 2 WLR 924[7], although cases such as **Freemantle v
R** [1994] 1 WLR 1437, PC and **Shand v R** [1996] 1 WLR 67, PC
have suggested that if the jury would have convicted anyway because
the evidence was so strong and failure to give a warning would have
made no difference then the conviction will not be overturned.[8]

However, there is a suggestion that Siobhan is lying and trying to
frame Iona for the offence. In the case of **R v Courtnell** [1990]
Crim LR 115 the Court of Appeal held that if the sole issue is the
veracity of the witness then the only question for the jury is whether
or not they believe the witness. However, the Privy Council case of
Beckford v R (1993) 97 Cr App R 409 suggests that if the jury will
have to go on to also consider that an honest mistake could have
been made then a **Turnbull** warning will have to be given.[9]

The audio recording

The audio recording can be played to the jury to compare with Iona's voice and the case of **R v Robb** (1991) 153 JP 538 confirmed that expert evidence is admissible to assist the jury. Because there is still a risk of error in voice identification the jury must be given a warning which is analogous to a **Turnbull** warning. In **R v Flynn** [2008] EWCA Crim 970 the Court of Appeal held that the judge should carefully direct the jury about the danger of mistakes being made in voice identification evidence.

In the circumstances the prosecution should be advised that there is a possibility that the evidence of Meghan will be regarded as a mere description and admissible only as circumstantial evidence. Catherine's evidence may be excluded due to the breaches of Code D of PACE and whilst Siobhan's evidence is likely to be admissible without a **Turnbull** warning much will turn on whether the jury believe her version of events. The audio recording is likely to be admissible but with a qualified **Turnbull** warning being given.[10]

[10] By summing up the nature of your advice you demonstrate an ability to draw all the issues together and this is required to provide a good structure to your answer.

✓ Make your answer stand out

- Discuss miscarriages of justice cases such as *R v Mattan (Deceased)* (1998) *The Times*, 5 March when discussing potential unreliability of visual identification evidence.
- Briefly mention the Criminal Law Revision Committee's Eleventh Report (Cmnd 4991, 1972).
- Refer to specific sections of Code D when discussing Catherine's identification in a crowd, namely Code D-3.2.
- Discuss additional cases such as *R v Trew* [1996] Crim LR 441, CA when discussing identification procedure under Code D – namely that the judge could sum up to the jury that it is possible that the witness (Meghan) made a mistake by picking out someone other than Iona at the identification procedure.

! **Don't be tempted to...**

■ Ignore the facts when considering the nature and weakness of the evidence of Meghan and Catherine – you need to explain what makes the identification unreliable.

■ Forget to discuss the issue of supporting evidence when discussing Catherine's evidence – weak and unsupported identification evidence must be withdrawn from the jury.

■ Forget to discuss identification procedures under Code D when discussing Catherine's identification evidence.

■ Fail to discuss the judicial discretion under s.78 PACE to exclude improperly obtained identification evidence when discussing Catherine's evidence – s.78 PACE 1984 can apply if the breach of Code D is considered 'significant and substantial'.

◆ Question 3

'There is a risk that, if the full *Turnbull* warning is given where it is not appropriate, the jury's attention will be distracted from such relevant issues. Distraction is not in the interests of justice neither is it necessarily in the interests of the accused.' (*R* v *Slater* [1995] Crim LR 244, commentary by Professor Birch at p.245)

Assess the extent to which a direction to the jury is necessary in the case of identification evidence.

Answer plan

→ Explain the nature of the *Turnbull* warning.

→ Discuss the circumstances in which a *Turnbull* warning is not necessary and analyse whether this is justified.

→ Identify the extent to which a warning remains necessary.

Diagram plan

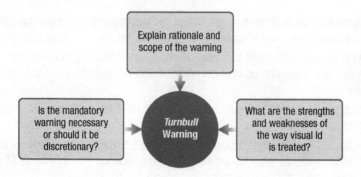

Explain rationale and scope of the warning

Is the mandatory warning necessary or should it be discretionary?

Turnbull Warning

What are the strengths and weaknesses of the way visual Id is treated?

A printable version of this diagram plan is available from www.pearsoned.co.uk/lawexpressqa

Answer

[1] Early reference to the quotation in the question shows that you are tackling the issues at an early stage and will give the examiner a good first impression of your answer.

[2] Reference to committee reports shows wider reading on your part and also a good level of knowledge. This will help to earn you additional marks.

[3] It is important to refer to the leading case in this area as that would be expected in a basic answer and there will be marks awarded for this.

[4] An ability to recognise areas omitted from the *Turnbull* guidelines will show the examiner that you have knowledge of the historical development of the guidelines and are able to appreciate the original recommendations made by the Devlin Committee. This will earn you extra marks.

Identification evidence has been accepted as one of the risks of miscarriages of justice and it is therefore right that it should be the subject of a judicial warning to the jury. However, as identified in the quotation of Professor Birch in the case of **R v Slater** [1995] Crim LR 244, a warning is not required in every case where identification evidence is given.[1]

Because identification is direct evidence it is given more probative value by the jury. The Devlin Committee in their report, *Evidence of Identification in Criminal Cases* (1976) Cmnd 338 proposed changes to the law which would involve removing the possibility that a conviction could be based solely or mainly on identification evidence.[2] They recommended a judicial direction to the jury reminding them of the dangers of convicting solely on identification evidence and suggesting that the jury look for supporting evidence. In the case of **R v Turnbull** [1976] 3 WLR 445 the Court of Appeal took the opportunity to provide guidelines for such a warning.[3] However, the **Turnbull** warning did not include the Devlin Committee's recommendation that there should be a mandatory direction to the jury to look for supporting evidence in the case of identification.[4]

Instead, the **Turnbull** warning restricted the issue of supporting evidence to weak identification evidence. In **R v Akaidere** [1990] Crim LR 808 the court held that, where supporting evidence is required, the judge should explain to the jury the evidence that is capable of supporting the identification but stress that it was for the jury to decide whether it actually did support the identification evidence.

The **Turnbull** warning as a whole does, however, require the judge to stress the strengths and weaknesses of the identification to the jury in the summing-up and draw the jury's attention to any circumstances that might undermine the identification. **R v Nash** [2004] EWCA Crim 2696 also stated that the court's experience of miscarriages of justice should be stressed by the judge to the jury when explaining the need for caution.

Lord Widgery CJ in **Turnbull** made it clear that a **Turnbull** warning should be given 'wherever the case against an accused depends wholly or substantially on the correctness of one or more identifications of the accused' and it is alleged that the witness is mistaken. The warning is considered to be mandatory in the case of mistaken identification and will usually lead to a conviction being overturned (see **Reid v The Queen** [1990] Cr App R 121) unless the identification was so strong that a **Turnbull** warning would have had no effect on the outcome of the trial (see **Freemantle v R** [1994] 1 WLR 1437).

[5] This shows that you are referring your answer back to the subject matter of the quotation. This ensures that your answer remains focused and will earn you available marks.

However, it has been accepted that there may be circumstances in which a **Turnbull** warning is not appropriate and would merely act to confuse the jury as mentioned by Professor Birch in the quotation.[5] The first example can be found in the case of **Turnbull** itself, where Lord Widgery CJ stated that poor and unsupported evidence should be withdrawn from the jury and no **Turnbull** warning would be needed. An example was given of a 'fleeting glance'.

Additionally, whilst a **Turnbull** warning is needed for identification evidence based on recognition, the case of **Beckford v R** (1993) 97 Cr App R 409 held that very good recognition evidence might justify no **Turnbull** warning being given to the jury if that recognition evidence could be considered to be reliable. In **R v Taal** [2002] EWCA Crim 1953 the Court of Appeal accepted that a qualified **Turnbull** direction might be appropriate in these circumstances.

The case of **R v Slater** [1995] Crim LR 244 provides another example of when a **Turnbull** warning is not needed. In this case the defendant did not dispute his presence at the scene. The witness identified the defendant as the man who had carried out the assault. The Court of Appeal held that a **Turnbull** warning

[6] As the quotation refers to the case of *R v Slater* you need to show the examiner that you are aware of the legal principles arising from the case and discuss this. It is OK to refer briefly to the facts in such a situation as long as you also mention the legal principle arising from the case. There will be marks for referring your answer back to the case mentioned in the quotation.

[7] An ability to compare and contrast conflicting case law such as *R v Slater* and *R v Thornton* shows a deeper level of understanding on your part and will earn you additional marks.

[8] Reference to further examples of when a *Turnbull* warning is not needed will add depth to your answer and earn you additional marks.

[9] A discussion of cases in which the *Turnbull* warning is varied or adapted helps build on your arguments with regard to the limitations of the warning. This ensures that your answer remains focused and will continue to earn you the available marks.

was required where there was an issue of mistaken identity and the issue is therefore whether or not the defendant was present. However, where the defendant admits their presence then a **Turnbull** warning is not needed because it is the conduct that is in dispute. A **Turnbull** warning would only serve to confuse the jury.[6] However, much will turn on the facts of the case and the judge will have to give careful consideration as to when a warning is necessary. This can be seen in the case of **R v Thornton** [1995] 1 Cr App R 578. In this case the defendant did not admit his presence at the scene but an issue of mistaken identity did arise because the defendant was in costume and there were other people in similar costumes at the party. The trial judge failed to give a **Turnbull** warning and the conviction was overturned on appeal.[7]

A **Turnbull** warning is only required for visual identification of facial features but is not required for identification of clothing worn by a suspect (see **R v Hassan** [2004] EWCA Crim 1478). A **Turnbull** warning is also not required if the witness merely gives a general description of the suspect rather than a detailed identification (see **R v Gayle** [1999] 2 Cr App R 131) as this can only be regarded as circumstantial evidence rather than direct evidence.[8]

Another example of when a **Turnbull** warning is not needed can be seen in the case of **R v Courtnell** [1990] Crim LR 115. In this case whilst the defendant denied being present at the scene, he also claimed that the witness was lying. The main issue therefore became the truthfulness of the witness rather than whether the witness was mistaken. The court held that in these circumstances a **Turnbull** warning was not necessary. In **Beckford v R** (above), however, the Privy Council disagreed and held that a **Turnbull** warning might still be necessary even if the issue was whether or not a witness was lying. This is because if the jury accepts that the witness is telling the truth, they would then have to go on to assess whether the witness could still be mistaken in the identification. In the case of **R v Giga** [2007] EWCA Crim 345 the Court of Appeal confirmed that a qualified **Turnbull** warning might be appropriate in some cases where the issue was whether the identification witnesses were lying.[9]

Whilst a **Turnbull** warning is considered necessary where the defence suggests that the witness is mistaken, if other issues such as the witness's veracity are also involved then a **Turnbull** warning is not considered necessary. However, the cases differ as to whether a qualified **Turnbull** warning should be given in such circumstances and ultimately this will be a matter for the judge to decide based on the facts of the case. Even if a judge decides that a **Turnbull** warning is not necessary where identification is in dispute this will not always lead to the conviction being overturned as later cases have accepted that the quality of the evidence can be high enough to ensure reliability. In the circumstances whilst a **Turnbull** warning remains an important requirement, it is accepted that there are circumstances in which it would merely serve to confuse the jury and so some flexibility must exist to avoid giving unnecessary and confusing directions to the jury on the quality of the evidence when the quality is clearly high.

 Make your answer stand out

- Refer to the Criminal Law Revision Committee's Eleventh Report (1972, Cmnd 4991) when discussing the dangers of identification evidence.
- Refer to views in journal articles such as A. Roberts 'The perils and possibilities of qualified identification: *R* v *George*' (2003) 7 E & P 130.
- Refer to additional cases such as *R* v *Fergus* (1993) 98 Cr App Rep 313 on the issue of withdrawal of poor and unsupported identification evidence.

! Don't be tempted to...

- Ignore the quotation in the question – you must offer some assessment of when a *Turnbull* warning is not necessary.
- Give an answer that is purely descriptive and simply describes the elements of a *Turnbull* warning without assessing decisions in subsequent cases about the need for a *Turnbull* warning.
- Ignore the fact that *R* v *Turnbull* includes an example of when a *Turnbull* warning will not be necessary, namely in the case of poor and unsupported identification evidence.

❓ Question 4

Christina is charged with assaulting Katya at a nightclub. Christina denies being at the nightclub on the date in question and says that Katya is lying. The prosecution have a number of witnesses who claim to have identified Christina as the person who carried out the assault on Katya:

(a) Jacob, an off-duty police officer, who says he saw Christina in a crowd raise her hand and slap the victim. Jacob says he had previously seen Christina and Katya arguing outside the toilets in the club and had heard Christina threaten Katya. He says he had therefore kept a close eye on Christina and although he was standing 6 metres away when the assault happened he is sure that it was Christina who hit Katya.

(b) Ben, who was the manager of the nightclub, who saw Christina push Katya to the ground before Christina ran out of the club. Ben has given a description of Christina as white, aged approximately 20 years, with brown hair. Ben was able to pick Katya out in an identification parade.

(c) Hassan, who was just entering the nightclub as Christina ran out and caught a fleeting glimpse of her before she left. Jacob was also running after Christina and asked Hassan in which direction she had gone because she was wanted for assault.

(d) Katya, who identified Christina as her assailant and says that they have been friends for five years but had argued at the club because Christina was drinking heavily.

Advise the prosecution about how each piece of identification evidence will be dealt with at trial.

Answer plan

→ Discuss the need for a *Turnbull* warning in relation to Jacob's evidence.

→ Mention that a *Turnbull* warning is not needed in relation to Ben's description.

→ Assess whether Hassan's evidence is poor and unsupported and whether it should be withdrawn from the jury.

→ Examine whether Katya's evidence requires a *Turnbull* warning given that it is recognition evidence and there is an issue of her untruthfulness.

Diagram plan

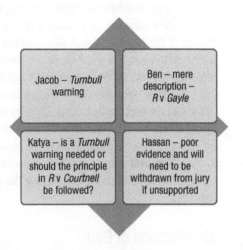

Jacob – *Turnbull* warning	Ben – mere description – *R* v *Gayle*
Katya – is a *Turnbull* warning needed or should the principle in *R* v *Courtnell* be followed?	Hassan – poor evidence and will need to be withdrawn from jury if unsupported

A printable version of this diagram plan is available from www.pearsoned.co.uk/lawexpressqa

Answer

The prosecution should be advised that, as their case depends substantially on the correctness of the various pieces of identification evidence, the trial judge will have to consider whether or not to give a warning to the jury in relation to the identification evidence and consider whether any of the evidence needs to be supported or withdrawn from the jury altogether.

Identification by Jacob

With regard to Jacob's identification the judge will have to give a **Turnbull** warning to the jury (see **R v Turnbull** [1976] 3 WLR 445). Cases such as **R v Bowden** [1993] Crim LR 379 have confirmed that a **Turnbull** warning is necessary even if the prosecution witness is a police officer, as they can also make mistakes like any other witness.[1] However, the case of **R v Tyler** (1992) 96 Cr App Rep 332 accepted that the judge could also direct the jury to the fact that the training and experience of police officers in observation techniques could be taken into account when assessing the reliability of their evidence. As part of the **Turnbull** warning the judge will need to tell the jury of the need to be cautious when considering

[1] An ability to spot clues in the question such as the fact that Jacob is a police officer and apply relevant case law shows a greater level of knowledge and awareness of the issues and will earn you extra marks.

[2] It is important to apply the *Turnbull* warning by using the facts to help you do this. In particular, you need to assess the strengths and weaknesses of the identification and the circumstances in which the identification was made by following Lord Widgery CJ's guidelines. This shows the examiner that you understand the practical implications of the *Turnbull* warning. This in turn shows a good level of understanding and will earn you the available marks.

Jacob's evidence because an honest witness can still be a mistaken one. The judge will have to explain the circumstances in which the identification evidence was made and this would involve pointing out to the jury that Jacob was standing 6 metres away from Christina and Katya at the time of the identification and that the identification was made in a crowded nightclub where the lighting would have been dimmed. The judge should also point out that Jacob had the opportunity to keep Christina under observation for a period of time because he had been watching her since hearing the argument outside the toilets between Christina and Katya.[2] A failure to give a **Turnbull** warning in these circumstances could lead to the conviction being overturned (see **Reid v The Queen** [1990] Cr App Rep 121).

Identification of Ben

An issue arises as to whether Ben has in fact given evidence of identification. Ben's description of Christina is one that could apply to a number of women, as such it cannot be considered to be direct evidence. In the case of **R v Gayle** [1999] 2 Cr App R 130 it was held that a general description could only act as circumstantial evidence in these circumstances.

[3] Marks will be awarded for spotting that the description does not merit a *Turnbull* warning and for also applying a relevant case to back up this principle.

However, Ben subsequently picks Katya out in an identification parade and evidence of the person selected by Ben during the identification procedure can itself be used as identification evidence. However, the correct procedure under Code D of the Police and Criminal Evidence Act 1984 must have been complied with.[3] The procedure, which should have been adopted under Code D, was a video identification procedure. However, Ben took part in an identification parade. This is the second procedure prescribed under the Code and should only take place if a video identification procedure is not reasonably practicable. Breaches of Code D may be taken into consideration at the trial and the court has discretion to exclude the evidence under s.78 of the 1984 Act if its admission would 'have such an adverse effect on the fairness of the proceedings'.[4] However, in **R v Forbes** [2001] 1 AC 473 the House of Lords held that non-compliance with Code D will not necessarily lead to the identification evidence being excluded and each case will have to be looked at on its facts. Minor breaches are unlikely to lead to exclusion and it is likely that the breaches will need to be

[4] As identification procedure has been mentioned in the facts you will be expected to discuss the implications of this issue to identification and there will be available marks awarded for this and for recognising that there has been a potential breach of Code D.

'significant and substantial' (see **R v B** [2008] EWCA Crim 1524). It is unlikely on the facts that exclusion of the evidence would be justified under s.78.

Identification by Hassan

According to Lord Widgery CJ in the case of **R v Turnbull** (above), poor and unsupported identification evidence should be withdrawn from the jury. Lord Widgery gave a 'fleeting glance' as an example of poor identification evidence. Hassan's identification evidence will therefore have to be supported. The trial judge should indicate to the jury the evidence that is capable of acting as support.[5] The supporting evidence must itself identify Christina. Cases such as **R v McConnell** [2004] EWCA Crim 1358 illustrates that identification by one witness can support the identification by another. Therefore, Hassan's identification could be supported by Jacob's identification of Christina. However, according to **R v Weeder** (1980) 71 Cr App Rep 228 the judge should still stress to the jury that several honest witnesses could still be mistaken and therefore that both Hassan and Jacob could both be mistaken.

[5] A clue has been given in the facts of the question when you are told Hassan caught a 'fleeting glimpse' of Christina and this which relates back to Lord Widgery CJ's speech in R v Turnbull. An ability to spot this clue shows that you have a wider understanding of the case of R v Turnbull and this will earn you additional marks.

Identification by Katya

The identification evidence of Katya is based on recognition evidence. In **R v Turnbull** Lord Widgery CJ said that a **Turnbull** warning would still be needed in the case of recognition evidence. However, such evidence would not have to be supported. The judge would still need to warn the jury of the need to be cautious. The case of **R v Bentley** (1991) 99 Cr App Rep 342 illustrates that the **Turnbull** warning may need to be adapted so that it makes sense in the context of good recognition identification evidence. The judge should avoid giving the jury obvious or irrelevant instructions about how to treat the evidence. In **Freemantle v R** [1994] 1 WLR 1437 it was accepted that in very rare circumstances it might not be necessary for the judge to give a **Turnbull** warning in the case of very high quality recognition evidence.[6] There is also an issue as to whether a **Turnbull** warning is needed at all given that Christina claims that Katya is lying (see **R v Courtnell** [1990] Crim LR 115) although in **Beckford v R** (1993) 97 Cr App R 409 it was held that a warning might still be necessary as once the jury are satisfied

[6] An ability to discuss and explain conflicting cases shows a deeper level of understanding on your part and is an example of critical analysis. This will earn you any available extra marks.

that Katya was not lying they would then have to go on to consider whether the identification could be mistaken.

In summary the prosecution should be advised that the identification evidence of Jacob and Hassan is likely to be admissible but that the judge will give a **Turnbull** warning. The evidence of Ben will be admissible as a description and will be regarded as circumstantial evidence and no **Turnbull** warning will be needed. The evidence of Katya will be admissible and may still need a **Turnbull** warning although the judge may decide to give a qualified **Turnbull** warning in the circumstances.

 Make your answer stand out

- When discussing Ben, mention that weaknesses in the identification procedure might warrant some comment during the judge's summing-up (see *R* v *Trew* [1996] Crim LR 441).
- When mentioning Hassan's 'fleeting glimpse', mention further cases such as *R* v *Fergus* (1993) 98 Cr App R 313 which suggest that the judge can invite submissions of 'no case to answer' at the end of the prosecution case in such circumstances.
- Mention the JSB *Crown Court Bench Book* specimen direction on identification evidence and Hedley J's comments in *R* v *Nash* [2004] EWCA Crim 2696 that it should be regarded as the 'briefest permissible summary of the dangers inherent in identification evidence'.

! Don't be tempted to...

- Suggest that Ben's evidence amounts to identification evidence without considering *R* v *Gayle*.
- Assume that because a 'fleeting glance' is mentioned in relation to Hassan's evidence, the evidence would be automatically withdrawn from the jury – you have to go on to consider whether the evidence is supported.
- Ignore the fact that Christina has alleged that Katya is lying – this is relevant to the issue of whether a *Turnbull* warning is needed.

Denials and silence

How this topic may come up in exams

This topic is regarded as an important one in the law of evidence and is usually examined with reference to human rights issues when presented in essay form. However, silence as a topic is also a favourite for incorporation as part of a multi-issue problem question especially when considering other issues arising at a police station such as confessions and identification evidence. It is important to appreciate the different judicial directions given for both s.34 and s.35 of the Criminal Justice and Public Order Act 1994 as well as understanding the approach taken to legal advice given to the defendant to remain silent under s.34. However, it is also necessary to have a working understanding of ss.36 and 37 so that you can recognise these provisions when they appear in a problem question.

Attack the question

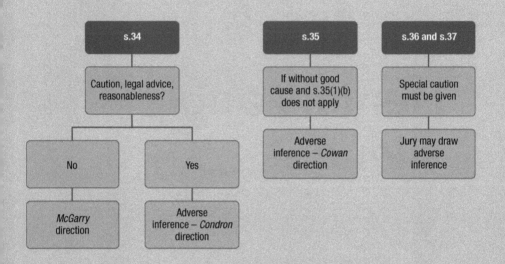

Question 1

'The drawing of inferences from silence is a particularly sensitive area. Many respected authorities have voiced the fear that s.35 and its sister sections may lead to wrongful convictions.' (Lord Bingham CJ in *R* v *Birchall* [1999] Crim LR 311)

Evaluate the above statement in the context of the exercise of the defendant's right to silence.

Answer plan

→ Consider the rationale for the right to silence and adverse inferences under s.34–37 of the 1994 Act.

→ Evaluate the strengths and weaknesses of the provisions.

→ Consider whether the provisions restrict the right to a fair trial or whether there are sufficient safeguards.

Diagram plan

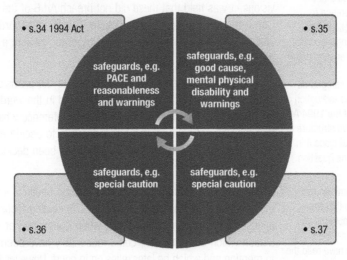

A printable version of this diagram plan is available from www.pearsoned.co.uk/lawexpressqa

Answer

The origins of a defendant's right to silence can be found in the general principle that the prosecution bears the burden of proving the accused's guilt. The accused need not co-operate with the police investigation (see **Rice v Connolly** [1966] 2 QB 414) or give evidence at trial.

One of the problems with this principle, however, is that unless the prosecution is given some notice of the defence to be put at trial they are prevented from producing evidence to disprove that defence. The Criminal Law Revision Committee in their Eleventh Report (Cmnd 4991, 1972)[1] took the view that not to allow the jury to draw whatever inferences they considered proper from an accused's silence would give 'an unnecessary advantage to the guilty'.

The Criminal Justice and Public Order Act 1994 introduced a qualification to the right to silence. Whilst the accused retained the right to silence before and during the trial, the jury can draw an adverse inference. In the case of **Murray v United Kingdom** (1996) 22 EHRR 29, which looked at Northern Ireland's silence provisions, it was held that these did not breach Art.6 of the European Convention on Human Rights. Article 6 was not regarded as an absolute right and safeguards were sufficient to prevent a breach of the right to a fair trial.[2]

A number of safeguards have been built into the provisions of the 1994 Act. The first safeguard[3] is to be found in the wording of the provisions. The jury 'may' draw an adverse inference which means that they do not have to. It is left to the jury to decide whether or not to draw an adverse inference once it has been decided that an adverse inference can be drawn.

Section 34[4] is the more controversial section because it relates to the accused's pre-trial right of silence. The section focuses on the accused's failure to mention a fact when questioned at the police station which the defendant could reasonably have been expected to mention and which he later relies on in court. However, s.34 does not require a suspect to answer every question put to them. It is in fact limited in scope to mentioning a 'fact' which is later used in the defence for example an alibi.[5] The suspect can also still provide a 'no comment' interview as long as a prepared statement is given to the police setting out the facts relied on (see **R v Knight** [2004] 1 WLR 340).

[1] Reference to committee reports such as the Criminal Law Revision Committee's Eleventh Report demonstrates wider reading and knowledge of the subject area and will earn you extra marks.

[2] Referring to human rights cases is a good way to show the examiner that you have appreciated that the quotation's reference to wrongful convictions has a human rights angle and this also gives your answer depth.

[3] Discussion of safeguards assists with your evaluation of the strengths of the 1994 Act and will help give structure to your answer and place it in the context of the question.

[4] Show the examiner that you understand that the question does not limit you to discussing only s.35. This shows that you have read the question carefully.

[5] Some explanation of s.34 demonstrates that you have a command of the topic and that your understanding is good.

Safeguards exist because the questioning must be done under caution whether this is during the interview itself or the charging process. In addition, under s.34(2A) of the Act no adverse inference can be drawn if the suspect has not had the opportunity to consult a solicitor. Reliance on the advice of a solicitor to remain silent will not prevent an adverse inference being drawn as indicated in cases such as **R v Beckles (No. 2)** [2005] 1 WLR 2829. The jury can still draw an adverse inference even if the defendant genuinely relied on the advice if the jury feel it was not reasonable for the defendant to have done so.[6]

[6] By analysing the weaknesses as you discuss the strengths you give a balance to your answer.

[7] By ensuring that you discuss all the provisions on silence in the 1994 Act, you ensure that your answer is a full one.

Sections 36 and 37 of the 1994 Act[7] present further difficulties in that, like s.34, these provisions apply to pre-trial questioning and silence but, unlike s.34, they do not include a provision relating to 'reasonableness'. Therefore, failure to give an explanation at the time of arrest for an object, substance or mark found on the suspect's person (s.36) or an explanation when the suspect is found at a particular place (s.37) can in itself trigger an adverse inference and few safeguards exist for these provisions other than that a special caution must be given at the time of arrest.

However, under s.38(3) of the Act an adverse inference cannot be the sole basis for a jury to make a finding of guilt. There must be evidence which supports that finding. This applies to ss.34–37 of the Act.

[8] Discussion of the positive direction in *McGarry* for s.34 is an important way to show the examiner that your knowledge of s.34 is much wider than the basic provisions set out in that section. This in turn shows a deeper level of understanding.

Judicial directions are also a safeguard. For example, for s.34 if the judge decides from the circumstances existing at the time that it was not reasonable for the accused to have mentioned the fact that he later relies on in his defence, the judge must direct the jury not to draw an adverse inference (see **R v McGarry** [1999] 1 Cr App Rep 377).[8]

[9] Discussing additions to the *Cowan* direction as a result of subsequent case law shows that your knowledge is up to date and will help to earn you additional marks.

If the jury can draw an adverse inference under s.34, the judge must still specifically direct them. **R v Condron** [1997] 1 WLR 827 states that the judge should explain to the jury matters such as the basis for drawing the inference and that the burden of proof remains with the prosecution. The European Court of Human Rights held in the case of **Condron v United Kingdom** (2001) 31 EHRR 1 that the direction should also include reference to the fact that the jury can only draw an adverse inference once they have concluded that the accused's silence can only sensibly be attributed to the defendant having no answer or none that would stand up to cross-examination.[9] Failure to give this direction would mean that the defendant's rights had been breached under Art.6. Before an adverse inference can be drawn under s.35 the judge should give the jury a warning according to the case of **R v Cowan** [1995] 3 WLR 818 which is similar in nature to that under s.34.

Further safeguards are built into s.35 relating to silence during the trial. Under s.35(1)(b) no adverse inference can be drawn if the physical or mental condition of the accused makes it 'undesirable' for him or her to give evidence. For example, in the case of **R v Friend (No. 2)** [2004] EWCA Crim 2661 the appeal was allowed on the basis that the judge should not have allowed the jury to draw an adverse inference since the defendant was suffering from attention deficit and hyperactivity disorder at the time of the trial.

[10] By reaching a view in your conclusion as to whether or not you agree with the quotation, you ensure that your structure flows and remains relevant to the question. You are not assessed on whether your view is right or wrong in a question such as this. You must simply be able to support your view with convincing arguments.

In conclusion, it is important to note that the defendant's right of silence remains protected despite the provisions in the 1994 Act. A number of safeguards exist such as judicial directions to ensure that the right is not eroded. Article 6 is a qualified right and therefore does not prevail over the proper administration of justice. The disclosure requirements placed on a defendant means that there should be an expectation that if the defendant has an explanation it will be given at the earliest opportunity.[10]

✓ Make your answer stand out

- Refer to journal articles such as D. Birch 'Suffering in silence' [1999] Crim LR 769, I. Dennis 'Silence in the police station' [2002] Crim LR 25 to add depth to your answer.
- Refer to the Royal Commission on Criminal Justice Report (1993) Cm. 2263 for historical context to the 1994 Act.
- When discussing safeguards argue that the 'reasonableness' requirement in s.34 is in itself a safeguard and mention cases such as R v Argent (1996) 161 JP 190 which gives examples of the matters that would affect reasonableness such as age, health, tiredness, lack of legal advice, etc.
- Mention cases such as R v Goodsir [2006] EWCA Crim 852 in relation to s.34's limitations namely only applicable if suspect questioned in an 'authorised place of detention'.
- Mention further ECtHR cases such as Averill v United Kingdom (2000) App. No. 36408/97 when discussing Art.6.

> **!** **Don't be tempted to...**
>
> ■ Ignore the safeguards – they are important to addressing the quotation in the question.
>
> ■ Fail to discuss important ECHR cases such as *Murray* v *UK* – these are also important in addressing the quotation in the question.
>
> ■ Concentrate only on s.35 because it is mentioned in the quotation – the quotation also mentions 'sister provisions'.

❓ Question 2

Marvin, aged 15, Curtis, aged 23 and Don, aged 27 are arrested for burglary. They are all taken to the police station.

(a) Marvin is interviewed in the presence of his solicitor but no caution is given. On the advice of his solicitor, Marvin gives a 'no comment' interview on the basis that the police appear to have no evidence against him. Marvin intends to plead not guilty on the basis that, although he accompanied Curtis and Don, he did not take part in the burglary.

(b) Curtis is interviewed in the presence of a solicitor. He answers police questions in which he denies any knowledge of the burglary. At trial he intends to disclose as his alibi that he was out of the country at the time of the burglary.

(c) At the time of his arrest Don was found with a crowbar in his hand. When asked about the crowbar he failed to give an explanation. Don does not intend to give any evidence at trial because he suffers from a speech impediment and is worried about speaking publicly in court.

Advise Marvin, Curtis and Don of any evidential issues arising from the above set of facts.

Answer plan

→ For Marvin consider s.34 Criminal Justice and Public Order Act 1994 and whether the jury can draw an adverse inference from his silence at the police station and the appropriate judicial warning.

→ For Curtis consider the application of s.34 and the judicial direction under *Condron*.

→ For Don consider both s.36 and s.35 silence and whether an adverse inference can be drawn.

→ Reach a conclusion as to how the jury are likely to be directed on the issue of silence at trial.

Diagram plan

> Marvin – consider s.34 reasonableness and legal advice

> Curtis – consider s.34 alibi

> Don – consider s.36 re crowbar and s.35 re speech impediment

A printable version of this diagram plan is available from www.pearsoned.co.uk/lawexpressqa

Answer

[1] By summarising the evidential issues in your introduction you demonstrate an ability to recognise the legal issues at the outset and to put your answer in the correct legal context. You also avoid irrelevant general statements about the right to silence and this enables you to tackle the issues in the question at an early stage. This avoids wasting time and helps to ensure your answer is focused.

In order to advise Marvin, Curtis and Don it is necessary to consider the effect their failure to give information or testify will have on their trial. Whilst a suspect has a right of silence under the Criminal Justice and Public Order Act 1994, this right is qualified.[1]

Marvin

Marvin fails to answer police questions or to give a written statement to the police during the interview. Under s.34 of the 1994 Act if Marvin fails to mention a fact which he could reasonably be expected to mention and which he later relies on in his defence then the jury can be invited to draw an adverse inference at his trial. However, under s.38(3) an adverse inference alone is not enough for a finding of guilt.

[2] By identifying Marvin's failure to give an explanation you show the examiner that you understand how s.34 works and that you are able to apply it in the context of the problem. This demonstrates application of the law to the facts and therefore shows your ability to take a practical approach to the problem question. This will gain you higher marks.

Marvin has an explanation to give, namely that he was present but did not take part in the offence but he fails to give this explanation at the time of the interview.[2] Section 34 provides that the 'fact' must be something which he could reasonably have been expected to mention. The case of **R v Argent** (1996) 161 JP 190, CA suggests that 'reasonableness' could be affected by such matters as the age of the defendant, health and legal advice. Martin is only 15 years of age and may not have appreciated the importance of cooperating with the police at the time. It is also important to note that

3 Show the examiner that you have appreciated the importance of clues given in the question such as Marvin's age and reliance on legal advice both of which will affect the issue of 'reasonableness' under s.34. This demonstrates a good level of understanding which will earn you the available marks.

4 It is permissible, although not essential, to refer to journal articles in a problem question but if you do so you must ensure that you tie it in to the facts that are under consideration.

5 This shows the examiner that you are able to take your discussion further and recognise when s.34 may not apply and therefore ensures that your discussion of this statutory provision is a full one and this will earn you more of the available marks.

6 This shows the examiner that you understand that the absence of the s.34 criteria still has consequences and this shows a deeper understanding on your part.

7 By dealing with other ways in which an adverse inference can be drawn under s.34, you show a deeper understanding of the subject matter and this can gain you more marks.

Marvin had legal advice and he relied on this legal advice in giving a 'no comment' interview.[3] In **Condron v UK** (2001) 31 EHRR 1 the European Court of Human Rights held that the fact that the solicitor advised the defendant to remain silent is an important consideration as there may be good reason for such advice. In **R v Howell** [2003] EWCA Crim 1, however, the Court of Appeal held the fact that the defendant relied on legal advice is not enough to stop an adverse inference being drawn. The jury could still consider whether the defendant still remained silent because he had no explanation to give. The issue was clarified in **R v Hoare** [2005] 1 WLR 1804 and **R v Beckles (No. 2)** [2005] 1 WLR 1804, which held that the issue was not simply whether the defendant genuinely believed in the advice but whether it was reasonable for him to do so. The solicitor had valid reasons for advising on a 'no comment' interview, as the police have not advanced any evidence and so the solicitor may have problems advising the client (see comments of Rose LJ in **R v Roble** [1997] Crim LR 449) so it may have been reasonable for Marvin to belive in that advice. Even if the solicitor's advice were ill-judged as Rosemary Pattenden points out in her article 'Inferences from silence' [1995] Crim LR 602 it would be unfair to penalise a defendant for the failings of the solicitor.[4]

In addition, in order for s.34 to apply Marvin must have been given a caution before the start of the police interview. This does not appear to have happened.[5] The case of **R v McGarry** [1999] 1 Cr App Rep 377 states that where the jury cannot draw an adverse inference because the circumstances of s.34 have not been met, the judge must positively direct them that they cannot draw such an inference otherwise there is a danger that they will.[6]

Curtis

In the case of Curtis, although he answers police questions, a s.34 inference can still be drawn. This is because he still fails to mention a fact which he later relies on at court, namely his alibi. Even if an alibi is mentioned during interviewing it must also be disclosed in a defence statement or the jury can still draw an adverse inference. This means the jury can draw an adverse inference under s.34 of the 1994 Act.[7]

The judge will have to direct the jury about drawing an adverse inference. **R v Condron** [1997] 1 WLR 827 states that the judge should explain the basis under which a s.34 inference can be drawn, that the burden of proof remains with the prosecution, that the defendant has a right of silence and that an adverse inference alone cannot be enough for a finding of guilt. In addition, **Condron v UK** (2000) App. No. 35718/97 held that the jury should only draw an adverse inference if they believe the silence is because the defendant does not have an answer to give or none that would stand up to cross-examination.[8]

[8] A discussion of the elements of the *Condron* warning is needed here and will show that you have a good level of knowledge which will mark you out from the weaker student who may mention but not explain the nature of the warning. This will earn you the available marks.

Don

Don's failure to provide an explanation for the crowbar falls under s.36 of the 1994 Act, which relates to a defendant's failure to provide an explanation on arrest where there is an object, substance or mark on his person. However, before s.36 can apply Don must have been given a special caution by the police officers on arrest in which they explain the basis of their suspicions and give him a chance to offer an explanation. He appears to have been offered a chance to give an explanation.

[9] Showing familiarity with the relevant statute to the extent that you are able to recognise when certain sub-sections apply demonstrates that you have a good all round knowledge of this area of the law.

Don will not be testifying at the trial. Under s.35 of the 1994 Act 'an adverse inference can be drawn if his failure to testify is without good cause'. Section 35(1)(b) of the 1994 Act provides that an adverse inference will not be drawn if the defendant's physical or mental condition makes it undesirable for him to give evidence.[9] Don suffers from a speech impediment and this may provide good reason for his refusal to testify.[10] It is within a judge's discretion to decide whether s.35(1)(b) is satisfied. If the judge decides that the jury can draw an adverse inference, he should still remind the jury of the defence's explanation for the failure to give evidence. The usual s.35 direction under **R v Cowan** would not apply to a s.35(1)(b) situation.

[10] Show the examiner that you have recognised that a legal issue arises from the facts and spotted an important clue in relation to Don's speech impediment. This shows good command of the material.

In the circumstances, Marvin should be advised that it is possible that the jury will be able to draw an adverse inference in his case because of the test in the cases of **Hoare** and **Beckles**. Curtis should be advised that an adverse inference is unlikely given that he did not have access to legal advice. Don should be advised that unless the judge accepts that his speech impediment is a relevant physical or mental condition under s.35(1)(b) the jury may be invited to draw an adverse inference.

✓ **Make your answer stand out**

- Mention the case of *Murray* v *DPP* [1994] 1 WLR 1, HL when discussing s.35(1)(b) and that if the judge does not exercise a discretion it is still necessary to remind the jury of the defence's explanation for failure to testify.
- When discussing Curtis's failure to mention his alibi in his defence statement, refer to the disclosure requirements under s.6 and s.11(5) of the Criminal Procedure and Investigation Act 1996.
- Introduce cases such as *R* v *Brizzalari* [2004] EWCA Crim 310 when discussing s.34 and how the courts dissuade prosecutors from relying on s.34.

! **Don't be tempted to...**

- Ignore the judicial warnings that must be given for s.34 and s.35 – in particular that a positive *McGarry* direction is needed in the case of Marvin.
- Confuse the provisions of s.36 and s.37 – you must correctly identify which aspects of arrest each covers.
- Ignore important facts such as the issue of legal advice, alibi and Don's speech impediment – these are all important clues in the question.

 Question 3

'... if a charge is made against a person in that person's presence it is reasonable to expect that he or she will immediately deny it, and that the absence of such a denial is some evidence of an admission on the part of the person charged ...' (Cave J in *R* v *Mitchell* (1892) 17 Cox CC 503, Assizes)

Critically evaluate the extent to which the above statement can be said to be true in the modern day.

Answer plan

→ Discuss the rule in *R* v *Christie* [1914] AC 545 on silence as an admission.

→ Explain the limitations to the rule in *Hall* v *R* [1971] 1 WLR 298.

→ Mention the developments since the passing of the Criminal Justice and Public Order Act 1994.

→ Summarise the extent to which you agree or disagree with the quotation.

Diagram plan

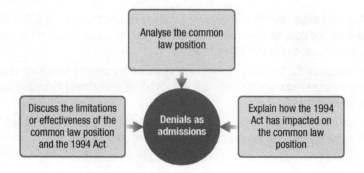

A printable version of this diagram plan is available from www.pearsoned.co.uk/lawexpressqa

Answer

[1] Discussing the rule in the case of *R* v *Mitchell* from which the quotation is taken shows the examiner that you have thought about the issues and that your answer is focused. This gives a good first impression and will earn you the available marks.

[2] Tackling the central issue of the correctness of the quotation and providing examples by contrasting case law and the modern day approach under statute shows that your answer is focused and that you have a good knowledge of the issues.

At common law it was generally accepted in **R v Mitchell** (1892) 17 Cox CC 503 that it was possible for silence to amount to an admission where an accusation was put to a defendant which he failed to directly deny. Cases such as **R v Cramp** (1880) 14 Cox CC 390 confirmed that in such cases the evidence of the silence could constitute 'supporting material'.[1]

The quotation of Cave J in **R v Mitchell** arguably reflects the modern day position with regard to silence generally, since s.82(1) of the Police and Criminal Evidence Act 1984 defines a confession as including any statement adverse to the maker 'whether made in words or otherwise'. This definition is wide enough to include demeanour as an admission, because demeanour could fall within the ambit of a 'statement' made otherwise than in words. However, it would be more difficult to argue that silence is a 'statement'.[2] The common law is expressly preserved in the silence provisions of the Criminal Justice and Public Order Act 1994, ss.34–37.

The requirement in **R v Mitchell** that an inference should only be drawn where a denial might have been expected is mirrored in the provisions of s.34 of the 1994 Act and reinforced in the case of **R v Argent** (1996) 161 JP 190. Before an adverse inference can be drawn under s.34, certain criteria must be met. These include the requirement that there must be proceedings against the defendant to which the silence relates and that the questioning by the police must have been under caution and that there must be a failure to mention a fact which is then relied on during those same court proceedings. Following the decision in **Murray v UK** (1996) 22 EHRR 29, s.34(2A) of the 1994 Act adds an additional requirement and that is that the defendant must have been offered access to legal advice.

[3] The ability to refer to academic opinion in this area of law will help to build upon and support your arguments and demonstrates to the examiner that you have undertaken wider reading and have a deeper level of understanding of the topic. This will help to earn you additional marks.

Ian Dennis in his article 'Silence in the police station: the marginalisation of section 34' [2002] Crim LR 25 argues that s.34 has been curtailed by recent cases including those decided in the European Court of Human Rights to such an extent that there is no longer justification for s.34 and that whilst the inferences under s.34 can amount to useful corroboration, the technical requirements of s.34 are a needlessly complicated way of achieving this purpose.[3]

[4] By breaking down each element of the rule in *R v Mitchell* and considering its relevance to the modern day provisions you continue a good analytical style and this shows the examiner that you have command of the material, all of which will earn you extra marks.

Cave J in the case of **R v Mitchell** identified an important limitation to the rule that silence could amount to an admission and that was that an inference of acceptance of an accusation should only be drawn in such circumstances where the parties were speaking 'on equal terms'.[4] The relationship between a suspect and a police officer who is questioning that suspect was not regarded as being on 'equal terms', as the police officer is in a position of authority over the suspect. This was confirmed in the case of **Hall v R** [1971] 1 WLR 298. Lord Diplock also cautioned that silence alone could not give rise to an inference that the accused had accepted the truth of the accusation.

The 'equal terms' requirement has caused difficulties. For example, in the case of **R v Chandler** [1976] 1 WLR 585 the Court of Appeal held that it was possible for a suspect and a police officer to be speaking on 'equal terms' if the suspect had a solicitor present during the interview. A distinction was made between the position before the police had administered a caution to the suspect when they could be accepted as speaking 'on equal terms' and after a caution had been administered when this would not be the case.

[5] This brings your answer back to the common law position and explains to the examiner that you are aware that the common law position has survived the 1994 Act. This shows that you have a deeper understanding of the issues and that you are able to keep on top of the material. This in turn will earn you extra marks.

Section 34(5) of the 1994 Act preserved the position in **Chandler** in respect of pre-caution silence. However, the suspect and the police officer must still be 'on equal terms', and this will occur if the suspect has a solicitor present.[5] Therefore the modern day approach once again mirrors the common law. The case of **R v Collins; R v Keep** [2004] 1 WLR 1705 confirmed that where

[6] This brings your answer back to the common law position and explains to the examiner that you are aware that the common law position has survived the 1994 Act. This shows that you have a deeper understanding of the issues and that you are able to keep on top of the material. This in turn will earn you extra marks.

[7] An ability to identify where the modern day approach differs shows you are evaluating the issues and helps you to build upon your arguments. This gives your answer good structure and creates an overall good impression that will distinguish you as a good student.

[8] The more safeguards you are able to identify and discuss, the greater will be the force of your arguments and this will create an overall impression of a quality answer and ensure that you continue to earn the available marks.

the parties were on equal terms there must still be some evidential basis for suggesting the silence is capable of amounting to an admission.[6]

The 1994 Act does go further than the decision in **R v Mitchell**, in that under s.34 inferences can be drawn from silence during questioning by the suspect by a police officer post-caution regardless of the issue of 'equal terms'.

However, the 1994 Act also imposes a safeguard under s.38(3), which addresses Lord Diplock's concern in **Hall v R** (above) that an adverse inference alone cannot be sufficient for a finding of guilt.[7] The **Condron** direction under s.34 of the Act and the **Cowan** direction under s.35 ensures that the s.38(3) provisions are drawn to the jury's attention, as well as reminding the jury that the defendant has a right of silence, that the burden of proof remains with the prosecution and that there must first be a case to answer. More importantly, the judge should direct the jury that they may only draw an adverse inference if they are satisfied that the reason for the defendant's silence is because he has no answer to give or none that would stand up to cross-examination.

A further safeguard was incorporated following the decision on **R v McGarry** [1998] 1 Cr App Rep 377, in which the Court of Appeal held that if the requirements of s.34 are not met the trial judge has a duty to positively direct the jury that they cannot draw an adverse inference.[8]

Sections 36 and 37 deal with circumstances relating to questioning outside of the police station and on arrest of a suspect. However, the police must still in these circumstances inform the defendant that they believe he has an object, substance or mark on his person or his presence at a particular place is related to the commission of an offence. As part of the caution they must give him an opportunity to provide an explanation and explain the circumstances of his failure to respond. It will be rare, given the stringent requirements under Code C of the Police and Criminal Evidence Act 1984, for a **Chandler** situation to arise whereby the defendant is questioned by the police before a caution has been administered.

In conclusion, whilst the quotation of Cave J remains true today in the sense that silence is an evidential factor that the jury can take into account in support of the case against the defendant the 1994 Act has introduced safeguards which mean that silence will not always be regarded as an evidential factor and much will depend on the circumstances of the silence.

✓ Make your answer stand out

- Refer to further cases on the issue of silence as an admission such as *R* v *O* [2006] EWCA Crim 556, whereas silence by a co-accused when accused was capable of suggesting that he had adopted the words used by his co-defendant at the time of the offence.

- Advance an argument that the provisions of s.115(3) and s.118 of the Criminal Justice Act 2003 could apply to admissions through demeanour rendering then admissible hearsay.

- Compare and contrast the *Condron* and *Cowan* directions and point out that, whilst the *Condron* direction does not specifically mention that the jury have to be satisfied that there is a *prima facie* case against the defendant, cases such as *R* v *Gill* [2001] 1 Cr App Rep 160 1 have now made it clear that this is a requirement for both s.34 and s.35.

- Discuss the Northern Ireland case of *Murray* v *DPP* [1994] 1 WLR 1, which demonstrates that the sensible approach to s.35 (which has similar provisions in Northern Ireland) is that an adverse inference under s.35 could be used towards a general inference of guilt rather than merely an inference about specific facts such as whether a defendant's alibi is true.

! Don't be tempted to...

- Simply give an answer that describes the law relating to silence but fails to focus on the quotation or the common law rule.

- Concentrate solely on the common law position without explaining how the 1994 Act has altered the right to silence.

- Focus only on one of the silence provisions of the 1994 Act without discussing the others.

? Question 4

Ayo is arrested for a public order offence during a student demonstration. He is alleged to have thrown a dustbin at a politician giving a speech on tuition fees. A fellow student grabs him and says 'you threw that, didn't you?' Ayo does not reply but instead runs away. He is then arrested in a neighbouring street. At the police station Ayo is not offered access to a solicitor. He decides to give a 'no comment' interview, as the police do not explain the exact nature of the charge to him. They tell him they have witnesses but do not give details of what the witnesses saw or heard. Ayo is released on bail and later tells his solicitor that he in fact took the dustbin away from a fellow protestor who was going to throw it at a police officer and Ayo had thrown the dustbin to one side of the crowd to avoid it being used as a weapon. He says if it hit anyone, this was accidental. Ayo does not want to testify at trial as he says he suffers from migraines that are brought on by stress and does not think he will perform well in the witness box.

Advise Ayo as to the approach the jury are likely to take in respect of his silence.

Answer plan

→ Consider issues relating to silence through conduct in respect of the accusation made by a fellow student.

→ Discuss whether s.37 silence is applicable under the Criminal Justice and Public Order Act 1994 on Ayo's arrest or s.34 when Ayo is questioned.

→ Examine the circumstances in which Ayo will be entitled to refuse to testify and whether s.35 will operate.

Diagram plan

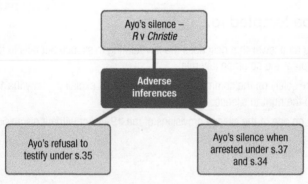

A printable version of this diagram plan is available from www.pearsoned.co.uk/lawexpressqa

Answer

In order to advise Ayo it will be necessary to consider issues relating to silence under ss.34–37 of the Criminal Justice and Public Order Act 1994.

[1] By dealing with the issues early on in your answer and avoiding general commentary you demonstrate an ability to keep your answer focused. You have also identified here that you are aware that Ayo's pre-trial silence arises much earlier than on arrest. This demonstrates good observation and will earn you the available marks.

The first issue that arises is in relation to whether Ayo's decision to remain silent when confronted by a fellow demonstrator can be considered to be an admission of guilt. The case of **R v Christie** [1914] AC 545 is authority for the principle that demeanour conduct or words are admissible as admissions[1] if the person can be taken to have accepted the truth of the statement put to him at the time of the alleged offence. Ayo and his fellow demonstrator can be said to be on 'even terms' (see **R v Norton** [1910] 2 KB 496). This rule has been preserved by s.34(5) of the Criminal Justice and Public Order Act 1994. It will be necessary to consider whether it would have been reasonable to have expected a reply from Ayo (see Cave J's comments in **R v Mitchell** (1892) 17 Cox CC 503). Given that he was being accused of something he later claims he did not do, it would have been reasonable to have expected some response from him when the accusation was made. In addition, according to **R v Mitchell** (above) the silence or conduct is more likely to be regarded as an admission if the accused and the person who made the statement were speaking 'on equal terms'. In the circumstances, Ayo's failure to answer the accusation coupled with his conduct in running away from the scene might be admissible at trial as evidence of an admission on his part.

[2] An understanding of when an adverse inference cannot be drawn shows that you have more than just a basic understanding of the statutory provisions. This will earn you the available marks as it shows good application of the law to the facts.

The next issue that arises is in relation to an arrest under s.37 of the Criminal Justice and Public Order Act 1994 when Ayo is found to be in a neighbouring street at about the time the offence is alleged to have occurred. The jury may draw an adverse inference from Ayo's failure to provide an explanation at this stage. However, the police officer must first have told Ayo that he is believed to be involved in the offence and then ask Ayo to explain his presence and warn him of the consequences of failing to do so.[2] This is a modified or special caution. It is unclear whether the arresting police officer complied with these requirements. If a caution was given then at trial the jury would be entitled to draw an adverse inference from Ayo's silence. However, under s.38(3) of

[3] Knowledge of s.38(3) is important to any question on silence as it demonstrates an understanding of the limitations of the jury drawing an adverse inference and there will usually be marks awarded for knowing this.

the 1994 Act a conviction can never be based solely on an adverse inference.[3]

Ayo is then interviewed at the police station and again fails to provide an explanation. Under s.34 an adverse inference can be drawn at trial where a suspect fails to mention a fact they could reasonably have been expected to mention at trial. However, Ayo must rely on the explanation that he subsequently gives to his solicitor as part of his defence at trial before an adverse inference can be drawn. Although Ayo does not intend to testify at trial if his legal representatives put forward the explanation on his behalf as part of his defence this can still trigger an adverse inference under s.34 (see cases such as **R v Webber** [2004] 1 WLR 404).

[4] The use of cases to illustrate your answer is necessary, especially if you can link the facts of the case to the issues in the problem question. This will earn you the available marks.

It is also necessary to examine whether it would have been reasonable for Ayo to have mentioned his explanation at the time. Ayo might rely on cases such as **R v Roble** [1997] Crim LR 449 on the basis that failure by the police to give details of the exact nature of the charge he faced meant that he could not put forward a satisfactory response.[4] Also the police have clearly breached Code C of PACE by failing to explain the nature of the charge at the start of the interview. In addition, under s.34(2A) of the 1994 Act, an inference cannot be drawn as Ayo was refused access to legal advice.[5] In the circumstances the requirements of s.34 have not been meant and the judge must according to the case of **R v McGarry** [1991] 1 Cr App Rep 377 give a direction to the jury that they should not draw an adverse inference.

[5] An ability to spot important clues in the question such as the fact that Ayo was refused access to legal advice demonstrates a good level of knowledge of the subject area and will earn you the available marks.

The final issue that arises is in relation to Ayo's refusal to testify at trial. Under s.35 of the 1994 Act the jury can draw an adverse inference from Ayo's refusal to testify if this is without good cause. Ayo suffers from migraines which bring on stress and affect his performance in the witness box. Under s.35(1)(b) the jury will not be able to draw an adverse inference if Ayo's refusal to testify is based on a physical or mental condition. In **R v Tabbakh** [2009] EWCA Crim 464 it was held that the mere fact that an accused might simply have difficulty giving evidence was not enough for the purposes of deciding whether the accused was suffering a physical or mental condition. In **R v Friend** [1997] 1 WLR 1433 it was accepted that s.35(1)(b) gave a wide discretion to the judge and this

[6] Using cases to help you illustrate the approach that the trial judge might take to the issues is another form of application of the law to the facts. Even if you are unable to reach any firm conclusions you will have demonstrated to the examiner that you are aware that there is no definitive approach and much will depend on how the judicial discretion is exercised. This will be enough in this situation to earn you the available marks.

[7] Reference to applicable practice directions demonstrates wider reading on your part and a deeper level of knowledge and will earn you additional marks.

discretion could only be challenged if it was '**Wednesbury** unreasonable'.[6] The trial judge will have to decide whether the migraines are severe enough to fall under s.35(1)(b). If a s.35 inference can be drawn the judge must ensure that Ayo understands the effect of failure to testify by asking Ayo's legal representative if the effect of s.35 has been explained to Ayo. This will be done in front of the jury and in accordance with the Practice Direction (Criminal Proceedings: Consolidation) [2002] 1 WLR 2870.[7]

The judge must also give a warning to the jury in accordance with the decision in **R v Cowan** [1995] 3 WLR 818 to remind the jury that Ayo has a right of silence and that the burden of proof is on the prosecution and they must have established a case to answer. The jury must also be reminded that they cannot convict solely on the basis of an inference drawn from silence but that they may draw an inference if the only explanation for Ayo not going in the witness box is that he has no answer to give or none that would stand up to cross-examination.

In summary, Ayo's silence following the accusation by a fellow student is admissible against him and it is possible that s.37 inferences could be drawn if he was properly cautioned at the time of the arrest. However, it is unlikely that a s.34 inference can be drawn by the jury given the operation of s.34(2A). Whether a s.35 inference can be drawn will be at the discretion of the judge when assessing whether Ayo's migraines are severe enough to be considered a physical condition within the meaning of s.35(1)(b).

 Make your answer stand out

- When discussing the rules on silence, mention cases such as *Murray* v *UK* (1996) 22 EHRR 29 which has confirmed that the use of silence to strengthen the prosecution's case does not make a trial unfair under Art.6 ECHR.

- When discussing s.34, explore Lord Bingham's speech in *R* v *Webber* (above) on the issue of the jury exploring the truth of any explanation the defendant gives for not mentioning a 'fact'.

- On the question of the police failure to disclose details of the case to Ayo at the interview, mention further cases such as *R* v *Imran*; *R* v *Hussain* [1997] Crim LR 754 and *R* v *Van Bokkum* [2000] 6 Archbold News 2.

! Don't be tempted to...

- Ignore the requirements for a judicial warning when discussing s.34 and s.35.
- Fail to discuss the fact that Ayo's silence following an accusation by a fellow student could be treated as an admission.
- Discuss only s.34 and s.35 silence and ignore s.37 – you are told Ayo was arrested in a neighbouring street at the time of the offence and gave an explanation to the police and therefore you must consider s.37.

10

Supporting evidence and lies

How this topic may come up in exams

Supporting evidence and lies link to each other because lies can act as supporting evidence. They are both favourites for inclusion as part of a multi-issue question in a problem relating to the evidence of witnesses (including the defendant). However, supporting evidence can equally be found in the form of an essay question which focuses on the historic development of the discretionary **Makanjuola** warning.

Attack the question

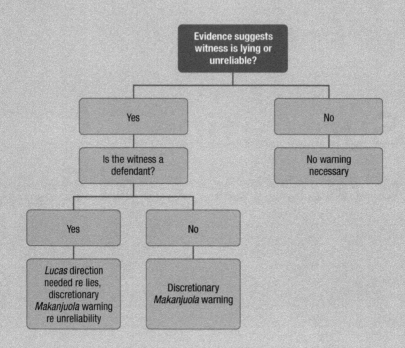

Question 1

In the case of *R* v *Makanjuola* [1995] 1 WLR 1348, CA Lord Taylor CJ said 'attempts to re-impose the straitjacket of the old corroboration rules are strongly to be deprecated'.

Analyse to what extent (if at all) this approach to supporting evidence is compatible with the trial judge's duty to put the case fairly to the jury?

Answer plan

→ Explain the old approach to corroboration and some of the difficulties.

→ Compare with current approach post-*Makanjuola*.

→ Assess whether the current approach allows the judge to give a fair and balanced summing-up.

→ Examine alternative approaches.

Diagram plan

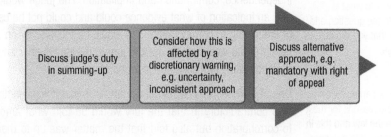

Discuss judge's duty in summing-up → Consider how this is affected by a discretionary warning, e.g. uncertainty, inconsistent approach → Discuss alternative approach, e.g. mandatory with right of appeal

A printable version of this diagram plan is available from www.pearsoned.co.uk/lawexpressqa

Answer

¹ As the question refers to the judge's duty to sum-up using summing-up cases such as *Marr* and *Bentley* shows the examiner that you are able to link your introduction to the question and provide supporting authority. You could also use other cases such as *R* v *Spencer* [1986] 3 WLR 147, as long as the legal principles are the same this will be acceptable.

² This shows the examiner that you have understood the focus of the question.

³ Referring back to the quotation shows the examiner that you are able to restrict your answer to what is relevant to the question and therefore that you are able to be concise.

⁴ This shows an ability to analyse the reasons for the change in the law and this in turn demonstrates a deeper level of understanding and will earn you additional marks.

Cases such as **R v Marr** (1989) 90 Cr App Rep 154 and **R v Bentley (Deceased)** [2001] 1 Cr App Rep 307 have confirmed that the trial judge has a duty to fairly sum-up the case to the jury[1] and that this should involve balancing both the prosecution and defence evidence. The issue is whether leaving a warning on supporting evidence to the discretion of the trial judge means that, in certain circumstances, the summing-up will not be balanced in terms of the strengths and weaknesses of the case.[2]

The quotation refers to the old corroboration rules. These rules provided that the judge had to give a full corroboration warning in relation to children, accomplices and complainants in sexual offence cases.[3] The full warning involved telling the jury that it was dangerous to convict on uncorroborated evidence of a witness, unless satisfied of the truth of the evidence. The judge would also have to give the jury an explanation of the technical meaning of corroboration taken from **R v Baskerville** [1916] 2 KB 658, namely independence, confirmation and implication. The judge would then give an indication of what evidence could and could not be capable of amounting to corroboration. This would be followed by an explanation that it was a matter for the jury to decide whether any such evidence did in fact constitute corroboration.

One of the criticisms of the full warning was that it was lengthy and also contradictory in that the jury would be told what amounted to corroboration but also told that the matter was up to them.[4] In addition, the old warning took no account of the circumstances of a particular case or the credibility of the witness giving the evidence. Section 32(1) Criminal Justice and Public Order Act 1994 abolished obligatory warnings in the case of accomplices and complainants in sex cases. Section 34(2) Criminal Justice Act 1988 abolished obligatory warnings in the case of children.

R v Makanjuola [1995] 1 WLR 1348 confirmed that whilst obligatory warnings had been abrogated the judge still had a discretion to give one if he saw fit. However, there would need to be some evidential basis for suggesting that a witness is unreliable or lying.

The strength of the discretionary warning can also vary with either a 'special need for caution' warning being given of acting on the unsupported evidence or a stronger warning (known as a special warning) where the judge suggests that it would be wise to look for some supporting evidence before acting on the unsupported evidence alone. The judge is no longer required to explain the technical meaning of corroboration or give a detailed full warning as existed before. Supporting evidence rather than technical corroboration is now sufficient. However, the case of **R v B (MT)** [2000] Crim LR 181 states that it is still incumbent on the judge to identify any independent supporting evidence.

[5] This shows an attempt to evaluate the effectiveness of the current law and shows the examiner that you have an ability to assess and sift through information.

One of the difficulties of a discretionary warning is that it can lead to inconsistencies, with some judges preferring a direction whilst others would view it as unnecessary.[5] For example, in the case of **R v Walker** [1996] Crim LR 742 the trial judge made no reference in his summing-up to the fact that the witness had previously retracted her allegation of sexual assault. The Court of Appeal held that a discretionary warning was appropriate. It is arguable that appeals act as a safeguard to any inconsistencies in approach. However, this is not always true because failure to exercise a discretionary warning cannot be automatically appealed. The case of **Makanjuola** confirms that lack of a discretionary warning can only be appealed if '**Wednesbury** unreasonable', namely that no reasonable judge given the same set of facts would have reached the same decision.

[6] A comparison with other judicial discretions shows the examiner that you are able to draw comparisons and therefore have a wider understanding of the module as a whole. This will mark you out as a good student and separate you from the weaker student who only has a knowledge of selective areas of the module.

Other judicial discretions such as those for good character, lies and identification evidence are mandatory in nature and require the judge to give the jury some direction on how to treat the evidence.[6] In particular, the **Turnbull** warning also deals with the special need for caution and the judge can direct the jury to look for supporting evidence. It is arguable, therefore, that directions relating to corroboration should also be mandatory.

[7] By balancing criticisms with suggestions you demonstrate an ability to provide solutions and this shows a deeper level of thought to your answer which will mark you out as a good student and earn you additional marks.

A solution would be a return to a mandatory warning but with the appeal process being flexible[7] as to whether a failure to give a warning should always lead to a conviction being quashed. This would be similar to **Turnbull** warnings where cases such as **Freemantle v R** [1994] 1 WLR 1437 have recognised that it may be acceptable in some circumstances for an identification warning not to be given. In addition, the wording of the warning need not be prescriptive and this would avoid some of the difficulties encountered with the old full warning.

[8] Giving examples strengthens your arguments and makes them more convincing.

This argument has some validity when one considers the problems encountered in relation to evidence given by fellow inmates[8] where a confession is made to them by a defendant. In **R v Causley** [1999] Crim LR 572, which was later supported by cases such as **Pringle v R** [2003] UKPC 9, it was held that a corroboration warning should be given wherever cell confessions are relied upon by the prosecution as a central plank of their case. However, the case of **R v Stone** [2005] EWCA Crim 105 the Court of Appeal took a more cautious approach and refused to recognise cell confessions as a special category. It was held that whilst cell confessions should prompt careful consideration by the trial judge such consideration should not be affected by fixed rules and it is for the judge to decide the strength of any warning in his summing-up.

[9] This shows the examiner what your final view is in relation to your arguments and leads into your conclusion. Whilst there is no correct view to a question like this, you must avoid 'sitting on the fence' and must form a clear view supported by convincing arguments.

A return to a mandatory warning would still leave a problem as to the strength of the warning to be given.[9] Lord Taylor himself gave some direction on this issue in the case of **Makanjuola** when he stated that for unreliable witnesses a special need for caution warning would be sufficient but a stronger warning would be necessary in the case of witnesses shown to have lied or who bear the defendant some grudge. Arguably, the trial judge is best suited to assess which applies and to do this on a case-by-case basis rather than being constrained by rigid rules.

In conclusion, it is arguable that in order to put the case fairly to the jury the judge needs to assess the evidence for each individual case rather than make assumptions based on a witness belonging to a particular category or be constrained by the nature of the direction to give to the jury. Therefore, a degree of flexibility is needed. A discretionary warning achieves a balance in that judges have some guidance on when it would be appropriate to give a warning whilst still being able to consider each case on its facts.

Make your answer stand out

■ Mention cases such as *R* v *Beck* [1982] 1 WLR 461, *R* v *Cheema* [1994] 1 All ER 639 and *R* v *Spencer* [1986] 3 WLR 348 and make the point that the old approach still involved an element of discretion as far as dealing with witnesses outside of the three categories was concerned.

■ When discussing the full warning, mention how the technical definition of corroboration was not always followed as far as independence of the evidence was concerned, by mentioning cases such as *R* v *McInnes* (1989) 90 Cr App Rep 99 and *R* v *Chauhan* (1981) 73 Cr App Rep 232.

■ Mention articles such as D. Birch, 'Corroboration: goodbye to all that?' [1995] Crim LR 525 or P. Mirfield, 'Corroboration after the 1994 Act' [1995] Crim LR 448 when comparing the old and current approach to corroboration.

❗ Don't be tempted to...

■ Simply write a descriptive answer about how the rules of corroboration have changed. You must relate your answer back to the quotation by discussing how this affects the judge's duty to put the case fairly to the jury.

■ Ignore the quotation from Lord Taylor CJ – you must attempt to analyse why there should not be a return to the old approach.

■ Fail to discuss the nature of the discretionary warning under *Makanjuola* – this is essential to the question.

❓ Question 2

In a trial of defendant A for rape the trial judge is presented with the following evidence:

(a) The evidence of complainant B that defendant A raped her. The complainant had initially made a complaint to police officers about defendant A and had then changed her mind and retracted her statement and then changed her mind again and stuck with her original statement.

(b) Defendant A, whilst on remand in prison, confessed to a prisoner that he had indeed raped B. The prisoner gives evidence at trial regarding the confession.

(c) Witness C, who will give evidence that shortly after the rape complainant B ran into her shop sobbing and said, 'a man just raped me'.

(d) Defendant A says in evidence that he was visiting his girlfriend at the time of the rape. However, his girlfriend has given evidence that she was not with him at the time of the rape and was in fact out of the country.

Discuss how the trial judge will deal with each of the above supporting evidence in his summing-up.

Answer plan

→ Discuss discretionary corroboration warning for complainant B.

→ Explore whether cell confessions require a warning in the case of defendant A's confession.

→ Examine whether witness C's statement can act as supporting evidence.

→ Consider the need for a *Lucas* direction in relation to defendant A's false alibi.

Diagram plan

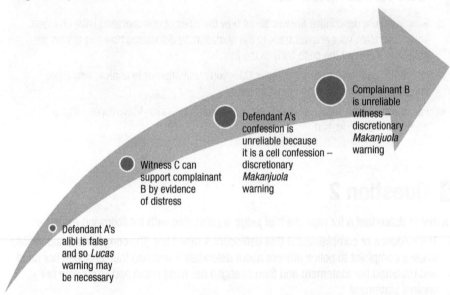

Complainant B is unreliable witness – discretionary *Makanjuola* warning

Defendant A's confession is unreliable because it is a cell confession – discretionary *Makanjuola* warning

Witness C can support complainant B by evidence of distress

Defendant A's alibi is false and so *Lucas* warning may be necessary

A printable version of this diagram plan is available from www.pearsoned.co.uk/lawexpressqa

Answer

[1] By mentioning that *Makanjuola* warnings are used in the summing-up and therefore stressing the importance of such warnings you provide a platform from which you can go on to explore the issues raised by the facts. In this way you provide a structured answer which ties in your introduction to the question.

In order to deal with supporting evidence in his summing-up the judge will have to consider whether an appropriate **Makanjuola** warning should be given to the jury and the form and strength of the warning.[1]

Evidence of complainant B

The judge will need to consider whether complainant B's oral evidence at trial should be supported, given that she has changed her mind about what happened and retracted and then stuck to her original statement. This may mean that she is an unreliable witness.

[2] Using leading cases such as *Makanjuola* to support your answer shows the examiner that you have a good grasp of the applicable law.

In the case of **R v Makanjuola** [1995] 1 WLR 1348[2] the Court of Appeal held that there must be some evidential basis for suggesting that the witness might be unreliable before a warning is given to the jury and whether or not to give a warning would be a matter for the judge. In the case of **R v Walker** [1996] Crim LR 742 the court held that a corroboration warning should have been given where a witness changes their story a number of times before the trial.

[3] By distinguishing between the two types of *Makanjuola* warnings you demonstrate more than just a basic knowledge of this area of law and will earn you the available marks.

It will be for the judge to decide whether the warning merely takes the form of telling the jury that there is a special need for caution when considering complainant B's evidence (i.e. a care warning) or whether the warning should be stronger warning suggesting that the jury look for supporting evidence before relying on complainant B's testimony.[3] The case of **Makanjuola** suggests that strong warnings will be appropriate where the witness has been shown to have lied or made previous false complaints or has a motive to serve. It is likely, therefore, that on these particular facts a special need for caution warning will be more likely here.[4] However, if the jury were directed to look for supporting evidence then the confession of defendant A and the evidence of witness C could all act as supporting evidence.

[4] This shows application of the law to the facts and demonstrates practical skills on your part.

[5] Reference to judge's speeches shows a greater understanding and knowledge of the case itself.

A failure by the judge to give a warning can only lead to the decision being appealed if it is regarded as '**Wednesbury** unreasonable'. This was confirmed by Lord Taylor CJ in **Makanjuola** and re-confirmed in cases such as **R v Whitehouse** [2001] EWCA Crim 1531.[5]

Defendant A's confession

This confession can be termed a 'cell confession', as it has been made to a fellow prisoner. In the Privy Council case of **Benedetto and Labrador v R** [2003] 1 WLR 1545, PC Lord Hope indicated that cell confessions are inherently unreliable evidence because of the advantage the fellow prisoner thinks they might get for themselves in providing the information to the authorities.[6] The case suggested that a special need for caution warning would be required and it should involve the judge drawing the jury's attention to the various factors that would lead to an inference that the evidence was unreliable. In the circumstances the trial judge should explain to the jury that they should be careful in accepting the prisoner's evidence and draw their attention to those factors that might suggest the evidence is motivated by self-interest. It is at the discretion of the judge as to the strength of the warning to be given based on all the circumstances of the case. However, in the case of **R v Stone** [2005] EWCA Crim 105 the Court of Appeal refused to accept that a warning must always be given for cell confessions.[7]

Witness C's evidence

Witness C's evidence is capable of supporting the evidence of complainant B because of the distressed state of the complainant following a sexual assault. This was confirmed by the Court of Appeal in **R v Venn** [2003] EWCA Crim 236. However, because the distress is not independent of the complainant it cannot be said to be truly independent evidence.[8] For this reason the circumstances in the case must first suggest that the distress is genuine before it should be left to the jury to consider. Therefore, any significant time delay between the rape and complainant B being seen by witness C may affect the issue of whether the distress was genuine. The jury must be told that they have to be satisfied that the distress was genuine before they take it into account. However, they do not first need to be satisfied that the distress did not arise from some other cause (see **R v Winter** [2008] EWCA Crim 3). As there is no suggestion that witness C is lying or unreliable, it will not be necessary to give a **Makanjuola** warning in relation to her evidence.

[6] This level of detail indicates a wider understanding of the case itself and will mark you out as a good student.

[7] Referring to a contrary view demonstrates an ability to compare and contrast cases and this will earn you additional marks.

[8] This shows the examiner that you understand a key requirement of corroboration and therefore demonstrates familiarity with the material.

Defendant A's alibi

Defendant A's girlfriend has given evidence which throws doubt on the correctness of his alibi. A false alibi can be used as supporting evidence to show that a defendant has lied. This may in turn support complainant B's account that defendant A was the person who raped her. However, lies alone cannot lead to a finding of guilt (see **R v Middleton** [2001] Crim LR 251) as there may be genuine reasons for the lie that are unassociated with guilt. In the circumstances the jury must also be given a warning as set out in the case of **R v Lucas** [1981] 3 WLR 120. The jury must still be satisfied that the prosecution have proved their case, although the lie cannot be the sole reason for returning a guilty verdict. The jury should also be reminded that people lie for all sorts of reasons and that there might be an innocent explanation for the lies. There must first be a risk that the jury will draw an inference from the lie before a **Lucas** warning is given. The lie must be deliberate and relate to a material issue and the motive for the lie must be a realisation of guilt. It must also be shown to be a lie by independent evidence (see **R v Goodway** (1993) 98 Cr App Rep 11).[9] This would apply on the facts as the evidence of the girlfriend shows the alibi to be false.

[9] A summary of the nature of the *Lucas* warning shows the examiner that you are able to provide a detailed answer to this part of the question and will earn you the available marks.

[10] This shows that you are continuing to relate the law back to the facts and are not inventing facts to suit your answer. This demonstrates an ability to deal only with relevant matters.

If there is any evidential basis to suggest that defendant A's girlfriend might be unreliable or lying then the trial judge would have to also give a separate **Makanjuola** warning in respect of her evidence. However, on the facts there is no evidence to suggest that she might be lying.[10]

In conclusion, the trial judge should give a care warning in respect of the evidence of complainant B because her evidence has been previously retracted, a care warning in respect of the prisoner's evidence about defendant A's confession and a **Lucas** warning in respect of defendant A's false alibi. The evidence of complainant B's demeanour as seen by witness C can be used to support complainant B's evidence.

✓ **Make your answer stand out**

- When discussing complainant B, briefly mention that s.32(1) Criminal Justice and Public Order Act 1994 abrogated mandatory warnings for complainants in sex offence cases.

- When discussing defendant A's cell confession, mention cases such as *R* v *Causley* [1999] Crim LR 572 which confirm the warning does not have to be as strong as in previous cases such as *R* v *Spencer* [1986] 3 WLR 147.

- For your discussion of complainant B, mention cases such as *R* v *B (MT)* [2000] Crim LR 181 on the guidance the judge should give to the jury about what evidence is capable of acting as supporting evidence.

❗ **Don't be tempted to...**

- Spend time on the historical development of the discretionary warning and the move away from the mandatory warning – you must discuss the current law and apply it to the facts.

- Ignore the potential for demeanour to act as supporting evidence when discussing witness C and be diverted into discussing issues of hearsay – the question specifically asks you to confine your answer to supporting evidence.

- Fail to spot that defendant A's evidence renders his confession a false one – this then raises the need for a *Lucas* direction (see *R* v *Burge and Pegg* [1996] 1 Cr App Rep 163).

Question 3

'Innocent people sometimes tell lies even when by doing so they create or reinforce the suspicion of guilt.' (Judge LJ in *R* v *Middleton* [2001] Crim LR 251)

Analyse the above statement in the context of the modern day approach to the treatment of lies as evidence.

Answer plan

→ Discuss the rationale for the cautionary approach to lies by referring to the quotation.

→ Use cases to illustrate the development of the courts approach to lies.

→ Consider whether the quotation reflects the modern day approach to lies.

Diagram plan

Lies of a defendant can be innocent → Lies may lead to jury infering guilt → *Lucas* warning is necessary but not in all cases and may need to be modified

A printable version of this diagram plan is available from www.pearsoned.co.uk/lawexpressqa

Answer

The lies of a defendant can often be used to challenge the credibility of the defendant and influence the 'ultimate issue' of the defendant's guilt. If a defendant is caught out in a lie during a trial this may have a serious effect on the way the jury view the defendant even though credibility of the defendant is regarded as a collateral issue.

[1] Referring to the quotation in the question at an early stage of your answer helps to draw the issues together and keeps your answer focused. This will distinguish your answer from that of a weaker student who merely provides a description of the evidential rules relating to lies.

As indicated in the quotation of Judge LJ taken from **R v Middleton** [2001] Crim LR 251, it is recognised that there may be all sorts of reasons why a defendant might lie and that a lie is not proof of guilt. Judge LJ went on to say that a judicial direction is needed to avoid the risk that the jury might adopt 'forbidden reasoning' that the defendant has lied and must therefore be guilty.[1]

[2] Reference to key cases such as *R v Lucas* is essential as it demonstrates relevant knowledge and will earn you the available marks.

Judicial direction to the jury is therefore considered important. The issue of how lies should be treated was considered in depth by the Court of Appeal in the case of **R v Lucas** [1981] 3 WLR 120.[2] The Court of Appeal held that lies could act as corroboration but that the trial judge should give a warning to the jury about the use they could make of the lie whilst also reminding the jury that people lie for innocent reasons. There are no mandatory words for a **Lucas** direction although suggested wording is set out in the Judicial Studies Board Specimen Direction No. 27 (as contained in the *Crown Court Bench Book*).

However, the cases of **R v Lucas** (above) and **R v Goodway** (1993) 98 Cr App R 11 also highlighted that not every lie will warrant a judicial direction to the jury. The lie must be considered deliberate and relate to a material issue. The motive for the lie must be the

[3] By explaining the requirement for a *Lucas* direction you show the examiner that you are aware that a *Lucas* direction is not necessary for every lie. This shows that you have an understanding of the legal principle arising from key cases, which is necessary to take your answer beyond a basic one.

[4] Comparisons with the approach taken in other countries will demonstrate to the examiner that you have read widely on the topic and this will give an overall impression of a good answer and earn you extra marks.

realisation of guilt and the lie must be shown to be a lie by evidence that is independent of the witness.[3] These two cases highlighted the instances when a direction would be necessary namely when lies are used as corroboration or are a central plank of the prosecution's case.

The case of **R v Burge and Pegg** [1996] 1 Cr App R 163 highlighted that the judge should also give a direction if there is a risk at any point in the trial that the jury will place too much reliance on the lie. However, this is regarded as the most difficult ground for a **Lucas** warning. This requires the judge to look into the minds of the jury. In Australia this aspect of the **Lucas** direction has been specifically rejected as can be seen in cases such as **R v Renzella** (1996) 88 ACR 65.[4] In **R v Burge and Pegg** (above) Kennedy LJ recognised the difficulties with this particular requirement for a **Lucas** direction and suggested that where the judge believed there was a danger the jury might rely on the lie as evidence of guilt he should consider with counsel whether a **Lucas** direction was in fact required.

The modern day approach to lies can also be seen from cases such as **R v Bullen** [2008] EWCA Crim 4, where the court indicated that when reminding the jury that lies can be innocent a judge should also direct the jury on the exact issue to which the lie is relevant. This presumably prevents the jury from leaping to the 'forbidden reasoning' feared by Judge LJ in **R v Middleton**. Cases such as **R v Faryab** [1999] BPIR 569 recognise that when a lie arises in separate proceedings, a **Lucas** direction may still be necessary and in some circumstances would be regarded as essential.

In addition, whilst the lie must be deliberate and relate to a material issue a mere assertion by the prosecution that the defendant is lying is not enough as the lie must be shown to be a lie (see **R v Barnett** [2002] EWCA Crim 454). However, once the jury have decided on the basis of other evidence that they do not accept the defendant's defence there is no need for a **Lucas** warning. Because of this fine line between lies and guilt, a **Lucas** warning can sometimes act to confuse the jury.

The use of **Lucas** warnings has also been restricted since the original decision, a **Lucas** warning is not needed if the only issue is whether the lie is relevant to the defendant's credibility as a witness (see **R v Smith** [1995] Crim LR 305). The lie must be about a

[5] It is appropriate to refer briefly to the facts of *R v Middleton* as the quotation in the question is taken from the case. This demonstrates to the examiner that you have a good understanding of a key case. However, you must ensure that you keep your discussion of the facts brief and that you also explain the legal principle arising from the case.

subsidiary matter which would then form a link to the central issues so that reasoning as to guilt can be drawn from it. In the case of **R v Middleton** (above) it was ultimately accepted on the facts of the case that a **Lucas** direction would have merely confused the issue. The defendant's defence was one of alibi but the alibi had not been proved to be false and so the issue was simply one of whether the jury believed his testimony or not.[5]

In summary, the modern day approach to the treatment of lies remains broadly in line with the guidelines in the case of **R v Lucas**. The **Lucas** direction remains important to ensure that a defendant receives a fair trial under Art.6 of the European Convention on Human Rights, particularly where the prosecution are relying on the defendant's lies as an independent part of their case. It is important that the burden of proof is seen to be discharged at the appropriate standard rather than simply by the jury reasoning guilt from lies. The quotation of Judge LJ remains important today as a reminder of the risks associated with the use of lies as evidence.

 Make your answer stand out

- Refer to more recent cases such as *R v Edwards* [2004] EWCA Crim 2102 to illustrate the fact that not all lies are relevant.
- Point out that *R v Lucas* (above) was decided on the issue of the old corroboration rules and therefore some of the conditions in the *Lucas* warning are of less importance today.
- When discussing the fine line between lies and guilt, refer to the decision in *R v Harron* [1996] 2 Cr App Rep 457 that a warning to the jury is not needed simply because the jury reject the defence and by doing so find the defendant guilty as long as they have not adopted the 'forbidding reasoning'.

! Don't be tempted to...

- Provide an answer that merely describes the *Lucas* direction without attempting any analyses of the strengths and weaknesses of the approach.
- Fail to refer to the quotation in your answer.
- Assume the *Lucas* direction also applies to the lies of a non-defendant.

? Question 4

Calista and Rhoda are sisters. Both are charged with handling stolen goods, namely £50,000-worth of gold jewellery found during a lawful police search. Calista denies the charge and says that she has never seen the jewellery before. However, at trial the prosecution produce a picture of Calista wearing one of the stolen necklaces at a charity gala. Calista claims that she found the necklace in Rhoda's room and wore it without her permission and had not mentioned it before because she thought Rhoda would be angry with her. She says that she and Rhoda have not been on speaking terms for six months, ever since she started going out with Rhoda's ex-boyfriend, David. Rhoda also denies the charge and says that Calista is in fact the guilty one as she agreed to look after the stolen goods for David. Rhoda says she did not know at the time that the jewellery was stolen. During the police search Calista's six-year-old son Louis volunteered information that his mother had told him not to tell anyone about the 'stuff under the bed because you will get Mummy into trouble if you talk about it'.

Advise the parties on the probative value of the evidence described above.

Answer plan

→ Discuss the need for a *Lucas* warning in relation to Calista's lie about knowledge of the jewellery.

→ Examine whether Rhoda's evidence can be regarded as 'suspect' and therefore require a *Makanjuola* warning.

→ Consider whether a *Makanjuola* warning is needed in respect of the evidence of Louis.

Diagram plan

Calista	Rhoda	Louis
• Calista has been shown to have told a material lie • A *Lucas* warning is necessary	• Rhoda has a motive to blame Calista • A *Makanjuola* warning may be necessary	• Louis is a young child whose evidence may be unreliable • A *Makanjuola* warning may be necessary

A printable version of this diagram plan is available from www.pearsoned.co.uk/lawexpressqa

Answer

The above scenario requires a discussion of the extent to which a witness's evidence can be accepted without the need for it to be supported by other independent evidence. The trial judge will also have to consider whether to give a judicial direction in respect of lies revealed at trial.

The first issue that arises is in relation to Calista's evidence that she had not seen any of the jewellery before. This has been shown to be a lie, as the prosecution have evidence of Calista wearing the offending article. As Calista has been caught out in a lie, there is a danger that the jury will attach too much importance to this lie and it is therefore necessary for the trial judge to give a **Lucas** direction to the jury (see **R v Lucas** [1981] 3 WLR 120).[1] In the case of **R v Middleton** [2001] Crim LR 251 Judge LJ highlighted the fact that even innocent people lie and this may be, for example, to deflect suspicion. The trial judge must therefore direct the jury to be cautious about how they treat Calista's lie and that the lie is not proof of guilt. The Court of Appeal in **R v Burge and Pegg** [1996] 1 Cr App R 163 confirmed that a **Lucas** direction does not have to be given every time a lie is revealed at trial but should be given in certain circumstances, such as where there is a risk that the jury might rely on the lie or where the prosecution relied on the lie as a central plank of their case. It is likely, therefore, that the trial judge will give a **Lucas** direction in respect of Calista's lie.

[2] An ability to spot important clues in the question shows the examiner that you have the necessary level of knowledge to detect the issues and this will earn you marks.

[3] This shows the examiner that you have an understanding that the law has moved on whilst also being able to apply the correct law. This will separate you from the weaker student and ensure that you continue to earn the marks.

The second issue relates to the fact that Calista and Rhoda appear to be running 'cut throat' defences, in which they blame each other. Rhoda will give evidence at trial that Calista had received the stolen goods from her boyfriend David. The issue here is whether the jury should be warned that, before they accept Rhoda's evidence as true, they should look for other supporting evidence of Calista's guilt.[2] This is because, as a co-accused, Rhoda may have a motive to blame Calista in order to lessen her own involvement. The judge no longer has to give a mandatory corroboration warning to the jury in relation to the evidence of a co-accused as this was removed by s.32(1) of the Criminal Justice and Public Order Act 1994.[3] The case of **R v Makanjuola** [1995] 1 WLR 1348 confirmed that the court still retains a discretion to give a warning to the jury however where there is an evidential basis for suggesting that a witness is lying or unreliable. There is some reason to suggest that Rhoda could be lying because there is evidence that she and Calista are not on good terms. In the case of **R v Porter** [2001] EWCA Crim 2699 a **Makanjuola** warning was considered necessary in relation to the evidence of a witness who had reason to lie in order to deflect suspicion from themselves. If a **Makanjuola** warning is necessary then the trial judge should first discuss this with counsel in the absence of the jury.

The trial judge can decide on the strength of the warning to give and this could either be in the form of a 'care warning' directing the jury to treat Rhoda's evidence with caution or the warning could be stronger and direct the jury to look for supporting evidence before accepting Rhoda's evidence. The case of **Makanjuola** suggests that the stronger warning would be warranted if the witness is shown to have lied. However, there is no evidence that Rhoda is definitely lying other than the claims made by Calista and so a care warning may be more appropriate here. The warning should be given during the summing-up.[4]

Depending on whether the evidence of Calista's six-year-old son Louis is accepted as reliable then this could act as supporting evidence. However, the reliability of the evidence of young children will depend on the level of maturity of the child. Whilst children as young as six can be regarded as competent to give evidence (see **R v CAZ** (1990) 91 Cr App Rep 203), for the purposes of reliability the trial judge will still have to consider whether a **Makanjuola** warning is necessary by considering whether Louis' age would make his evidence unreliable because, for example, he cannot tell fact from fiction.[5] Louis volunteered the information without prompting and the evidence is clear and may therefore be admissible without the need for a **Makanjuola** direction, although this is ultimately at the discretion of the trial judge.

In conclusion it is likely that Calista will be entitled to a Lucas direction in respect of her lie and that a **Makanjuola** warning will be necessary in respect of Rhoda although Louis' evidence may be admissible without a need for a warning. However, if the judge decides not to give a **Makanjuola** warning in respect of Rhoda or Louis this decision would not be appealable unless it could be shown to be '**Wednesbury** unreasonable' in that no trial judge given the same circumstances could have arrived at the same decision (see **R v Whitehouse** [2001] EWCA Crim 1531).

[4] An ability to select the most likely form of *Makanjuola* warning using the facts demonstrates that you are able to apply the relevant law to the facts and that you have a practical approach to the problem question and this will earn you extra marks.

[5] An ability to recognise that age does not necessarily mean the evidence is unreliable demonstrates that you have knowledge of the case law in another part of the subject (competence and compellability) and that you are able to link topics and have an overall knowledge of the subject. This in turn will earn you additional marks.

Make your answer stand out

- When discussing that corroboration warnings are no longer mandatory, refer to the Law Commission's Report No. 202, *Corroboration Requirements Reconsidered* [1984] Crim LR 316, in which they called for the abolition of the mandatory warning.

- When discussing the need for a discretionary warning in the case of Rhoda's evidence, consider old common law rules such as *R* v *Beck* [1982] 1 WLR 461, as upheld in *R* v *Jones and Jenkins* [2003] EWCA Crim 1966, which suggests that a 'care warning' should be given where a co-accused is running a 'cut-throat' defence.

- When discussing the need for warnings in respect of Rhoda's evidence, refer to the Criminal Law Revision Committee's Eleventh Report, *Evidence (General)* (Cmmd 4991), in which it was recognised that there was no obligation to give a warning if the accomplice's evidence was likely to be reliable.

! Don't be tempted to...

- Ignore the need to discuss a *Lucas* direction on the issue of Calista's lie – you are clearly told that pictures in the possession of the prosecution have disproved Calista's evidence.

- Be sidetracked into discussing whether or not the search of Calista and Rhoda's premises was lawful – you are told that the police had a warrant.

- Ignore the issue of Louis' age – this has a bearing on whether his evidence can be considered to be reliable.

11

Disclosure, privilege and public interest immunity

How this topic may come up in exams

Disclosure, privilege and public interest immunity link together because they relate to when evidence can be legitimately withheld and these topics tend to appear in the form of essay questions (but this can vary between institutions). Human rights issues are important in this area of law. An essay question can address privilege or public interest immunity separately or combine them to be compared and contrasted. It is always best to learn these topics together rather than in isolation. The privilege against self-incrimination can appear within the topic of privilege but can equally be examined in the context of examination of witnesses (Chapter 3).

Attack the question

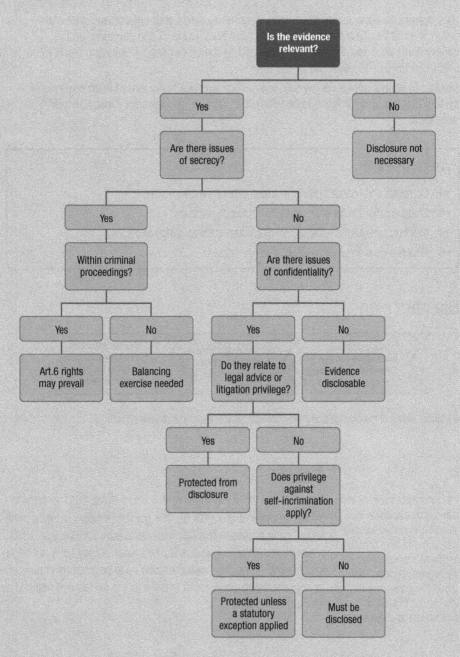

Is the evidence relevant?

Yes → Are there issues of secrecy?

No → Disclosure not necessary

Are there issues of secrecy?
- Yes → Within criminal proceedings?
- No → Are there issues of confidentiality?

Within criminal proceedings?
- Yes → Art.6 rights may prevail
- No → Balancing exercise needed

Are there issues of confidentiality?
- Yes → Do they relate to legal advice or litigation privilege?
- No → Evidence disclosable

Do they relate to legal advice or litigation privilege?
- Yes → Protected from disclosure
- No → Does privilege against self-incrimination apply?

Does privilege against self-incrimination apply?
- Yes → Protected unless a statutory exception applied
- No → Must be disclosed

A printable version of this diagram is available from www.pearsoned.co.uk/lawexpressqa

Question 1

'The right to an adversarial trial means, in criminal cases, that both prosecution and defence must be given the opportunity to have knowledge of and comment on the observations filed and the evidence adduced by the other party.' (*Rowe and Davis* v *UK* (2000) 30 EHRR 1 at 60)

Discuss to what extent it can be said that justice is properly dispensed in an adversarial system that enables evidence to be withheld in criminal proceedings irrespective of relevance.

Answer plan

→ Compare and contrast privilege and public interest immunity.

→ Discuss rationale for each and when rules do not apply.

→ Mention safeguards against non-disclosure such as a stay and s.78.

→ Reach a view on whether Art.6 is still protected.

Diagram plan

Discuss how prosecution can use PII and whether this is fair

Discuss defence's use of privilege and whether this is also fair

Are safeguards in place to ensure these rights are not abused and Art.6 is protected?

A printable version of this diagram plan is available from www.pearsoned.co.uk/lawexpressqa

Answer

[1] By setting out the general principle on disclosure you start with a good structure to your answer before proceeding to discuss the exceptions to the general principle. This shows the examiner that you can put together a well-structured answer.

Rules 21 and 22 of the Criminal Procedure Rules 2011 govern disclosure in criminal proceedings. The guiding principle is that parties should have access to relevant material in advance of a trial, which prevents parties being ambushed by evidence they have not seen in advance.[1] In criminal cases disclosure is particularly important, as non-disclosure could mean that the jury is misled and result in a wrongful conviction.

2 Identifying that non-disclosure is usually discouraged and then going on to explain the rationale for the exclusionary policy of PII and privilege shows the examiner that you can build an argument and this will help to gain you marks.

Ordinary safeguards are built into the criminal process,[2] in that non-disclosure of relevant information can be treated as an abuse of process leading to a stay of proceedings as occurred in **R v Birmingham** [1992] Crim LR 117. In addition, non-disclosure can be protected by excluding any evidence originally withheld but obtained by trickery. The court can exercise its statutory discretion under s.78 PACE 1984 to exclude such evidence or treat the issue as one of an abuse of process and stay proceedings.

3 This shows the examiner that you have recognised the need to discuss human rights issues because this ties in with the case from which the quotation is taken. This shows an ability to focus on the issues.

However, in the UK adversarial system certain documents and information are protected from disclosure on the grounds of confidentiality or public interest whether this is in relation to protecting the confidential relationship between legal adviser and client, protecting national security, or ensuring the proper administration of justice. This exclusionary approach is regarded as necessary despite its potential to affect the appearance of fairness during a trial and thereby contravene Art.6 of the European Convention on Human Rights and the principle of equality of arms.[3]

4 As the quotation is taken from this case, an explanation of the legal principles from the case shows the examiner that you have relevant knowledge and a deeper understanding of the case law surrounding this area and will help to earn you additional marks.

The case of **Rowe and Davis v UK** (2000) 30 EHRR 1, which is referred to in the quotation,[4] reiterated that Art.6 is not an absolute right and that countervailing interests may prevail which would enable Art.6 to be breached. In certain circumstances non-disclosure may be necessary for the protection of a witness, such as the rule in **Marks v Beyfus** (1890) 25 QBD 494 that an informant's identity will not be disclosed unless it is necessary to prevent a miscarriage of justice.

5 This introduces the arguments you intend to advance and therefore provides a good structure for the remainder of your answer.

Documents may be withheld by the prosecution on the grounds of public interest immunity (PII). This relates to the protection of sensitive or secret information and is a question of law to be determined by the court (see **Conway v Rimmer** [1968] 2 WLR 998). However, this protection is not automatic and certain criteria must be met before disclosure can be withheld.[5]

6 This alerts the examiner to the fact that you understand that the PII rule was historically developed in civil proceedings but applies equally to criminal proceedings. Your ability to support this knowledge with case law demonstrates a good level of understanding of this are of law and will earn you the available marks.

Consideration of PII applications involves a balancing exercise and requires the judge to consider the nature and content of the document or information. In **R v Governor of Brixton Prison, ex parte Osman** (1990) 93 Cr App Rep 202 it was held that public interest immunity could apply to criminal proceedings. However, unlike in civil proceedings, greater emphasis is placed on Art.6 when considering whether applications for PII should stand.[6]

In **R v Keane** [1994] 1 WLR 746 Lord Taylor stated that 'if the disputed material may prove the defendant's innocence or avoid miscarriages of justice, then the balance comes down resoundingly in favour of disclosing it'.

In **R v H** [2004] 2 WLR 335 the House of Lords set out guidelines that a judge should take into account when deciding issues of PII. If the material is such that it would weaken the prosecution case or strengthen the defence's case then disclosure should be ordered. If necessary, an anonymised version of the document can be disclosed.

[7] Having discussed protections, going on to discuss potential difficulties shows a balance to your answer and demonstrates an ability to evaluate the issues.

One area of difficulty is the use of so-called secret hearings to decide the issue of PII in the absence of the defence. The case of **Jasper v UK** (2000) App. No. 27052/95 held that the use of secret hearings which excluded the defendant from considerations of public interest immunity applications were permissible.[7] The court had to weigh up competing interests such as national security and the need to protect witnesses against the rights of the defendant. Cases such as **R v C; R v H** [2004] 2 WLR 355 also held that the use of 'special counsel' to represent the interests of the absent defendant was not an automatic right but had to be decided on a case-by-case basis. In addition, the judge can continue to monitor the issue of disclosure during the trial as new issues emerge.

[8] Advancing a counter-argument such as the fact that the defendant has similar rights to withold information will earn you extra marks as it shows good analysis.

The prosecution's right to withhold relevant information is balanced by the defendant's own right to withhold information also.[8] Unlike PII, legal professional privilege is a personal right and can be waived. However, no adverse inferences can be drawn if a defendant refuses to waive the privilege (see **R v P** [2002] EWCA Crim 1388). Section 10(1) PACE 1984 recognises the existence of legal professional privilege in criminal proceedings.

The privilege encompasses the separate rights under legal advice privilege and litigation privilege. Litigation privilege covers not just the client and legal adviser but also includes third parties. It is restricted in that any communications must have been prepared for the purpose of pending or contemplated legal proceedings.

Legal advice privilege covers communications passing between client and legal adviser for the purposes of advice and is seen as an absolute right (see **R v Derby Magistrates' Court, ex parte B** [1995] 3 WLR 681). The rationale for this is to protect the candour between a client and legal adviser to ensure the proper functioning of justice. The protection of this right can be justified on the basis that it is analogous to Art.8, which is the right to have one's private life respected.[9] However, there are some restrictions; for example, the right will not apply where the legal adviser is complicit in criminal activity (see **R v Cox** (1884) 14 QBD 153).[10]

[10] Identifying restrictions such as this is a good way to evaluate the effectiveness of the principle of privilege and helps you to build on your arguments.

Privilege against self-incrimination may allow both prosecution and defence witnesses to withhold information if it would expose them to a criminal charge, penalty or forfeiture of property (see **Blunt v Park Lane Hotel** [1942] 2 KB 253). The rationale for this is that it encourages witnesses to speak freely and is intended to avoid incidents of perjury. However the right cannot be relied upon where there are statutory exceptions such as s.172(2)(a) of the Road Traffic Act 1988 (see **Brown v Stott** [2001] 2 WLR 817). The right can be understood in the context of the defendant's own right of silence. The defendant's right to silence means that there may still be a situation in which information is withheld regardless of privilege or PII issues.

[11] Stating a final view completes your answer and shows that you are able to address the question in full.

In summary, there are sufficient safeguards to ensure that in criminal proceedings the rights of the defendant are still sufficiently protected and cases such as **R v H** (above) show that the courts are likely to favour the rights of a defendant when considering prosecution applications to withhold relevant information. In addition, the defendant also has similar rights of non-disclosure which arguably provides more of a level playing field in relation to pre-trial investigation.[11]

✓ Make your answer stand out

- When discussing public interest immunity mention the fact that the move away from the Crown considering whether evidence should be held to one in which the court decides the issue arguably is a safeguard against abuse of Art.6 rights and mention the cases of *Duncan* v *Cammell Laird & Co Ltd* [1942] AC 624 and *Conway* v *Rimmer* [1968] 2 WLR 998.

- Briefly summarise the series of questions a court might ask before deciding on disclosure of PII documents as identified by Lord Bingham in *R* v *H*; *R* v *C* [2004] 2 WLR 335.

- Discuss with reference to cases such as *Makanjuola* v *Commissioner of the Metropolis* [1992] 3 All ER 617 the fact that public interest immunity normally cannot be waived.

- Consider other means by which relevant evidence is held, e.g. s.17 Regulation of Investigatory Powers Act 2000.

! **Don't be tempted to...**

- Discuss PII and privilege in the context of civil proceedings – the question specifically refers to criminal proceedings.
- Ignore the issue of Art.6 – the quotation is taken from a case on the impact of Art.6.
- Discuss only one of the topics of PII and privilege without considering both – the question does not direct you to consider one topic only.

❓ Question 2

As a result of exposure to a virus during routine testing in the university laboratories, Professor Tyler contracts a viral infection which leads to partial brain damage. Professor Tyler brings a civil claim against the university and also the Department of Health who instructed the university to test the virus.

(a) Professor Tyler has obtained a memorandum prepared by the Department of Health that he wishes to use in his civil action. The memorandum reads: 'the effect of the virus on humans is thought to be safe although it has only been tested on a small human sample.'

(b) Kemi is employed as a secretary at the university and is also a local activist in the group 'Planet Matters'. She photocopies a letter that the Vice-Chancellor of the university has written to the university solicitors, Meads & Dhesi LLP, in which he states 'the University were involved in the testing of the original human sample and we informed the department of health that the results were not conclusive'. Kemi sends a copy of this letter to Professor Tyler.

(c) Simon, the director of the company XL plc which manufactured the virus, will be called to give evidence in court about the formulation of the virus. Simon says that he will refuse to answer any questions because this may prejudice a licence for the manufacture of the virus in the United States.

(d) Professor Tyler is aware of the existence of an expert report written by a leading chemist for the Department of Health which states that the virus is dangerous and should be destroyed immediately. It was written after the virus was tested. The Department of Health are refusing to disclose the contents of this report.

Advise Professor Tyler as to how the above evidence may be obtained and used in his civil action.

Answer plan

→ Consider the issue of public interest immunity for the Department of Health in the memorandum.

→ Discuss the issue of legal advice privilege for the letter written to the solicitors.

→ Examine whether the privilege against self-incrimination applies to Simon's evidence.

→ Discuss litigation privilege in relation to the expert's report.

Diagram plan

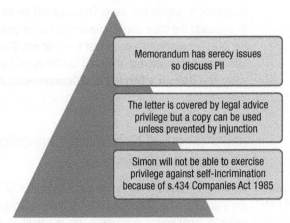

Memorandum has serecy issues so discuss PII

The letter is covered by legal advice privilege but a copy can be used unless prevented by injunction

Simon will not be able to exercise privilege against self-incrimination because of s.434 Companies Act 1985

A printable version of this diagram plan is available from www.pearsoned.co.uk/lawexpressqa

Answer

In order to advice Professor Tyler it will be necessary to consider whether any of the evidence is protected from disclosure as a result of privilege and public interest immunity.

Memorandum prepared by Department of Health

[1] This shows the examiner that you have recognised that the memorandum relates to public interest immunity and therefore that you are able to spot the relevant issue.

The issue here is whether the Department of Health (DOH) can claim that there should be non-disclosure of the memorandum on the basis of the secrecy of the information contained in it and that it is sensitive in nature.[1] This is a question of law to be decided by a judge following the decision in **Conway v Rimmer** [1968] 2 WLR 998. The DOH may rely on public interest immunity (PII) and claim that disclosure would damage the public interest as it would hinder proper research and testing of viruses. The Minister for Health can issue a public interest immunity certificate in relation to the memorandum and apply under r.31.19 of the Civil Procedure Rules 1998[2] without notice to Professor Tyler and it will then be for the judge to decide whether non-disclosure is necessary for the 'proper functioning of the public service' (per Lord Reid in **Conway v Rimmer**). This means that the judge should also consider the interests of Professor Tyler in needing to use the information to assist his case, particularly in light of a right to a fair trial under Art.6 of the European Convention on Human Rights. This requires a balancing exercise. The judge would be entitled to inspect the document to decide the issue. The onus will be on Professor Tyler to persuade the court that disclosure should be ordered rather than the DOH persuading the court that it should not. This is because the Minister's public interest immunity certificate will be taken at face value (see **Balfour v Foreign and Commonwealth Office** [1994] 2 All ER 588).

[2] Reference to relevant procedural rules shows the examiner that you have more than a basic understanding of the area and will gain you more marks.

Letter prepared by the Vice-Chancellor of the University of Westland

As the letter was written by the Vice-Chancellor (VC) to the university's solicitors the letter would be protected from disclosure as a result of legal advice privilege.[3] This is based on the confidential nature of the client/legal adviser relationship. Protection from disclosure will apply if the purpose of the letter was to obtain legal advice or was a continuum of such advice (see **Balabel v Air India** [1988] 2 WLR 1036, CA). The facts suggest that the VC was providing the solicitors with information as to the extent of the university's involvement and this would be necessary information for the solicitors to advise the university fully. In the circumstances the original letter is likely to be protected from disclosure.[4]

[3] This shows the examiner that you have identified that the letter relates to privilege and therefore that again you can spot relevant issues.

[4] Supporting your view with cases such as *Balabel* v *Air India* and then applying the legal principle from the case to the facts is an example of good application and procedural rules, demonstrates a wider knowledge of the subject area and will gain you the available marks.

However, Professor Tyler has obtained a copy of this letter rather than the original. The case of **Calcraft v Guest** [1898] 1 QB 759 confirms that copies of privileged documents can be used in evidence even if they have been stolen. However, under r. 32.1 of the Civil Procedure Rules 1998 the judge has a discretion to exclude such evidence.[5] In addition, cases such as **Goddard v Nationwide Building Society** [1986] 3 WLR 734, CA confirm that where a document has been obtained by improper means an injunction can be granted by the court to prevent use of the document. It is unlikely on the facts that Professor Tyler will be successful in using the copy of the letter because it was obtained by Kemi without her employer's knowledge.

Simon's refusal to give evidence

[6] Specific reference to commentary from judges in a particular case such as *Blunt* v *Park Lane Hotel* demonstrates wider reading on your part which will also gain you more marks.

Simon could refuse to answer questions at trial by relying on the privilege against self-incrimination. However, such questions must be capable of exposing him to 'any criminal charge, penalty or forfeiture of property' according to Lord Goddard in the case of **Blunt v Park Lane Hotel** [1942] 2 KB 253, CA.[6] It is doubtful that loss of a licence to manufacture the virus would fall within the definition. In any event, even if it were regarded as forfeiture of property or penalty such property or penalty must be in the United Kingdom (see s.14(1)(a) of the Civil Evidence Act 1968). In addition, the privilege cannot be relied upon if there are statutory powers requiring a person to produce documents or provide information, for example s.434 of the Companies Act 1985.[7] Simon is a director of the Company XL plc. In the case of **Allen v United Kingdom** (2002) App. No. 76574 it was held that the privilege against self-incrimination did not prevent the use of statutory powers to require a person to provide information about their own or their company's affairs.[8]

[7] Reference to relevant statutory exceptions such as s.434 of the Companies Act 1985 shows the examiner that you have a wider understanding of the subject area and that you can apply that exception and this will earn you additional marks.

[8] A discussion of relevant human rights cases such as *Allen* v *UK* shows the examiner that you understand the wider issues surrounding the privilege of self-incrimination and this will mark you out as a good student and help to earn you additional marks.

Expert report

The report of the chemist which was prepared for DOH could be protected from disclosure under litigation privilege. This covers confidential communications passing between the client and a third party. On the facts, the expert will be regarded as a third party and the DOH as a client. However, according to **Wheeler v Le Marchant** (1881) 17 ChD 675, CA the report must have been prepared for contemplated or pending legal proceedings. The report was written after a cause of action arose, as Professor Tyler had already contracted the

[9] An ability to offer solutions to circumvent the principle of privilege shows that you have taken a considered approach to the problem and this also shows the examiner that you are able to take your arguments further than just the basics.

viral infection. There may therefore be some validity to the DOH's claim that it was prepared for pending litigation. However, if Professor Tyler can argue that the report was also obtained for another purpose, for example, to assess how to avoid future exposure to the virus, then the 'dominant purpose' test in **Waugh v British Railways Board** [1979] 3 WLR 150[9] can be used. If the need to avoid future exposure is considered equally important to the creation of the report then it will not be protected by litigation privilege as this cannot be regarded as the dominant purpose.

[10] A reasoned conclusion shows the examiner that you have grasped the important issues and that your answer is focused.

In the circumstances Professor Tyler is entitled to see the memorandum prepared by the DOH. Even if disclosure is not ordered, the court must keep this decision under review. It is unlikely that Professor Tyler will be able to use the letter from the VC because of the way in which it was obtained. The court is likely to compel Simon to answer questions if these arise as a result of s.434 of the Companies Act 1985 and the report of the expert is unlikely to be covered by litigation privilege if Professor Tyler can show that it was prepared for the dominant purpose of trying to prevent future exposure.[10]

 Make your answer stand out

- Mention Lord Scott's speech in *Three Rivers DC* v *Governor of the Bank of England* [2005] 1 AC 610 when discussing the importance of legal advice privilege.
- Mention *Ashburton* v *Pape* [1913] 2 Ch 469 when discussing documents obtained in an improper manner.
- When discussing Simon's reliance on the privilege of self-incrimination, mention cases such as *Westinghouse Electric Corporation Uranium Contact Litigation MDL Docket No. 235 (No. 2)* [1978] AC 547 which confirm that controlling shareholders or directors cannot hide behind the fact that a company is a separate entity when being asked to provide information or answer questions.
- Mention *Saunders* v *UK* (1996) 23 EHRR 313 when discussing privilege against self-incrimination and s.434 of the Companies Act 1985.

> **! Don't be tempted to...**
>
> ■ Discuss the historical move away from Crown Privilege – you must deal with the current law.
> ■ Ignore the Civil Procedure Rules – these are important in this area of disclosure.
> ■ Ignore important facts such as the fact that the letter is obtained by improper means and is a copy and that the purpose for obtaining the expert report is unclear.

Question 3

'It is one thing for someone to make a statement to the police or anyone else which he might afterwards try to retract. It is quite another for him sometime later to be made to repeat any admission on oath ... It makes the potentially retractable impossible to retract.' (Waller LJ in *Den Norske Bank ASA* v *Antonatos* [1999] QB 271)

Analyse the extent to which the privilege against self-incrimination can be said to hamper the proper administration of justice.

Answer plan

→ Explain the privilege and discuss the rationale with reference to the quotation.

→ Use case law to give examples of the extent of the privilege and examine the impact of the decisions in the European Court of Human Rights.

→ Give examples of the ways in which the privilege can be said to hamper the proper administration of justice.

→ Formulate a final view as to whether the privilege can be defended.

Diagram plan

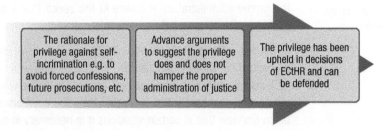

The rationale for privilege against self-incrimination e.g. to avoid forced confessions, future prosecutions, etc.	Advance arguments to suggest the privilege does and does not hamper the proper administration of justice	The privilege has been upheld in decisions of ECtHR and can be defended

A printable version of this diagram plan is available from www.pearsoned.co.uk/lawexpressqa

Answer

¹ A definition of the privilege against self-incrimination is a necessary requirement for your answer in order to show the examiner that you understand the principle under discussion. Marks will usually be awarded for providing a proper definition.

The privilege against self-incrimination as expressed by Lord Goddard in **Blunt v Park Lane Hotel** [1942] 2 KB 253 is a right of a witness to refuse to answer questions which 'have a tendency to expose the deponent to any criminal charge, penalty or forfeiture'.[1] The privilege relates to both oral testimony and the production of documentary evidence.

² A reference to the quotation ensures that your answer remains focused on the question and that you continue to earn the available marks.

The rationale for the protection is that it would be contrary to the principles of fairness to require a witness under oath to be forced to give an answer where such answers could lead to prosecution and this is reflected in the above quotation of Waller LJ in the case of **Den Norske Bank ASA v Antonatos** [1999] QB 271.[2] Lord Templeman in the case of **AT & T Istel Ltd v Tully** [1992] 3 All ER 523 gave further reasons for the justification of the privilege as discouraging the ill-treatment of suspects and the production of dubious confessions. He felt, however, that the privilege was less justified in the context of civil proceedings.

Adrian Zuckerman in his article 'The principle against self-incrimination may not confer a right to refuse disclosure of incriminating evidence that come into existence independently of the disclosure order' [2007] CJQ 395 agrees that the rationale for the privilege against production of documents in civil proceedings seems nonsensical. This is because documentary evidence is admissible independently of a witness and even when a witness is compelled to produce a document they are not required to authenticate the document.

³ An early attempt at addressing the question shows the examiner that you have an ability to select only relevant information and that you are able to focus on the issues raised by the question. This is essential to a good answer and will ensure that you continue to earn the available marks.

The privilege has the potential to hamper the proper administration of justice if it prevents the court from receiving important and relevant evidence but equally if the privilege is removed it risks affecting the proper administration of justice in the sense that a witness could be made to expose themselves to criminal liability.[3]

In **Brown v Stott** [2001] 2 WLR 817 Lord Steyn said that the privilege is not absolute and can be infringed as long as a particular legislative provision was enacted 'in pursuance of a legitimate aim' and is 'necessary and proportionate'. The government has taken the view that in certain situations it is necessary in order to ensure the proper administration of justice to force witnesses to

give incriminating evidence or produce documents. An example is
s.172(2)(a) of the Road Traffic Act 1988, which requires the regis-
tered owner of a car to reveal the identity of the driver of the vehicle
at the time of the commission of an offence.[4] In the case of **Brown
v Stott** (above) it was held that this statutory exception was a proportionate interference with the privilege against self-incrimination
and this was further confirmed in the case of **O'Halloran v United
Kingdom** [2007] Crim LR 897.

4 An ability to include and
explain some of the exceptions
to the rule of privilege against
self-incrimination shows that
you have more than just a
basic understanding of the
subject matter, which in turn
will separate you from the
weaker student.

In fact, the use of legislation to limit the privilege was in itself seen
to have the potential to affect the proper administration of justice,
particularly in terms of ensuring fairness to the defendant. Statutes
that required the witness to provide answers or information which
might tend to incriminate them and then which allowed the material to be used against the witness in subsequent proceedings were
of particular concern. An example is s.434 of the Companies Act
1985. This provision was challenged in the case of **Saunders v UK**
(1999) 23 EHRR 313 and the court held that there had been an
infringement of Art.6.

Following the decision in **Saunders v UK** (above), s.59 of the Youth
Justice and Criminal Evidence Act 1999 was enacted and in the case
of statutes such as s.434 answers provided during non-judicial investigation cannot be used in a criminal trial.[5] The privilege also does not
extend to documents or other pieces of evidence that were independent from 'the will' of the witness. Therefore, in the case of **C plc v P
(Attorney General Intervening)** [2007] 3 WLR 437 pornographic
images found on a computer which was searched by police under a
lawful warrant was not protected by the privilege as the evidence was
regarded as 'real' and 'independent' evidence.

5 Reference to s.59 shows the
examiner that you are aware
of changes made to this
area of law and the reasons
for those changes. This
demonstrates that you have
more than a basic knowledge
of the area. This is important
to ensure that you continue to
earn any marks awarded for
the question.

Further, in the case **Brannigan v Davison** [1997] AC 238 it was
held that any criminal charge must relate to the jurisdiction in which
the privilege is being claimed. Section 14(1)(a) of the Civil Evidence
Act 1968 imposes the same requirement for civil cases.

The privilege was upheld by the European Court of Human Rights in
the case of **Funke v France** (1993) 16 EHRR 297 and **Saunders
v UK** (1996) 23 EHRR 313 on the basis that a legal compulsion to
produce evidence would infringe the right of silence.[6]

6 An awareness of the impact
of the ECHR in this area shows
that you have wide knowledge
and an appreciation of the
controversial nature of the
provisions. An understanding
of the important human rights
cases in this area will earn
you additional marks if applied
in the context of the question.

Crucially, the final issue as to whether a question might expose a witness to a criminal charge is a matter for the judge. Cases such as **Khan v Khan** [1982] 1 WLR 513 have indicated a criminal charge must at least be 'a realistic possibility' (or 'reasonably likely', as expressed in **Blunt v Park Lane Hotel**). The trial judge will therefore have to look at factors such as the gravity of the offence or the length of time since it occurred. In addition, if a witness relies on the privilege no adverse inference can be drawn (see **Wentworth v Lloyd** (1864) 10 HLC 589).

The privilege against self-incrimination like legal professional privilege is necessary to ensure fairness to the defendant regardless of the consequential restriction of information at trial. However, there are sufficient safeguards in place to ensure that the proper administration of justice is not impeded altogether.

Make your answer stand out

- Refer to views in journal articles such as C. Theophilopoulos, 'The Anglo-American privilege against self-incrimination and the fear of foreign prosecution' [2003] *Sydney Law Review* 14 or M. Redmayne, 'Rethinking the privilege against self-incrimination' (2007) 27 OJLS 209 when discussing refusal to answer questions.

- Mention the case of *Allen* v *United Kingdom* (2002) App. No. 76574/01, which confirmed that the privilege does not prevent the court using powers to require a person to provide information about their financial affairs or that of their company.

- Mention that whilst the statutory exceptions restrict the privilege s.14(1)(b) of the Civil Evidence Act 1968, has, on the other hand, extended the privilege in civil cases to include questions which would incriminate a claimant's spouse or civil partner.

- Point out that the case of *R* v *K (A)* [2010] 2 WLR 905 confirmed that the privilege can also be relied on if the answers themselves would start a process which would lead to incrimination or the discovery of incriminating evidence.

- Give examples of other statutory exceptions such as s.31 Theft Act 1968, s.9 Criminal Damage Act 1971, s.72 Senior Courts Act 1981 and s.98 Children Act 1989.

- Include a discussion of s.1(2) of the Criminal Evidence Act 1898 which provides that a defendant may be asked any question on cross-examination regardless of whether it would tend to incriminate him when discussing issues of whether privilege against self-incrimination hampers the proper administration of justice.

Don't be tempted to...

- Confuse the privilege of self-incrimination with the right of silence – the privilege extends to witnesses other than the defendant.
- Ignore the impact of decisions in the European Court of Human Rights such as *Saunders* v *UK* (above).
- Ignore the issue of whether privilege hampers the proper administration of justice – this is the essence of the question and must be addressed by you.

? Question 4

Patrick is charged with criminal damage to the value of £10,000. During pre-trial disclosure Patrick's solicitors discover that the police have a witness statement from a person who has admitted to the criminal damage. However, the police decide not to disclose the witness statement as the witness is a person of low intelligence and the police have decided that they do not believe the confession. Patrick's solicitors prepare a defence statement in which details of Patrick's alibi are given (the police were made aware of the existence of the alibi during the police interview with Patrick). However, the defence statement is served late. Patrick believes that he has been deliberately targeted by the police because he is a member of an environmental group called 'the warriors' who the police currently have under surveillance. Patrick believes the police want to discredit members of that group. Patrick's solicitors would like the police to disclose video evidence of the surveillance of the group to show that all of the group's demonstrations have been peaceful. The police have refused disclosure on the basis that this would be contrary to the public interest. The police also believe that Patrick has previously confessed to his solicitor about being involved in the criminal damage offence and would like disclosure of all relevant attendance notes of meetings between Patrick and his solicitor.

Advise the prosecution as to likelihood of the court ordering disclosure of the evidence discussed in the above scenario.

Answer plan

→ Discuss the prosecution's duty of disclosure under s.3 Criminal Procedure and Investigations Act 1996 in relation to the third party confession.

→ Consider whether an adverse inference can be drawn as a result of the late service of the defence statement under s.11(5) of the 1996 Act.

→ Examine whether the prosecution can rely on public interest immunity to withhold information about the surveillance.

→ Consider whether the solicitor's attendance notes can be said to be privileged.

Diagram plan

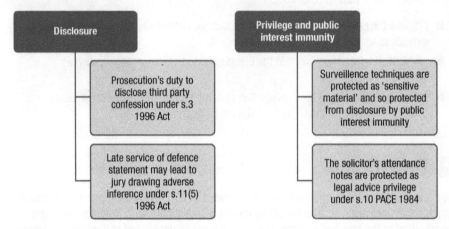

A printable version of this diagram plan is available from www.pearsoned.co.uk/lawexpressqa

Answer

The issues raised in relation to the above scenario require consideration of the rules of disclosure and the circumstances in which evidence can be legitimately withheld. In order to ensure a fair trial under Art.6 of the European Convention on Human Rights, a defendant should have access to all relevant information, which might assist his case to ensure 'equality of arms'.

[1] An ability to refer to relevant statutory provisions and rules governing disclosure such as the Criminal Procedure Rules 2011 will show the examiner that you have a good level of knowledge of the subject area and this will mark your answer out as a detailed one and earn you extra marks.

The first issue that arises is in relation to the pre-trial disclosure. The prosecution have a duty under s.3 Criminal Procedure and Investigations Act 1996 and Part 21 of the Criminal Procedure Rules 2011 to disclose evidence which 'might reasonably be considered capable of undermining the case for the prosecution against the accused or of assisting the case for the accused'.[1] The prosecution have a witness statement from a third party confessing to the criminal damage and this can therefore be considered capable of undermining the prosecution case against Patrick. The Attorney General's Guidelines on Disclosure (2005) provide examples of the type of information which might be considered relevant under s.3 and this includes any material which might point to another person being involved in the commission of the offence (para. 12.ii).[2] The test is an objective one. In the circumstances if the prosecution refuse to disclose the witness statement in question the defence

[2] Reference to any guidelines in this area, such as the Attorney General's Guidelines on Disclosure, is also a good way to demonstrate you have read around the subject and takes your answer beyond a basic one. This will earn you additional marks as it shows a deeper level of knowledge.

3 As the question has
specifically asked you to advise
the prosecution, it is important
that you do this at each stage
of your answer. This will show
the examiner that your answer
is focused and will earn you
the available marks.

4 It is important to act on
the clues in the question
such as the late service of
the defence statement and
apply the relevant law to the
facts. This demonstrates an
understanding of the practical
issues involved and this will
earn you the available marks.

5 Having recognised that an
adverse inference can be
drawn it is also necessary
to consider the limitations
of drawing an adverse
inference. This will ensure
that your answer for this part
of the problem question is
complete and this in turn will
mean that you pick up all of
the available marks.

should be advised to make an application under s.8 of the 1996 Act for specific disclosure but should first serve a defence statement so that the prosecution can properly assess whether this undisclosed evidence should now be disclosed as part of their continuing duty under s.7A to keep disclosure under review. The prosecution should therefore be advised that it is likely that disclosure of the witness statement will be ordered and so to avoid costs disclosure should be made now.[3]

The next issue relates to the late service of Patrick's defence statement. Patrick is obliged to serve a defence statement under s.5 of the 1996 Act once the prosecution have complied with their duty under s.3. This must set out the nature of the defence as well as points in dispute and include alibi details. The prosecution should be advised that if Patrick's defence statement is served late then, under s.11 of the Act, the court or any party may comment on this and the jury may draw an adverse inference. However, under s.11(5) it is within the discretion of the judge as to whether to allow a comment to be made and so allow the jury to consider the option of drawing an adverse inference.[4] Therefore, the judge will have to consider whether the late service of Patrick's defence statement warrants some comment. However, the defence should be advised that under s.11(10)) Patrick cannot be convicted solely as a result of an adverse inference being drawn.[5]

With regard to the question of whether Patrick is entitled to disclosure of video evidence of the surveillance of the group this will depend on whether the prosecution are able to successfully argue that the information is protected by public interest immunity. According to the case of **Conway v Rimmer** [1968] 2 WLR 998, this is a question of law for the courts to decide. In **R v Governor of Brixton Prison, ex parte Osman** (1990) 93 Cr App R 202 it was held that public interest immunity could apply in criminal proceedings. However, the test in criminal proceedings is more stringent and, according to the cases of **R v Keane** [1994] 1 WLR 746 and **R v Dervish** [2001] EWCA Crim 2789, disclosure will be ordered if the evidence is necessary for the defence to have a fair trial or would otherwise avoid a miscarriage of justice. The defence could argue that the details of the surveillance are important to the defence to show that Patrick is not capable of causing criminal damage. However, the prosecution may also argue a need to

[6] An ability to refer to the key cases setting out the test for public interest immunity shows a good level of knowledge on your part. Going on to apply key facts such as the reasons why the surveillance details are needed shows good practical knowledge of the issues and an ability to assess the problem and find solutions using supporting case law. This is good application and will earn you marks.

protect details of different surveillance techniques because revealing this information could impede the police ability to carry out future surveillance undetected.[6] The Code of Practice issued under s.23 of the 1996 Act gives examples of 'sensitive material' which might justify protection on the basis of public interest immunity and this includes surveillance techniques. In the circumstances the prosecution should be advised to make an application to the court for a public interest immunity order in relation to details of the surveillance.

Finally, the police seek disclosure of all relevant attendance notes of meetings between Patrick and his solicitor. Under s.10 Police and Criminal Evidence Act 1984 confidential communications passing between a solicitor and legal adviser will be privileged as long as they relate to the giving of legal advice. In the case of **Minter v Priest** [1930] AC 558 it was held that it is the nature of the comments rather than the meeting itself which is privileged.[7] This principle applies equally to criminal proceedings. The fact that the prosecution are seeking attendance notes dealing with a confession they believe Patrick has made means that the prosecution are unlikely to succeed in their request for disclosure. Any advice the solicitor has given Patrick about his confession and how his case should be dealt with will come under the heading of legal advice for the purposes of s.10. The case of **R v Seaton** [2010] EWCA Crim 1980 confirms that the privilege is paramount and it is not a question of balancing other considerations of public interest. The prosecution should be advised that they will be unable to obtain the attendance notes in question.

[7] Using the statutory provisions and case law to explain the scope of legal advice privilege shows the examiner that you have relevant knowledge of the subject area. This is important to distinguish your answer from a basic one. It is the kind of level of detail which will earn you extra marks.

Make your answer stand out

■ When discussing Patrick's entitlement to video evidence of the surveillance, refer to Lord Taylor CJ's guidelines in the case of *R v Davis* [1993] 1 WLR 613 relating to the procedure to be adopted by the prosecution for applying for immunity from disclosure.

■ When referring to the prosecution's obligation of disclosure under s.3 of the 1996 Act, refer to Lord Bingham's speech in *R v H*; *R v C* [2004] 2 WLR 335 to the effect that the golden rule is full prosecution disclosure and derogation from the rule will require the court to ask itself a series of questions.

■ When referring to the prosecution's failure to disclose the third party confession, also refer to cases such as *Mills v Poole* [1998] AC 382, HL, which stated that the duty to disclose extended to statements of witnesses whom the prosecution did not regard as credible.

■ Refer to the Protocol for the Control and Management of Unused Material in the Crown Court *Archbold*: *Criminal Pleading, Evidence & Practice* (2006), when discussing the prosecution's obligations of disclosure following service of the defence statement.

■ Refer to views in journal articles such as D. Omerod, 'Improving the disclosure regime' [2003] 7 E & P 102 and M. Redmayne, 'Criminal Justice Act 2003: disclosure and its discontents' [2004] Crim LR 44 when discussing the disclosure rules.

! Don't be tempted to...

■ Ignore the issue of late service of the defence statement.

■ Confuse the criminal test for disclosure of public interest immunity material with the civil test.

■ Fail to mention s.10 PACE 1984 when discussing privilege and rely only on the common law rules.

Mixed problem questions

How this topic may come up in exams

Mixed problem questions are a popular form of assessment in many institutions because they can test the students' lateral thinking and ability to recognise evidential issues across the law of evidence. This makes it much harder for students to engage in selective revision where they limit themselves to revising a certain number of topics. The topics in mixed problem questions can appear in any combination.

■ Attack the question

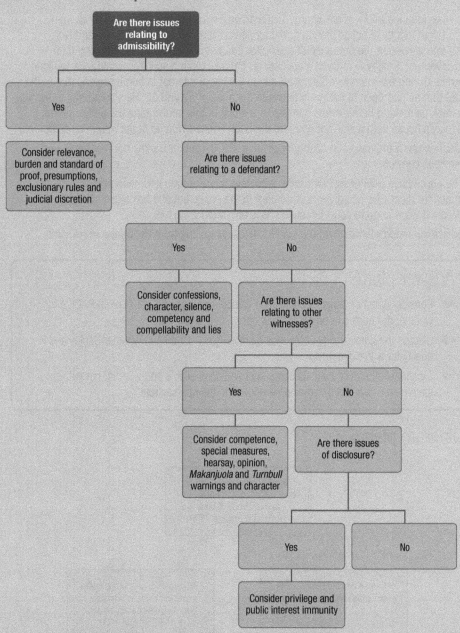

A printable version of this diagram is available from www.pearsoned.co.uk/lawexpressqa

❓ Question 1

Sanjay, Maurice and Ivor are charged with arson. Following their arrest all three men are taken to a local police station and interviewed separately. Both Maurice and Ivor are interviewed in the presence of a solicitor and both give statements denying their involvement. Sanjay is refused a solicitor on the basis that a solicitor would take too long to arrive. During the interview Sanjay admits to having in interest in bomb making due to the fact that he had been in the army between the ages of 22 and 25. He also admits to owning a book on making home-made bombs. As a result of this information the police search Sanjay's house with a warrant and find the book entitled *How to Make Home Made Bombs*.

Maurice has a previous conviction for arson in 2000. Neither Sanjay nor Ivor have any previous convictions.

The police have a witness, Ivor's wife, who says that the men had been planning the arson attack for days. She has given a statement to the police but she has since stated that she does not want to go to court because she is afraid of facing Ivor.

Advise all three defendants of the evidential issues arising from the above set of facts.

Answer plan

→ Consider whether Sanjay's confession can be excluded under s.76(2)(b) PACE and whether the book can be admitted under s.76(4) and s.78.

→ Discuss the admissibility of Maurice's previous conviction and whether Sanjay and Ivor qualify for a *Vye* direction.

→ Explain whether Ivor's wife is competent and compellable and whether her witness statement can be admitted as an exception to the hearsay rule.

Diagram plan

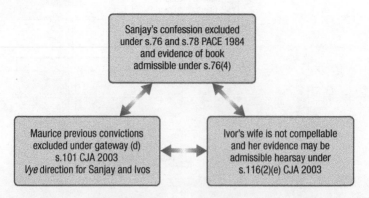

Sanjay's confession excluded under s.76 and s.78 PACE 1984 and evidence of book admissible under s.76(4)

Maurice previous convictions excluded under gateway (d) s.101 CJA 2003 *Vye* direction for Sanjay and Ivos

Ivor's wife is not compellable and her evidence may be admissible hearsay under s.116(2)(e) CJA 2003

Answer

Show the examiner that you are able to recognise the multiple issues at the outset as this shows good overall knowledge and an ability to spot the issues. This gives a good first impression of your answer. This style of introduction is preferable to one that is a commentary on the law of evidence generally as it shows you are focused on the issues.

This shows the examiner that you are able to apply the definition of a confession and therefore demonstrates a sound knowledge of the material.

Supporting your observations of the breach with the relevant statutory provisions shows both an ability to apply the law to the facts in the question and a good grasp of the subject area. This will gain you the available marks.

By spotting important clues in the question, such as the fact that the police knowledge of the books arose from facts mentioned in Sanjay's evidence, and then applying the correct statutory provisions under s.76(4) supported by case law, you demonstrate that you have a wider knowledge and understanding of the provisions of s.76 and this will earn you more of the available marks.

In advising Sanjay, Maurice and Ivor it is necessary to consider issues relating to confessions, competence and compellability, bad and good character and hearsay.[1]

Sanjay

Sanjay has made a confession during his interview because the definition of a confession under s.82(1) Police and Criminal Evidence Act 1984 includes anything which is adverse to the maker. Sanjay has admitted to having an interest in bomb making and this can be said to be adverse to him because he is charged with arson.[2] The issue is whether the confession is admissible. Sanjay has been refused access to a solicitor. This is a breach of his rights under s.58 of the 1984 Act this right can be delayed but not denied altogether.[3] This may be grounds for the defence to argue that the confession is unreliable due to the breach of the Act and should therefore be inadmissible under s.76(2)(b) of the same Act due to things said and done by the police officers, which renders the confession unreliable. As an alternative, the defence can ask the judge to exercise his discretion under s.78 of the Act to exclude the confession on the basis that its admission would have an unfair effect on the proceedings. In the case of **R v Samuel** [1988] 2 WLR 920, CA the court was willing to exclude a confession under s.78 where access to legal advice had been denied.

Even if Sanjay's confession is excluded it will not affect the admissibility of the books found at his home. This is because under s.76(4) of the 1984 Act any facts discovered as a result of a confession is admissible independently of the confession. However, the evidence must still be relevant before it can be admitted. As the police believe that the books are capable of showing that Sanjay would have the knowledge and ability to make the type of home-made bombs used in the arson then the books may be admissible. However, according to the case of **Lam Chi-Ming v R** [1991] 2 WLR 1082 no reference can be made to how the police knew where to look for the books, as this would be inadmissible.[4]

As Sanjay does not have any previous convictions he will be entitled to a **Vye** direction according to the case of **R v Vye** [1993] 1 WLR 471. He will be entitled to the first limb of the direction relating to credibility because he has made a pre-trial statement during a police interview. He will also be entitled to the second limb of the direction on propensity, as this is given regardless.[5]

Maurice

Maurice has a previous conviction for arson and the prosecution may seek to use this as evidence of bad character at his trial, as previous convictions satisfy the definition under s.98 of the Criminal Justice Act 2003. The prosecution would have to show that one of the gateways under s.101 of the 2003 Act applies. As the previous conviction is the same description as the present charge then gateway (d), which relates to 'an important matter in issue' between the defence and the prosecution, may apply.[6] Section 103 states that an important matter in issue includes whether a defendant has a propensity to commit offences. The case of **R v Hanson** [2005] 1 WLR 3169 stated that a single conviction would not normally show propensity unless it shows a tendency towards unusual behaviour or has probative force in relation to the present offence. If, for example, there are similarities in the way Maurice carried out the offence previously and now, then it may be more likely that the conviction will be admitted. The defence can, however, ask the judge to exercise discretion under s.101(3) of the 2003 Act on the fairness principle. When exercising the discretion under s.101(3) the judge must also have regard to the length of time between the previous conviction and the present charge. Also under s.103(3) the judge must consider the length of time since the conviction occurred. As the conviction occurred in 2000 it is arguable that it is too old to have any probative value.

[6] By showing the examiner that you understand why gateway (d) is applicable on the facts this again shows a good level of knowledge of the subject area coupled with practical application skills.

As bad character evidence can be used for both credibility and propensity, the judge would have to direct the jury on how the bad character evidence is to be used in this case (see **R v Highton** [2005] 1 WLR 3472).[7]

[7] This demonstrates a wider understanding of the use of bad character and thus takes your answer beyond a basic one of simply discussing the method of admissibility. This will earn you additional marks.

Ivor

Like Sanjay, Ivor will be entitled to both limbs of the **Vye** direction. Ivor's wife has given key evidence against all three men. She is a competent but not a compellable witness on behalf of the prosecution because the offence of arson is not a 'specified offence' under s.80(3) PACE. However, she can voluntarily agree to give evidence, although the judge would have to ensure that she understands that she does not have to. As Ivor's wife is afraid to give evidence the prosecution might seek to admit her witness statement as evidence rather than calling her to testify. This would technically be hearsay but the prosecution may seek leave of the court to rely on the s.116(2)(e) exception found in the Criminal Justice Act 2003 on the basis that she is in fear. The judge will have to exercise a discretion under this provision by considering the factors in s.116(4). The factors include whether special measures would be a suitable alternative. The judge will consider the fact that the defence will want the opportunity to question Ivor's wife. In the circumstances the judge can order special measures to allow Ivor's wife to give evidence, for example behind a screen (s.26 Youth Justice and Public Order Act 1999). The judge would have to give a warning to the jury under s.32 of the Act to ensure that a special measures direction does not prejudice the defendant.[8] If the judge does allow the admission of the witness statement under s.116(2)(e) the defence will still be able to call other evidence to challenge the credibility of Ivor's wife under s.124 of the 2003 Act.

[8] Giving at least one example of a special measure here shows the examiner you understand what special measures are and so gives your answer more detail, which will in turn earn you additional marks.

[9] Drawing your answer together in a conclusion allows the examiner to check you have picked up and applied all the multiple issues covered in the question.

In conclusion,[9] Sanjay's confession is likely to be ruled inadmissible under s.76(2)(b) or s.78 of the 1984 Act. The book obtained during the search is relevant and reliable evidence and so potentially admissible under s.76(4). Maurice's previous conviction is likely to be admissible at trial unless the judge exercises judicial discretion to exclude on the basis of the age of the conviction and that it is a sole conviction with little probative value. However, both Sanjay and Ivor will be entitled to a good character direction. Ivor's wife is likely to testify at trial but probably under a special measures direction.

Make your answer stand out

- Discuss cases such as *R* v *Cain* (1993) 99 Cr App Rep 208 on the effect of admitting bad character evidence for Maurice while giving good character directions for Sanjay and Ivor.
- Mention Art.6 and the right to a fair trial when discussing the admission of bad character evidence.
- Discuss further cases on whether a single conviction is enough for propensity such as *R* v *M* [2006] EWCA Crim 3408 and that even old convictions can establish propensity (see *R* v *Sully* [2007] All ER (D) 421.

! **Don't be tempted to...**

- Ignore the fact that the admission to having an interest in bomb making is capable of amounting to a confession under s.82(1).
- Forget to mention s.76(4) in relation to the admissibility of evidence discovered as a result of an inadmissible confession.
- Fail to mention the importance of s.78 to confessions as well as s.76.
- Discuss illegal searches in the context of the discovery of the book – you are told that the search was carried out under a warrant.
- Ignore the importance of the fact that neither Sanjay nor Ivor have any previous convictions. This is important to good character *Vye* direction.
- Forget to discuss issues of the competence and compellability of Ivor's wife.

? Question 2

Pedro is charged with theft from his local branch of Nesco Supermarket. He suffers from learning difficulties and has an IQ of 63. He is cautioned, and interviewed with a solicitor and an appropriate adult present. Pedro's solicitors intend to call Pedro to testify at the trial.

Pedro's solicitor also wishes to call medical evidence from a psychiatrist, Mr Pang, to the effect that Pedro's learning difficulties means that he would have trouble distinguishing truth from fiction and therefore his confession is unreliable.

The prosecution have a statement from the manager of Nesco, who has provided a detailed description of Pedro whom he says he recognises as a frequent customer of Nesco. The identification was made during the day. However, the manager had recently undergone laser surgery on his eyes, shortly before the robbery, and admits that his vision was 'somewhat hazy'. He was able to pick Pedro out during a formal video identification procedure under Code D of Police and Criminal Evidence Act 1984.

Advise the prosecution of the evidential issues arising from the above facts.

Answer plan

→ Discuss competency of Pedro.

→ Consider whether expert evidence can be given at his trial relating to his confession.

→ Consider the admissibility of identification evidence by the manager.

Diagram plan

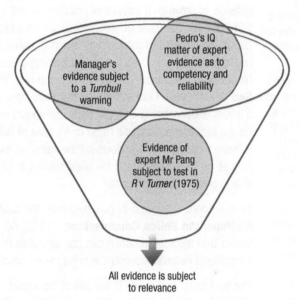

Manager's evidence subject to a *Turnbull* warning

Pedro's IQ matter of expert evidence as to competency and reliability

Evidence of expert Mr Pang subject to test in *R* v *Turner* (1975)

All evidence is subject to relevance

A printable version of this diagram plan is available from www.pearsoned.co.uk/lawexpressqa

Answer

In advising Pedro it is necessary to consider evidential issues relating to competence and compellability of witnesses, opinion and identification evidence.

Pedro

[1] This shows the examiner that you are able to spot the clues in the question such as Pedro's low IQ and discuss their significance. This shows a grasp of the material and will gain marks.

Pedro's interview appears to have been carried out in accordance with Code C of the Police and Criminal Evidence Act as he was cautioned and had both a solicitor and appropriate adult at his interview. However, as Pedro has a low IQ the first issue that arises is his competence to give evidence at trial.[1]

[2] By referring to specific statutory provisions such as s.53 of the 1999 Act you demonstrate a detailed knowledge of the subject area and this will earn you the available marks.

[3] Discussion of the procedure involved in challenging competency demonstrates a deeper level of knowledge and will gain you additional marks.

[4] By using cases such as *R v Sed* to illustrate your argument about the extent of Pedro's competency you demonstrate an ability to apply relevant case law to the facts and this will continue to help you to gain the available marks.

[5] Show the examiner that you are able to examine all possibilities as this ensures your answer is a full one.

[6] Dealing with the issues as they arise makes your answer easy to follow and demonstrates a logical structure with a clear thought process in the answer. This will impress the examiner and help to gain you marks.

Under s.53(1) of the Youth Justice and Criminal Evidence Act 1999[2] all persons are presumed competent to give evidence. It will therefore be for the opposing party, in this case the prosecution, to raise the issue of Pedro's competency. The test in s.53(3) of the 1999 Act is whether Pedro is able to understand questions put to him as a witness or give intelligible answers. Under s.55(2) Pedro will be presumed to have sufficient understanding if he is able to give intelligible testimony. It is for the party calling Pedro, in this case the defence, to prove on a balance of probabilities that s.55(2) is satisfied (s.54(2)). The issue of competency will be dealt with at a *voir dire* in the absence of the jury and expert evidence can be called[3] relating to whether Pedro's low IQ and learning difficulties will affect his ability to understand the questions put to him. The case of **R v Sed** [2004] EWCA Crim 1294 held that there does not have to be a 100% understanding and that the judge should make allowance for the fact that a witness's recall or it's level of detail could vary. If Pedro were unable to understand the nature of the oath then as long as he could understand the questions put to him he would be able to give unsworn evidence.[4]

Even if Pedro is allowed to give evidence, the case of **Toohey v Metropolitan Police Commissioner** [1965] AC 595, HL confirmed that medical evidence can still be called to challenge the credibility of Pedro's evidence due to his mental condition.[5]

The next issue that arises is the use of the expert evidence of Mr Pang.[6] Expert evidence provides an exception to the general rule that opinion evidence is admissible due to its irrelevance and potential bias. Following the decision in **R v Turner** [1975] 2 WLR 56, CA expert evidence is not admissible for those matters which are within the capability of the jury to decide, such as the credibility of the defendant. The key issue is whether Pedro's condition amounts to an identifiable psychiatric condition. The level of a person's IQ, however, is something that is considered as capable of being assessed by the jury if it is still at a normal but unintelligent level. However, if it falls within the realm of abnormality and comes into the realm of a pathological disorder then the jury will need some assistance from a psychiatrist or psychologist. In **R v Masih** [1986] Crim LR 395 it was held that IQ below 70 would usually be an indicator of abnormality. Therefore, Pedro's IQ of 63 would permit some expert evidence by Mr Pang. However, a potential problem is

⁷ Your ability to spot a separate aspect to the facts such as the issue of reliability of the confession demonstrates a good grasp of the material and will earn you more marks.

⁸ By finding solutions to the admissibility of the evidence and supporting this with case law you demonstrate to the examiner that you possess problem-solving skills and a wider understanding of the subject area and this is exactly the level of detail that will earn you extra marks.

⁹ By applying the *Turnbull* guidelines to the facts in this way you show the examiner that you have a good level of understanding of how the guidelines work and this is necessary to earn you the available marks.

¹⁰ Show the examiner that you are able to spot important clues in the question such as the manager's poor eyesight and apply the clues to the *Turnbull* guidelines. This is good application and will help you to gain marks.

¹¹ By identifying what evidence can be used to support disputed identification evidence you make the examiner aware that you can distinguish that *Turnbull* requires weak identification evidence to be supported. This separates you from the weaker student who may not spot the significance of weak identification evidence.

that Mr Pang's evidence appears to focus on the reliability of the confession, which would usually be a matter for the jury assisted by warning from the judge.[7] In the case of **R v Reynolds** [1989] Crim LR 220, CA expert evidence that the defendant could not distinguish between reality and fantasy was held to be inadmissible. However, according to cases such as **R v Ward** [1993] 1 WLR 619, if Pedro is found to be suffering from a personality disorder severe enough to be categorised as a mental disorder then expert evidence will be admissible on whether the confession is reliable.[8]

Evidence of the manager of Nesco

The manager at Nesco is able to give identification evidence of Pedro. Visual identification requires the judge to give a **Turnbull** warning to the jury in accordance with **R v Turnbull** [1976] 3 WLR 445, CA as long as the evidence is not poor and unsupported, in which case it would be withdrawn from the jury. The manager has provided a detailed description of Pedro and the identification is based on recognition. The **Turnbull** warning requires the judge to warn the jury of the special need for caution before convicting on the correctness of the identification evidence and explain that a mistaken witness can still be a convincing one. As the identification was made during the day, the visibility would have been good assuming the manager saw Pedro face on.[9] In addition, the manager recognised Pedro but the jury should be reminded that mistakes can still be made with recognition evidence. Finally, the judge should draw the jury's attention to any specific weaknesses in the identification. The fact that the manager's eyesight had been affected by recent laser surgery on his eye is important for the jury to know.[10] It is then left to the jury to decide how much weight to attach to the identification evidence. As the disputed identification evidence has been supported by a formal identification procedure in accordance with Code D of the Police and Criminal Evidence Act 1984, this can be regarded as supporting evidence in respect of the identification.[11]

With regard to Pedro it is possible that he may be a compellable witness if he is able to understand most questions put to him and give intelligible answers. Whilst Mr Pang's evidence is useful on any application regarding Pedro's competency, it is unlikely to be admissible at trial on the issue of the reliability of Pedro's evidence or his credibility as these are matters for the jury unless it can be shown

Pedro is suffering from a mental illness. The evidence of the manager of Nesco will be subject to a **Turnbull** warning at trial. It is unlikely to be excluded but due to some weak features will probably need to be supported.

✓ Make your answer stand out

- Discuss further cases on the use of expert evidence on the question of reliability of a confession such as R v O'Brien [2000] Crim LR 676.
- Discuss further cases such as R v VJS [2006] EWCA Crim 2389 when discussing the use of expert evidence to bolster credibility.
- Discuss the potential for miscarriages of justice when discussing the manager's identification evidence.

! Don't be tempted to...

- Discuss confessions, as there is no suggestion that the defendant has made a confession or that there were any breaches of PACE 1984.
- Invent possible breaches of PACE when the question is directing you to the fact that the interview has been conducted correctly.
- Ignore the issue of Pedro's IQ when discussing competence and also the admissibility of expert evidence.

? Question 3

Meredith is involved in divorce proceedings in which she seeks a divorce and financial settlement from her husband Albert. Albert alleges that the divorce is not lawful because Meredith was previously married to Dermott and that this marriage was never annulled. Meredith alleges that she and Dermott married in a private beach ceremony in Mauritius which was not a religious or recognised ceremony in either England or Mauritius. Albert claims Meredith is lying and says he has witnesses who are former neighbours of Meredith and Dermott who will say that Meredith and Dermott held themselves out to be married. Albert also alleges that Meredith had been having an affair with Vincent and that she was named in the divorce petition brought by Vincent's wife. Albert would like to use the decision in Vincent's divorce case to help show that Meredith has been unfaithful to him. Meredith wrote a letter to her solicitor in which she admits the affair with Vincent. In the same letter she says that she was also seeing Vincent at the time of her first marriage but wants this kept secret from Albert and for the solicitor to advance a case that she has not committed adultery. Unknown to Meredith, she sent this letter to Albert's solicitor by mistake. Albert's solicitor returned the original letter but made a copy and put it in Albert's file.

Advise both Meredith and Albert.

Answer plan

→ Discuss whether the presumption of marriage arises in relation to the marriage ceremony between Meredith and Dermott.

→ Explain whether the decision in Vincent's divorce proceedings can be used in Meredith and Albert's divorce.

→ Analyse issues of legal advice privilege in relation to Meredith's letter.

Diagram plan

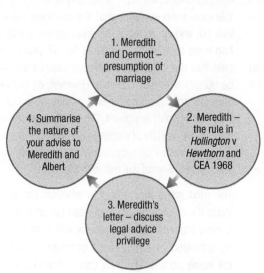

1. Meredith and Dermott – presumption of marriage

2. Meredith – the rule in *Hollington* v *Hewthorn* and CEA 1968

3. Meredith's letter – discuss legal advice privilege

4. Summarise the nature of your advise to Meredith and Albert

A printable version of this diagram plan is available from www.pearsoned.co.uk/lawexpressqa

Answer

In order to advise Meredith and Albert it will be necessary to consider the evidential rules relating to presumptions, previous judgments and privilege.

The first issue that arises is in relation to the claim that Meredith's marriage to Albert is a bigamous one because she was previously married to Dermott. It is necessary to consider whether it is possible for Albert to allege that, despite Meredith's claims, a presumption of marriage exists. Cases such as **Piers v Piers** (1849) 2 HL Cas 331 have confirmed that for a presumption of marriage to exist it must be shown that the parties, namely Meredith and Dermott, went through a valid marriage ceremony. Some minor technicality with the marriage will not necessarily make it invalid, however; most of the formalities of a marriage ceremony must be in existence.[1] If Meredith is able to show that the ceremony in Mauritius was not a valid ceremony then she will be able to rebut the presumption of marriage. Albert further alleges that he has witnesses who can support his allegation that Meredith was married to Dermott. Cases such as **Chief Adjudication Officer v Bath** [2000] 1 FLR 8 suggests that a man and woman who live together and hold themselves out as being a married couple will raise a persuasive presumption of marriage.[2] In this case even evidence that the marriage ceremony was not valid was not enough to rebut the presumption of marriage, as the couple had lived together as a couple for 37 years. The Court of Appeal held that the validity of marriages entered into in good faith should be upheld wherever possible. However, on the facts of this case as Meredith may have committed a criminal act of bigamy if her marriage to Dermott is upheld, the court may look more closely at the issue of the validity of marriage and whether the presumption of marriage can in fact be rebutted, as this would be in Meredith's favour. The burden of proof will rest with Meredith.[3]

The next issue that arises is whether the finding of adultery in Vincent's divorce proceedings can be used as evidence in Albert's divorce proceedings. The general rule is that civil judgments cannot be admitted in subsequent proceedings which do not involve the same parties. This rule comes from the case of **Hollington v Hewthorn** [1943] KB 587. The rationale for the rule is that such judgments are not relevant or could arguably amount to opinion evidence. However, one of the exceptions to this general rule can be found at s.12 of the Civil Evidence Act 1968 and this would apply to the facts of Meredith and Albert. Under s.12 any findings relating to adultery or paternity can be used in civil proceedings. If, therefore, the court hearing the divorce petition of Vincent's wife gave a decision confirming the adultery between Vincent and Meredith then

[1] Spotting the correct evidential issue and then using case law as authority gives depth to your answer. Applying the facts in the problem with reference to case law is an example of good application and this will ensure that you earn the marks awarded for the question.

[2] Use of more recent relevant cases in this area of law such as *Chief Adjudication Officer* v *Bath* demonstrates that your knowledge is up to date and will earn you additional marks.

[3] Some attempt on your part to predict the likely outcome at trial based on case law shows practical skills on your part, gives an overall good impression to the examiner of the quality of your answer and will earn you additional marks.

[4] An ability to identify and apply relevant exceptions to the exclusionary rule on previous judgments such as s.12 Civil Evidence Act 1968 demonstrates a good level of understanding and will earn you the available marks.

[5] The use of cases to help you define and explain legal advice privilege illustrates that you are aware of the important cases in this area which is necessary for a good answer.

[6] Where it is not clear on the facts whether the solicitor is involved in an act of deception then you should consider both sides of the argument. This shows the examiner that you are able to apply the relevant law to all eventualities and this in turn will earn you additional marks.

[7] Reference to relevant civil procedure rules in this area shows a greater level of knowledge and gives depth to your answer. This will earn you additional marks.

this could be used in the current proceedings involving Meredith and Albert.[4] However, this raises a persuasive presumption and it is then open for Meredith to prove on a balance of probabilities that she did not in fact commit adultery.

The next issue that arises is in relation to the letter written by Meredith to her solicitor which contains an admission of the adultery. However, the letter is covered by legal advice privilege as it is communication between Meredith and her solicitor. The contents of the letter are clearly confidential. The purpose must be for the obtaining and giving of legal advice. Cases such as **Three Rivers Council v Governor of the Bank of England (No. 6)** [2004] 3 WLR 1274 confirmed that this extends to 'advise as to what should prudently and sensibly be done in the relevant legal context'.[5] However, the difficulty here is that Meredith is not asking for advice but is requesting that her solicitor lie in court. The privilege is lost if the solicitor or client or both of them are involved in criminal or fraudulent activities according to the rule in **R v Cox** (1884) 14 QBD 153. According to cases such as **Crescent Farm (Sidcup) Sports v Sterling Offices Ltd** [1972] 2 WLR 91, fraud is given a wide meaning and can include any dishonesty and the test will be an objective one requiring the court to look at what a reasonable solicitor might have done in the circumstances. However, if Meredith's solicitor writes back to advise Meredith against lying about the adultery then, according to the case of **Butler v Board of Trade** [1970] 3 WLR 822, the privilege will not be lost.[6]

The next issue that arises is in relation to whether Albert can use a copy of the letter that Meredith mistakenly sent to his solicitor. If the privilege has not been lost by the actions of Meredith or her solicitor then privilege would apply only to the original letter. The copy on the file would not be covered according to the case of **Calcraft v Guest** [1898] 1 QB 759. Whilst the copy of the letter was obtained by honest mistake the case of **Guinness Peat Properties v Fitzroy Robinson Partnership** [1987] 1 WLR 1027 confirms that an injunction can still be granted. In addition, r. 31.20 of the Civil Procedure Rules 1998 would also prevent Albert's solicitors relying on a privileged document which has been inadvertently disclosed.[7] However, the solicitors would be entitled to assume that privilege has been waived but would need permission of the court to use the document and cases such as **Al Fayed v Commissioner of Police of the Metropolis** [2002] EWCA Civ 780 suggests this would not be granted where there has been an obvious mistake.

In the circumstances Meredith should be advised that there is a good chance that she will be able to rebut the presumption of marriage in respect of her marriage to Dermott. However, it is likely that the decision in Vincent's divorce proceedings will be used to prove her adultery if she is unable to show that she did not commit the adultery. Albert is unlikely to be able to use a copy of the letter written by Meredith to her solicitor unless it can be shown that Meredith has committed an act of deception.

✓ Make your answer stand out

- When discussing the presumption of marriage, refer to additional cases such as *Blyth* v *Blyth* [1966] 2 WLR 634 and *Re H (Minors)* [1996] 2 WLR 8, which confirm that the standard of proof remain on a balance of probabilities and compare with *Mahadervan* v *Mahadervan* [1964] 2 WLR 634 which suggested the standard was beyond reasonable doubt.
- When discussing privilege in respect of Meredith's letter mention that according to cases such as *Wentworth* v *Lloyd* (1864) 10 HLC 589 no adverse inference can be drawn if she fails to waive the privilege attaching to the original letter.

! Don't be tempted to...

- Ignore s.12 of the Civil Evidence Act 1968 – you are specifically told that the issue in Vincent's divorce proceedings was his adultery with Meredith.
- Assume that the presumption of marriage does not apply simply because there was not a valid marriage ceremony between Meredith and Dermott – you must examine all the case law in this area.
- Assume that copies of privileged documents are also privileged and therefore fail to discuss cases such as *Calcraft* v *Guest* (above).

❓ Question 4

Joseph is on trial for grievous bodily harm against his wife, Matilda, which he denies. The prosecution have a witness, Anita, who is a neighbour who says that she saw the assault taking place from her bedroom window. Joseph alleges that Anita has only recently fabricated her claim that she saw the assault and that she only went to the police a few days before the trial after Matilda had put pressure on her. Anita claims that she did not fabricate her claim and that whilst she was initially reluctant to get involved she did give a statement to Matilda's solicitor shortly after the assault and it was the solicitors who finally persuaded her to go to the police. Joseph also alleges that Matilda made a previous complaint of domestic violence against him in 2008 but withdrew the allegation and admitted to the police that she had lied. This is confirmed by the police files. No charges were brought against Joseph. Matilda says that she only withdrew the charges because Joseph threatened her in a letter and the prosecution produce a copy of that letter at trial. The defence wish to call Mr Nabokov, who is an academic and an amateur handwriting expert, to show that the handwriting on the letter is not Joseph's.

Discuss the evidential issues that are likely to arise during the trial.

Answer plan

→ Discuss the use of previous consistent statements under s.120(2) Criminal Justice Act 2003 to disprove allegations of fabrication by Anita.

→ Examine whether Matilda's false complaint meets the definition of bad character under the 2003 Act and whether it is admissible under s.100(1)(a).

→ Assess whether Mr Nabokov's evidence is admissible under the rules of opinion evidence and the rule of finality.

Diagram plan

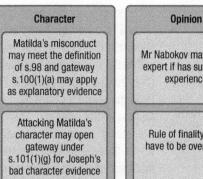

Rule against narrative	Character	Opinion
Use of a previous consistent statement to rebut allegation that Anita has fabricated her evidence	Matilda's misconduct may meet the definition of s.98 and gateway s.100(1)(a) may apply as explanatory evidence	Mr Nabokov may be an expert if has sufficient experience
Admissible under s.120(2) 2003 Act as proof of the matters stated	Attacking Matilda's character may open gateway under s.101(1)(g) for Joseph's bad character evidence	Rule of finality may have to be overcome

A printable version of this diagram plan is available from www.pearsoned.co.uk/lawexpressqa

Answer

A number of evidential issues are likely to arise in the trial of Joseph, which will require the trial judge to consider the admissibility of evidence and to give various directions to the jury during the summing-up.

Anita's evidence is attacked by the defence as a fabrication. This allows the prosecution to admit evidence of a previous consistent statement made by Anita to Matilda's solicitor under s.120(2) of the Criminal Justice Act 2003. This falls into one of the exceptions to the rule against narrative.[1] However, if during cross-examination a witness's evidence is challenged as fabricated then a party may adduce evidence in rebuttal. As can be seen in the case of **R v Sekhon** (1986) 85 Cr App R 19 the rebuttal evidence must show that Anita's version of events was the same before a particular incident or date as the version given at court when the fabrication is alleged.[2] The question of whether there has been an allegation of recent fabrication and whether the previous statement rebuts the allegation is a matter of discretion for the judge. In those circumstances this will not be subject to appeal unless the judge's decision can be held to be '**Wednesbury** unreasonable'.[3]

[2] Using case law such as R v Sekhon to illustrate the approach that will be taken to Anita's evidence is a good example of application and will earn you the available marks.

[3] By taking your answer further and looking at whether the judge's decision on recent fabrication could be challenged, you demonstrate a wider knowledge of the issues involved and this will earn you additional marks.

Matilda's alleged misconduct also raises the issue of bad character. The defence can seek permission of the court to use evidence of this misconduct as long as it satisfies the meaning of bad character under s.98 and s.112 of the Criminal Justice Act 2003 and also falls into one of the three gateways under s.100. Bad character is defined under s.98 as 'a disposition towards misconduct'. Misconduct is further defined in s.112 as 'the commission of an offence or other reprehensible behaviour'. The defence will have to show that Matilda's actions amounted to 'reprehensible behaviour' within the meaning of bad character. In **R v Riley** [2006] EWCA Crim 2030 the court accepted that mere allegations under s.100 might be relevant where the witness is the complainant,[4] such as Matilda in this scenario. The defence will have to show that the allegations are admissible under one of the three gateways under s.100. Gateway (a) may be applicable here if the defence can show that the evidence is important explanatory evidence 'without which a court or jury would find it impossible or difficult to properly understand the other evidence in the case'. It is also necessary to show

[4] Being able to define bad character using the statutory provisions and then applying the definition to the facts demonstrates that you have a good understanding of the 2003 Act and this is necessary to ensure that you pick up the available marks. However, using case law such as R v Riley gives added authority to your arguments.

that its value for understanding the case as a whole is substantial. In the case of **R v Anthony Weir** [2005] EWCA Crim 2866 evidence about the dishonesty of an alibi witness fell into gateway (a). Similarly, the dishonesty of Matilda relating to past allegations of domestic violence could be regarded as important explanatory evidence in relation to the charge of grievous bodily harm,[5] especially as Joseph claims that Matilda is lying. However, the defence must get permission of the judge to rely on this ground (see s.100(4)).[6]

Mr Nabokov's evidence

[6] You have shown the examiner that you understand that the gateways under s.100 are not automatic (unlike s.101) and this shows a deeper level of knowledge and will earn you additional marks.

[7] Being able to spot important clues in the question that would lead you to query the length of Mr Nabokov's experience and use case law to help illustrate how a trial judge might approach the problem shows good application of the facts to the law and will earn you the available marks.

The issue here is whether Mr Nabokov can be regarded as a handwriting expert, if so his evidence would be admissible as an exception to the exclusionary rule against the use of opinion evidence at trial. The trial judge will have to decide the issue of the suitability of Mr Nabokov to be an expert and this can be done in a *voir dire*. It is not necessary for Mr Nabokov to have any formal qualifications but he must have the relevant experience and be impartial. We are told that Mr Nabokov is an 'amateur' handwriting expert. In the case of **R v Silverlock** [1894] 2 QB 766 the amateur study of handwriting allowed a solicitor to act an expert, as the study had been conducted over ten years. Therefore, much will depend on how long Mr Nabokov has studied handwriting.[7]

[8] Being able to spot the applicable exclusionary rule and assess whether any exceptions apply and then to go on to dicuss how the rule itself might not apply shows a good level of knowledge, detailed application and a considered approach to the problem, all of which will earn you extra marks.

However, as the evidence is to be used to prove the issue of credibility, which is a collateral rather than a central issue, the rule of finality would apply. This means that if Matilda is cross-examined on the authenticity of the letter then any answer she gives should be regarded as final in the sense that further evidence intended to challenge her answer would not be admissible unless one of the exceptions to the exclusionary rule apply. On the facts Mr Nabokov is not being asked to comment on Matilda's general reputation for untruthfulness and so the evidence would not fit into the exception highlighted in the case of **R v Richardson** [1963] 3 WLR 15, neither is the evidence being used to prove a previous conviction. As such, the evidence does not fit easily into any of the exceptions. The defence may be able to argue using the test in **Attorney-General v Hitchcock** (1847) 1 Exch 91 that the evidence would have been admissible in evidence-in-chief as the letter was introduced in the first half of the trial as part of the prosecution's case. As such, it can be regarded as part of the central issue introduced by the prosecution themselves.[8]

In the circumstances it is likely that the prosecution will be allowed to use Anita's previous consistent statement to show that she has not fabricated her claims. Matilda's bad character evidence may be admissible under s.100 of the Criminal Justice Act 2003. Mr Nabokov's evidence is also likely to be admissible at trial if the defence can argue that it relates to a central issue in the case.

 Make your answer stand out

■ When discussing the allegation of fabrication in respect of Anita's evidence, also mention cases such as R v Wilmot (1989) 89 Cr App R 341 which would allow the person to whom the earlier statement was made to be called to give evidence (this is assuming litigation privilege is waived in respect of Matilda's solicitor).

■ When referring to the fact that, under s.120(2) of the 2003 Act, the previous consistent statement of Anita is admissible as evidence of matters stated, refer to the fact that this amendment came about as a result of calls for reform made by the Law Commission in their Report No. 245.

■ When discussing whether Matilda's allegations fall into the definition of 'misconduct' under s.112 of the 2003 Act, mention R v Bovell [2005] EWCA Crim 1091, in which the Court of Appeal said that the approach to this question could vary depending on whether the bad character fell under s.100 or s.101.

! Don't be tempted to...

■ Ignore a discussion of s.98 and s.100 of the 2003 Act in relation to Matilda's previous allegation of domestic violence.

■ Discuss a Lucas direction in relation to Matilda's false allegations – a Lucas direction only applies to defendants.

■ Argue issues of hearsay relating to the letter – both Matilda and Joseph are available as witnesses to give evidence about the letter.

❓ Question 5

Lady Justice Barrett is presiding over various fictional appeals against conviction where the trial judges have given the following summing-up:

(a) 'The defendant's alibi has been shown to be false. This is persuasive evidence as to the defendant's guilt and is a matter that you should take into account, members of the jury.'

(b) 'The co-accused has given evidence that it was the defendant who committed this vile offence. You have heard that the co-accused and the defendant have been arch-enemies for many years. It is entirely up to you whose evidence you accept.'

(c) 'The police officers should be commended for having caught a notorious criminal and it is unlikely that police officers of this calibre would have engaged in any trickery. In any event the only matter I have to take into account in deciding whether the police entrapped the defendant is whether they took an active or passive role in the commission of the offence. My view is that they took a passive role and that there is no evidence of entrapment.'

(d) 'The defendant's legal representatives sought to cross-examine various prosecution witnesses and I refused to allow this. The defendant claims that the complainant is biased in that he previously ended a longstanding relationship with her and that she therefore has a motive to lie and his request to cross-examine her was based on this claim. I do not think the claim has any merit.'

Discuss whether the above appeals are likely to succeed and explain the basis for your answer using relevant cases and statutory authority.

Answer plan

→ For the first extract discuss failure by judge to give a *Lucas* direction.

→ The second extract relates to the issue of whether a discretionary *Makanjuola* warning should have been given in relation to the co-accused's evidence.

→ Discussion of whether the judge's comments about the police officers were prejudicial and whether the correct test for entrapment has been applied is needed for extract three.

→ The final extract relates to whether the trial judge correctly applied s.41 of the Youth Justice and Criminal Evidence Act 1999.

Diagram plan

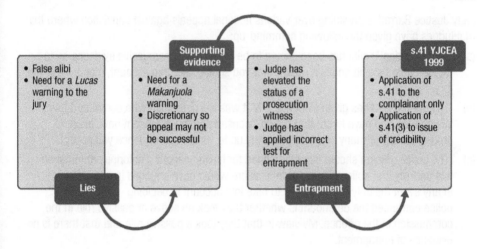

A printable version of this diagram plan is available from www.pearsoned.co.uk/lawexpressqa

Answer

In order to decide whether to grant the various appeals Lady Justice Barrett and the other Lord Justices of Appeal will have to consider whether the trial judge in each case gave the appropriate judicial directions to the jury and whether the correct law was applied.

(A)

With regard to the first summing-up the trial judge states that the false alibi is persuasive evidence as to the defendant's guilt and that the jury must take it into account. The appeal is likely to succeed because the trial judge has misdirected the jury on this occasion. According to the case of **R v Lucas** [1981] 3 WLR 120, it would be possible in these circumstances for a lie to be used as corroborative evidence in the prosecution's case. However, the judge must give a direction to the jury to remind them that the lie may not necessarily be indicative of guilt.[1] As indicated by Judge LJ in **R v Middleton** [2001] Crim LR 251, 'innocent people sometimes tell lies'.[2] If the lie can be said to be deliberate and relate to a material issue then a warning to the jury to exercise caution would be appropriate. However, the jury must also be satisfied that the motive for the lie was the realisation of guilt and that the lie has been shown to be a

[1] You have done two things here: you have made a decision as to whether or not the appeal will succeed (as required by the question) and you have explained why using relevant case law and applying this to the facts. This will earn you the available marks.

[2] The more cases you use to illustrate your answer the better and the ability to quote from judges in this way will add depth to your answer. It also gives the impression that you have a good level of knowledge of the subject area.

lie by independent evidence (see **R v Goodway** (1993) 98 Cr App R 11). Whilst there is no mandatory warning for a **Lucas** direction the judge clearly has not followed the spirit of the **Lucas** guidelines, as he does not balance his comments by pointing out to the jury that the defendant's lie may have been for innocent reasons and that they are not bound to consider the lie when deciding on guilt. The trial judge should have pointed out the exact issue to which the lie is relevant, namely whether the alibi can be considered to be true (see **R v Bullen** [2008] EWCA Crim 4) and the jury should not make an assumption that this would also be proof of guilt but should consider all other prosecution evidence when deciding this ultimate issue.[3]

[3] By going on to point out how the judge should have dealt with his summing-up and supporting this with case law you show that you are able to apply your wider knowledge to the facts. This will earn you additional marks.

(B)

The trial judge has referred to the fact that the co-accused and the defendant have been 'arch-enemies' for many years but has left it to the jury to decide whether they accept the evidence of the co-accused which implicates the defendant. This is unsatisfactory, as the jury require more guidance. Whilst it remains within the trial judge's discretion to decide whether to give a warning to the jury, the case of **R v Makanjuola** [1995] 1 WLR 1348 confirms that a warning should be given to the jury to exercise caution in accepting the unsupported evidence of a witness who can be regarded as unreliable or who has been shown to be lying. In cases such as **R v Petkar** [2003] EWCA Crim 2668 it has been held that where a co-accused has an interest of his own to serve then the trial judge should at the very least direct the jury to examine the co-accused's evidence with care. The warning does not have to go as far as directing the jury to look for supporting evidence before accepting the co-accused's evidence, however.[4] This summing-up by the trial judge may not, however, be successfully appealed because, as cases such as **R v Whitehouse** [2001] EWCA Crim 1531 have reaffirmed, a judge's discretion will only be subject to appeal if it is '**Wednesbury** unreasonable'. This would require the defence to establish that no other judge given the same set of facts would reasonably have concluded that the jury did not need a direction.[5]

[4] It is not enough to simply identify the type of direction the judge should have given to the jury but you need to make some comment on the strength of the direction when discussing *Makanjuola* because Lord Taylor CJ stated in this case that the warning could be either a 'care warning' or a warning that the jury should look for supporting evidence. This demonstrates a more detailed application of the law to the facts and will earn you additional marks.

[5] An ability to recognise that the discretionary nature of a *Makanjuola* warning means that it will be harder to appeal the discretion shows the examiner that you can take your answer beyond a basic one and have a good understanding of the implications of a discretionary warning.

(D)

The judge has erred in his summing-up in the fourth extract because he has made reference to the police officers' standing as being indicative that their evidence should be accepted by the jury. The case of **R v Bentley (Deceased)** [2001] 1 Cr App R 307 held that the judge should not elevate the status of prosecution witnesses in this way. The judge goes on to state that in deciding whether the police officers have been involved in trickery the court need only consider whether their role was 'passive' or active'. This comes from the guidelines in **R v Smurthwaite** (1993) 98 Cr App Rep 437. However, this aspect of the guidelines have been held to be less important. In **R v Looseley** [2001] 1 WLR 2060 the House of Lords held that the correct test for determining whether their has been entrapment is that identified by McHugh J in **Ridgeway v The Queen** (1995) 184 CLR 19, namely whether the police presented the defendant with an exceptional opportunity to commit a crime.[6] If so, then the entrapment will be treated as an abuse of process and the test for whether proceedings should be stayed for entrapment is whether the conduct of the prosecuting authority or its agents was such as to bring the administration of justice into disrepute. The final decision of the judge may be the correct one but he may have arrived at that decision in an incorrect way.

[6] By spotting the key words 'passive' and 'active' and applying them back to the case of *Smurthwaite* you show the examiner that you have a good understanding of the case law in this area and, more importantly, that you are able to distinguish between previous approaches taken by the courts and the current approach that the courts will now take.

(E)

With regard to the final extract the trial judge has refused to allow the defendant to cross-examine a number of prosecution witnesses. Whilst s.41 of the Youth Justice and Criminal Evidence Act 1999 prevents the cross-examination of a complainant about their sexual behaviour without permission of the trial judge, this does not extend to all prosecution witnesses (see **R v Maynard** [2006] EWCA Crim 1509). Whilst s.41 gives the trial judge a degree of discretion in whether to grant leave, he must consider the factors under s.41(2)(a) – that either the question relates to a relevant issue in the case or the questions would allow the defendant to explain or rebut evidence about the complainant's sexual behaviour which has been adduced by the prosecution. The defendant's claims that the claimant is biased and lying because he ended their previous relationship would, on a strict interpretation of s.41(4), mean that the defendant could not cross-examine the complainant as questions relating to credibility are not regarded as relating to a relevant issue under s.41(3). However, in **R v Martin** [2004] EWCA Crim 916 it was held that if credibility is merely one issue but not the purpose or main purpose of the cross-examination then s.41(3) could still apply. The trial judge must also be satisfied under s.41(2)(b) that a refusal would render unsafe any conclusions reached on any issues in the case before allowing leave. On the facts it would appear that credibility is the main purpose for the defendant wishing to question the complainant and as such it would appear that the judge was right to disallow the questioning of the complainant but wrong to allow the questioning of other prosecution witnesses.[7]

[7] By spotting the clue in the question about credibility and explaining the strict interpretation of s.41(3) and identifying cases that have taken a more generous approach you show the examiner that you are able to analyse the issues and this will earn you additional marks.

In the circumstances all appeals are likely to be successful except for the summing-up relating to the second extract, where the judge's direction is discretionary and therefore more difficult to appeal.

✔ Make your answer stand out

- When discussing abuse of process in the fourth extract (d), refer to additional cases such as *Teixeira de Castro* v *Portugal* (1998) 28 EHRR 101 in arguing that failure to stay proceedings may be regarded as a violation of Art.6.
- Mention that, in relation to s.41 (extract e), whilst it might be regarded as a discretion the reality is that once the criteria for admissibility has been met under s.41(2)(a) and (b) the judge has no discretion as seen in cases such as *R* v *F* [2005] 1 WLR 2848.
- Also point out that, for extract (d), a *Makanjuola* warning may also be appropriate in respect of the complainant if there is evidential basis for suggesting she is lying because of her bias.

! Don't be tempted to...

- Ignore the fact that a false alibi is an example of a material lie for the purposes of a *Lucas* direction.
- Deal only with the entrapment issue in extract (b) and fail to discuss the judge's comments about the police officers.
- Focus only on the word 'bias' in extract (d), as this may lead you to discuss only the need for supporting evidence, the comments must be taken in the context of the defence's request to cross-examine prosecution witnesses including the complainant.

❓ Question 6

Fabio and Dwayne are both charged with attempted murder relating to a street stabbing. In addition Fabio is also charged under s.139(1) of the Criminal Justice Act 1988 with having a bladed article (a knife) in his possession in a public place. Fabio explained to the police that he had just bought the knife for his wife to use to carve the Sunday roast. There are no witnesses to the stabbing other than the victim. Both men are interviewed at a local police station using the correct procedures under Code C of the Police and Criminal Evidence Act 1984 and with solicitors present. Dwayne says that he was not involved in the stabbing and that it was Fabio who had carried out the attack. Fabio denies this and says it was Dwayne who carried out the attack. Fabio has no previous convictions. Dwayne has a previous conviction for assault against the same victim in 2007. Fabio and Dwayne are to be tried together.

Discuss the evidential issues arising from the above set of facts.

Answer plan

→ Mention reverse burden of proof when discussing Fabio.

→ Discuss whether a *Vye* direction will be given in relation to Fabio.

→ Discuss whether Dwayne's previous convictions are admissible under gateways (c) and (e) of s.101 of the Criminal Justice Act 2003.

Diagram plan

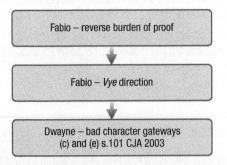

A printable version of this diagram plan is available from www.pearsoned.co.uk/lawexpressqa

[1] A summary of the relevant
evidential issues shows the
examiner at an early stage
that you have recognised the
relevant issues. This gives a
good first impression of your
answer.

Answer

The trial judge will have to decide on the admissibility of the evidence against Fabio and Dwayne and this will involve consideration of issues relating to burden and standard of proof and character evidence.[1]

With regard to the attempted murder charge the prosecution will bear the legal burden of proving the essential elements of the offence according to **Woolmington v DPP** [1935] AC 462. The standard will be beyond reasonable doubt and the jury should be directed as expressed in **R v Summers** [1952] 1 All ER 1059 to consider this as 'satisfied so that you are sure'. The prosecution will also bear the evidential burden of producing sufficient evidence to ensure that the charges can be left to the jury to consider.[2] At the half-way point of the trial the evidential burden will shift to the defence to produce sufficient evidence to support a defence although they are not obliged to prove anything and do not have to take up the evidential burden unless putting forward specific defences such as self-defence.

The next issue is that Fabio has been charged with an offence under s.139 of the Criminal Justice Act 1988. His defence is that the knife was in his possession for a legitimate reason. Under s.139(4) of the 1988 Act it is a defence for a person to show they had the bladed article for good reason or lawful authority. However, according to the case of **L v DPP** [2002] 3 WLR 863 this places a reverse legal burden on Fabio to show that he had the knife for a good reason or had lawful authority to carry it.[3] This was upheld in later cases such as **R v Mathews** [2003] 3 WLR 693 on the basis that the provision was necessary to protect members of the public. The standard of proof will be on a balance of probabilities (see **R v Carr-Briant** [1943] KB 607).

Finally, the issue of character evidence will have to be addressed at the trial. Fabio has no previous convictions and denies involvement in the current offence. He will be entitled to a probensity limb of the **Vye** direction (see **R v Vye** [1993] 1 WLR 471). He will only be entitled to the credibility limb of the **Vye** direction if he testifies at trial as he did not make any pre-trial statements at the police station.[4] The trial judge will effectively tell the jury that they can take the absence of previous convictions as something going towards

[2] You would normally be expected to recognise where the legal and evidential burden rests at the beginning of the trial and there will usually be available marks in a problem question for dealing with this.

[3] Recognising that s.139 of the 1988 Act is an example of a statutory exception to the general principle about where the burden of proof lies will set you apart from the weaker student who might not pick up on this. This shows that you have learnt the statutory exceptions and are aware of the applicable case law in this area such as *L* v *DPP*. You will therefore earn the marks awarded here.

[4] An ability to recognise and apply the appropriate limbs of the *Vye* direction by picking up on the clue that Fabio did not make pre-trial statements will show a good level of application on your part and will earn you additional marks.

Fabio's credibility and the issue of whether or not he is likely to have committed the offences.

Dwayne, however, has an offence for assault on the same victim in 2007. As the defendants are running 'cut-throat' defences, Fabio may seek to use the evidence of Dwayne's previous conviction to assist with his own defence. The previous conviction meets the definition of bad character under s.98 of the Criminal Justice Act 2003. Fabio's lawyers can try to have the conviction admitted under gateway (e) on the basis that it is an important matter in issue between the defence and the co-accused. However, the nature or conduct of Fabio's defence must be such that it undermines Dwayne's defence. This certainly applies on the facts, as the defendants are running 'cut-throat' defences and Fabio alleges that Dwayne carried out the attack. In addition, the case of **R v Lawson** [2007] 1 WLR 1191 held that gateway (e) could also be used if credibility was an important matter between the defendant and co-accused which again would apply on the facts.

The prosecution may also seek to adduce evidence of Dwayne's previous conviction but this time using gateway (c) on the basis that it is important explanatory evidence as it establishes motive because it shows that there was a prior relationship of violence between Dwayne and the victim and therefore goes to the issue of whether Dwayne is likely to have been involved in the present offence. In **R v Ball** [1911] AC 47 evidence of past rivalry between the defendant and the deceased was used to prove motive. In the case of **R v Haigh** [2010] EWCA Crim 90 the Court of Appeal confirmed that gateway (c) 'closely reflects the pre-existing common law'.[5]

The court must give a direction to the jury on whether the evidence is to be used for credibility or propensity or both. In **R v Davis** [2008] 3 All ER 461 the Court of Appeal held that evidence admitted under gateway (c) should be used towards credibility rather than propensity. However, Fabio can use the evidence under gateway (e) towards propensity as well as credibility.[6] There is no clear discretion that applies to gateway (e), whereas in **R v Highton** [2005] 1 WLR 3472 it was confirmed that s.78 of the Police and Criminal Evidence Act applied to any prosecution gateways under s.101. The trial judge therefore has a discretion to exclude bad character evidence under gateway (c), which is a prosecution gateway, using the general discretion under s.78.

[5] Applying recent cases that support the common law position demonstrates wider reading and also shows that your knowledge is up to date. This will earn you additional marks.

[6] Distinguishing the use to which the bad character evidence will be put marks your answer out as a good one and shows that you are able to fully apply the issues in the problem question. This will help you to gain extra marks.

In the circumstances Fabio will bear the legal burden of proving his defence under s.139 of the 1988 Act. It is likely that Fabio will be entitled to a **Vye** direction. However, Dwayne's bad character may be admissible against him under gateways (c) and (e).

✓ **Make your answer stand out**

- When discussing Fabio and reverse burdens, refer to Lord Bingham's 'moral blameworthiness' justification as set out in *Sheldrake* v *DPP* [2004] UKHL 43.
- Refer to views in journal articles such as I. Dennis, 'Reverse onuses and the presumption of innocence: in search of principle' [2005] Crim LR 90 and V. Tadros and S. Tierney, 'The presumption of innocence and the Human Rights Act' [2004] 67 MLR 402 when discussing reverse burdens.

❗ **Don't be tempted to...**

- Ignore the issue of reverse burdens – you are specifically referred to a statute and you should therefore consider whether a statutory exception applies to the *Woolmington* principle.
- Fail to discuss the application of gateway (e) – as the defendants are running 'cut-throat' defences it is clear that Fabio will benefit from using evidence of Dwayne's previous convictions.

Bibliography

Advisory Group on Video-Recorded Evidence (1989), Report ('Pigot Report'). London: Home Office

Auld LJ (2001), *A Review of the Criminal Courts of England and Wales*

Birch, D. (1995), 'Corroboration: goodbye to all that', Crim LR 525

Birch, D. (1999), 'Suffering in silence', Crim LR 769

Birch, D. (2004), 'Same old story, same old song', Crim LR 556

Blom-Cooper, L. (2002), 'Experts and assessors, past, present and future', 21 *Civil Justice Quarterly* 341

Butler-Sloss, E. and Hall, A. (2002), 'Expert witnesses, courts and the law', 95(9) *Journal of the Royal Society of Medicine* 431

Cooper, D. (2005), 'Pigot unfulfilled: video recorded evidence under section 28 of the Youth Justice and Criminal Evidence Act', Crim LR 456

Creighton, P. (1990), 'Spouse competence and compellability', Crim LR 34

Criminal Law Revision Committee (1972) Eleventh Report, Cmnd 4991

Criminal Law Revision Committee (1976) Eleventh Report, *Evidence (General)*, Cmnd 4991

Dennis, I. (2002), 'Silence in the police station: the marginalisation of section 34', Crim LR 25

Dennis, I. (2005), 'Reverse onuses and the presumption of innocence; in search of principle', Crim LR 90

Devlin Committee (1976), Report of the Committee on Evidence of Identification in Criminal Cases ('The Devlin Report'), Cmnd 338

Ellison, L. (1989), 'Cross-examination in rape trials', Crim LR 866

Faust, D. and Ziskin, J. (1988), 'The expert witness in psychology and psychiatry', *Science*, 24 July

Hofmeyr, K. (2006), 'The problem of private entrapment', Crim LR 319

Home Office (1998), Report, *Speaking Up for Justice*. London: Home Office

Home Office (2004), Research Study 283, *Are Special Measures Working? Evidence from Surveys of Vulnerable and Intimidated Witnesses*

Hoyano, L. C. H. (2010), 'Coroners and Justice Act 2009: Special measures directions take two: entrenching unequal access to justice?', 5 CLR 366

Jackson, P. (1986), 'The insufficiency of identification evidence', Crim LR 203

Jones, D. (1987), 'The evidence of a three year old child', Crim LR 677

Judicial Studies Board (2010), *Crown Court Bench Book*. London: Judicial Studies Board

Kibble, N. (2000), 'The sexual history provisions: charting a course between inflexible legislative rules and wholly untrammelled judicial discretion', Crim LR 274

Ladd, M. (1952), 'Expert testimony', 5 Vand LR 414

Law Commission (1984), Report No. 202, *Corroboration Requirements Reconsidered*, Crim LR 316

Law Commission (1996), Report No. 141, *Previous Misconduct of a Defendant*

Law Commission (1997) Report No. 245, *Evidence in Criminal Proceedings: Hearsay and Related Topics*, Cm. 3670

Law Commission (2009), Consultation Paper No. 190, *The Admissibility of Expert Evidence in Criminal Proceedings in England and Wales*

Mendonca, D. (1998), 'Presumptions', 11(4) *Ratio Juris* 399

Mirfield, P. 'Corroboration after the 1994 Act', Crim LR 448

Munday, R. (2007), 'The judicial discretion to admit hearsay evidence', 171 *JP News* 276

O'Brien, W. E. (2003), 'Court scrutiny of expert evidence', 7 Exp 172

Ormerod, D. (2003), 'Improving the disclosure regime', 7 E & P 102

Ormerod, D. and Birch, D. (2004), 'Evolution of the discretionary exclusion of evidence', Crim LR 138

Ormerod, D., Choo, A. L. T. and Easter, R. L. (2010), 'Coroners and Justice Act 2009: the "witness anonymity" and "investigation anonymity" provisions', 5 CLR 380

Pattenden, R. (1995), 'Inferences from silence', Crim LR 602

Pattenden, R. (2009), 'Pre-verdict judicial fact-finding in criminal trials with juries', 29 LJLS 1

Redmayne, M. (2004), 'Criminal Justice Act 2003: disclosure and its discontents', Crim LR 44

Redmayne, M. (2007), 'Rethinking the privilege against self-incrimination', 27 OJLS 209

Richardson, J. (ed.) (2006), *Archbold: Criminal Pleading, Evidence and Practice 2007*. London: Sweet & Maxwell.

Roberts, A. (2003), 'The perils and possibilities of qualified identification: R v George', 7 E & P 130

Roberts, A. (2004), 'The problem of mistaken identification: some observations on process', 8 E & P 100

Roberts, A. (2009), 'Rejecting general acceptance, confounding the gate-keeper: the Law Commission and expert evidence', Crim LR 551

Royal Commission on Criminal Justice (1993), Report, Cm. 2263

Royal Commission on Criminal Justice (2001), Report, *A Review of the criminal courts of England and Wales*

Squires, D. (2006), 'The problem with entrapment', 26 OJLS 351

Stone, M. (1991), 'Instant lie detection? Demeanour and credibility in criminal trials', Crim LR 821

Swift, E. (2000), 'One hundred years of evidence law reform: Thayer's triumph', *California Law Review* 88

Tadros, V. and Tierney, S. (2004), 'The presumption of innocence and the Human Rights Act', 67 MLR 402

Thayer, J. B. (1898), *A Preliminary Treatise on Evidence at the Common Law*. Boston, MA: Little, Brown

Theophilopoulos, C. (2003), 'The Anglo-American privilege against self-incrimination and the fear of foreign prosecution', *Sydney Law Review* 14

Ward, T. (2009), 'Usurping the role of the jury? Expert evidence and witness credibility',
    13 E & P 83

Whitting, C. (2001), 'Res ipsa loquitur: some last words', 117 LQR 392

Wigmore, J. (1974), *Evidence*, revised ed. Boston, MA: Little, Brown

Williams, G. (1976), 'Evidence of identification: "The Devlin Report"', Crim LR 407

Young, G. (2001), 'The sexual history provisions in the Youth Justice and Criminal Evidence
    Act 1999 – a violation of the right to a fair trial', 41 *Medicine, Science and the Law* 217

Index